ALSO EDITED BY LOUISE KAPP HOWE

The White Majority

The Future of the Family

The American Family:

MOTHERS, FATHERS AND CHILDREN —

SEX ROLES AND WORK —

COMMUNITIES AND CHILD CARE —

REDEFINING MARRIAGE AND PARENTHOOD

edited by Louise Kapp Howe

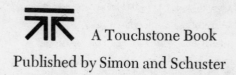 A Touchstone Book

Published by Simon and Schuster

Acknowledgment is gratefully extended to the following for permission to reprint from their works:

Simon and Schuster for material from *Up the Sandbox!* by Anne Richardson Roiphe, copyright © 1970 by Anne Richardson Roiphe.

Leviathan for "We May Not Have Much But There's a Lot of Us" by Myrna Wood, Vol. II, No. 1; copyright © 1971 by *Leviathan*.

The Sterling Lord Agency for "Divorced Mothers as a Political Force" by Gail Sheehy, originally published in *New York* magazine, copyright © 1971 by Gail Sheehy.

Harper & Row for material from *Uptown: Poor Whites in Chicago* by Todd Gitlin and Nanci Hollander, copyright © 1970 by Todd Gitlin and Nanci Hollander.

Margarita Donnelly for "Alternate Culture: Mirror America," originally published in *Women's Press,* copyright © 1972 by Margarita Donnelly.

Cowles Communications, Inc. for "Motherhood—Who Needs It?" by Betty Rollin, from the March 16, 1971, issue of *Look* magazine, copyright © 1971 by Cowles Communications, Inc.

Kids' Publishers, Inc. for "Questions to a Father" by Rochelle Joffe, reprinted from KIDS, *the Magazine by Kids for Kids,* Issue No. 5; copyright © 1971 by Kids' Publishers, Inc.

Up from Under for "My Father" by Madeline Belkin, copyright © 1970 by Up from Under Magazine, Inc.

Social Policy for "Confusions of a Middle Class Husband" by S. M. Miller, copyright © 1971 by Social Policy Corporation.

Little, Brown and Company for material from *Tally's Corner* by Elliot Liebow, copyright © 1967 by Little, Brown and Company, Inc.

Coward-McCann & Geoghegan, Inc. for material from *The American Male* by Myron Brenton, copyright © 1966 by Myron Brenton.

Urie Bronfenbrenner for "Who Cares for America's Children?," address presented at the 1970 Conference of the National Association for the Education of Young Children, reprinted by permission of the author.

Robert Lescher Literary Agency for "Male Chauvinist Spock Recants—Well, Almost" by Benjamin Spock, originally published in *The New York Times Magazine;* copyright © 1971 by Benjamin Spock.

E. J. Brill for material in "The Breadwinner Trap" by Erick Grønseth, which also appears in a different form under the title "The Husband Provider Role: A Critical Appraisal" in Andrée Michel (ed.), *Family Issues of Employed Women in Europe and America,* E. J. Brill, Leiden, 1971.

Johns Hopkins Press for material from *Sex in the Marketplace* by Juanita Kreps, copyright © 1971 by Juanita Kreps.

Issues in Industrial Society for "Changing Family Lifestyles" by Jessie Bernard in the special issue on "Woman's Place in the Workforce," Vol. 2, No. 1, published by the New York State School of Industrial and Labor Relations, Cornell University; copyright © 1971 by Cornell University.

The Urban Review, a publication of the Center for Urban Education, for "Child Care Communities: Units for Better Urban Living" by John Platt, April 1969 issue; copyright © 1969 by the Center for Urban Education.

American Journal of Orthopsychiatry for "Women in the Kibbutz" by Menachem Gerson from the July 1971 issue and for "Getting It All Together: Some Group Issues on Communes" by Rosabeth Moss Kanter from the July 1972 issue; copyright © 1971 and 1972 by the American Orthopsychiatric Association, Inc.

New Woman magazine for "The Case Against Marriage" by Caroline Bird from the September 1971 issue, copyright © 1971 by Allied Publications, Inc.

Acknowledgments

A nice thing about working on a book about the family is that most everybody you meet has definite opinions about your subject and, more than that, has firsthand knowledge to back them up. So many people gave me ideas and suggestions in the course of putting this book together that I'm unable to mention them all. But I'd like to single out with gratitude a few whose comments were particularly helpful: Vivien Leone, Tillie Olsen, Lillian Rubin, Ann Sachar, Nancy Baker Coe, Patricia Howe, Judy Lack, Eva Goodwin, Marja Hughes, Pauline Bart, Karen Jacobs, Karen Hurn, Sally Grieg, Susan Steinberg, Julie Pesonen—and, yes, I must admit a few men were helpful in their ideas, too, most of all Charles Howe, Adam Hochschild, Todd Gitlin, David Steinberg, David Rice, David Pesonen and Jim Goodwin. On the publishing side I'd also like to thank Alice Mayhew and Linda Healey at Simon and Schuster, and at the IBM electric, the indomitable Barbara Corso. Finally, my thanks most of all to the contributors, both those who let us reprint articles they had already written and those who wrote new material especially for the book.

FOR TESS

Contents

PART TWO: TRANSFORMING THE FAMILY

Sex Roles, Work and Income

Child Care

Community

Redefining Marriage and Parenthood

An Introduction

by Louise Kapp Howe

The one feeling that most clearly came out of our discussions . . . is a sense that in this society the family is shot through with contradictions, that it is perhaps as essential as it is damaging, as much a fulfillment of our needs as it fails them.
—Editorial in *Up from Under,* a magazine by, for and about women

I

This is a book about the American family, and the first thing to remember about the American family is that it doesn't exist. Families exist. All kinds of families in all kinds of economic and marital situations, as all of us can see. But the idea of the family —what it is supposed to be, what *we* are supposed to be in our roles as mothers or fathers or children—is invariably one of the strongest influences on our lives. That's the second thing.

When people say, as they have throughout history and lately do more and more, that it's breaking down, on the verge of death, or conversely that it's never been stronger, someone should ask them to define their terms. *The* American family? Just which American family did you have in mind? Black or white, large or small, wealthy or poor—or something in between? Did you mean a father-headed, mother-headed or child-less family? First or second time around? Happy or miserable? Your family or mine?

What is invariably in mind, we will find, is a white, middle-class, monogamous, father-at-work, mother-and-children-at-home family living in a suburban one-family house. This is a definition that now effectively excludes more than half the population. It is a family type that is increasingly being questioned by the women and young people who come out of it. Yet it remains the standard conception of what the American family is, the model against which all who live differently are still judged deviant.

And that, naturally, is no accident. The idea of the American family and what it should be is, after all, the most powerful image used by government and business to promote the values and goals of government and business, except for the image of the free-market economy, which, of course, also doesn't exist. Intimately related, the two distorted images walk hand in hand.

We all know what the American family is supposed to look like. We can't help it. The picture has been imprinted on our brains since we were tiny, through children's books, schools, radio, television, movies, newspapers, the lectures if not the examples of many of our parents, the speeches if not the examples of many of our politicians.

There they are, in the current television version, the four or five of them. Father, the Breadwinner, tall and lean and in a hurry ("Have to rush or I'll be late for the office"); Mother, the Homemaker, sweet and self-effacing ("Don't work too hard, dear"), athletic little Billy ("'Bye, Daddy"), adorable little Susie ("'Bye, Daddy"), and our optional third child, who unfortunately must be banished from our model portrait now because of overpopulation ("'Bye"); two children are quite enough these days.

And we know how they will spend their time. Father will work long and hard with great financial success all for the sake of Mother, Billy, Susie, the new car, house, refrigerator, washing machine, sailboat, and yearly vacation seeing-America-first. Mother will clean and shop and clean and, along with the schools, help Billy and Susie prepare for their future respective roles in American life as, naturally, breadwinner and homemaker. Late at night Mother will turn into Sophia Loren. And it will all be worthwhile. And the economy will flourish.

Now, the striking point about our model family is not simply the compete-compete, consume-consume style of life it urges us to follow. Nor even the isolation from the world of work it forces on the mother and children, the long hours away from home for the father. The striking point, in the face of all the propaganda, is how few Americans actually live this way.

Certainly a lot of us try. Many spend entire lives feeling not merely disappointed but defeated because Father did not get that big promotion, because Mother did not get that new house and new car. Ironically, if they only knew it, the fraction of the upper-middle-class population that most successfully duplicates the model set before us—where the husband is a demon occupationally and financially, while the wife stays home as a good woman should—are statistically the most likely of all middle-class couples to have their marriages sour. This, at least, has been the conclusion of a number of studies, one of them reported in this book by Jan Dizard. When the wife works and, even more to the point, the husband scales down his career drives, the statistical chances of a happy marriage are far higher.

Thus our American family model, with its emphasis on "success" on the one hand and "domesticity" on the other, appears to be actually a model for marital misery. Among the upper middle class, that is.

For better or for worse, for poorer but not for richer, most Americans never get to afford this kind of success-based misery, although many, of course, have no difficulty turning up the old-fashioned economic kind. The huge numbers of currently working mothers, of single-parent homes, of youth in communes, of retired old people, of, for that matter, unemployed fathers, makes it stereophonically clear that the old male-breadwinner, female-homemaker formula simply does not account for the majority of Americans anymore, if it ever did. Yet our government, in practically all of its policies related to the family, continues to act as if there were one and only one worthy way to run a household and refuses to give more than the stingiest support to the actual and growing variety of American family lives.

In this vein, in his famous government report, Daniel Patrick Moynihan was able to argue that the black family was "deteriorating" on the ground that about a fourth of black families did not have a male at the head. The fact that the mother-headed family, something we have known since the beginning of history and are now finding increasingly among whites, could be conceivably another legitimate form of the family—albeit often greatly in need of economic help precisely, as Erick Grønseth shows in this book, because of the male-breadwinner system—was something few of us then considered. In fact, Grønseth argues, it is the male-breadwinner system (and its intimidating effect on unemployed and underemployed men) that in the first place often *causes* the female-headed home.

And more recently, only months before his 1972 bid for re-election, President Nixon took the chance of losing the votes of over eleven million working mothers by vetoing major legislation for child care, because, in his words, its provision would impede his most important task: "to cement the family in its rightful role as the keystone of our civilization."

Cement the white, middle-class, male-breadwinner, female-homemaker family, he meant. Either that or the President must have had silly putty instead of cement in mind, since the very week following the veto he was back approving measures to provide child care for *welfare* mothers, so that they could be forced to work—obviously because they weren't careful enough to make sure there was a male breadwinner at home.

Actually, if all married women were now to stop working, the U.S. would experience a cataclysmic drop in family income such as hasn't been seen since the days of the Great Depression. The truth of most people's lives, according to the U.S. Bureau of Labor Statistics, is that it now usually *requires* a working wife to push family income into middle-class status. (Among husband-wife families with incomes of $10,000 or more in 1968, wives worked during the year in about 60 percent of the cases, compared with 24 percent in families with incomes under $2,000. And today two thirds of married women who are working are married to men who earn under $7,000 a year!) All the talk about "a woman's place" becomes almost surreal when you realize that the vast majority who work have no choice.

Nevertheless, as if the government couldn't read its own statistics, it is our old familiar male-breadwinner, female-homemaker, model nuclear family that is taken for granted in almost all of our domestic policies, whether they're on the state or national level, or concerned with education, child care, marriage, divorce, *man*power, taxes, social security or inheritance.

Once it was expected that women would work (as well as take responsibility for home and child care). In recent years, only in times of the greatest national crisis has the working mother been officially approved—the most prominent example being World War II, when mothers were told it was their "patriotic duty" to get out and work. To make it possible they were also told to leave their children at child-care centers which the government promptly set up and then just as quickly dismantled (to the chagrin of the majority of the mothers who wanted to stay on the job) as soon as the Johnny, the real breadwinner, came marching home.

We are, to be sure, not the only modern country to assume this male state of affairs. In this area we really do have a united nations. In those countries where the wife still works as a matter of official course, such as in Russia and in Poland, she is generally considered the secondary breadwinner and as such continues to have major responsibility for the home and children. Overworked, overburdened, it is no wonder that Eastern European women, like many U.S. working wives, have recently complained they need more time with their families at home. For although it has been sometimes true that women have been allowed entry into formerly male terrain, usually at the lowest levels, what has almost never been true is that men on any large scale have agreed to share responsibility for the home.

Even on the Israeli kibbutz (as Menachem Gerson shows), where sex roles were supposed to be abolished, and now on our own communes (see Bennett Berger *et al.*), any redivision of labor that has taken place has been an almost totally one-sided matter. Although you may be able to easily spot a woman working in the fields, you will have to travel to many a commune before you catch a man sorting out a pile of wet diapers.

Indeed, some people have observed a tendency for sex roles to be more rigid in collective living arrangements than in individual households. In the old extended family, in communes and on the kibbutz, it has been almost always other women (whether a grandmother or a fellow communard) who share the home and child care. In the nuclear family a husband usually has no choice but to help out when his wife is sick or away or simply exhausted. Given Choice A: the steady cooperation of other women in a collective, or Choice B: the sporadic help of a resentful or tired mate (assuming one has a mate), it is no wonder that increasing numbers of middle-class women as well as old people are joining youth in looking for alternatives to the isolation of nuclear-family life. Only in China and in Sweden, as Olof Palme shows, has any official effort been started by a government to not only provide equal work and child care, but to also involve men in that care and in domestic tasks generally. Started—far from achieved.

For these reasons among others, it is no wonder that many in the women's movement reject family life flatly. Despite some occasional promises, despite some token exceptions, women's fate in the end, whether in the extended or the nuclear family, has been to be left holding the broom and the baby or, more commonly, holding the broom and the baby and an outside job too. But if the present alternative, as many believe, is either to love the family (and be held back) or leave it (and compete in the male world), then I fear far more for the future of the women's movement than I do for the future of the family.

In reviewing the history of the original feminist movement and why it failed to alter the lives of most American women, William O'Neill (in *Everyone Was Brave*) concluded that the trouble was rooted in the movement's unwillingness to tackle the problems of the family. Most of the early American feminists either were young single women opposed to marriage and the family or else were married professional women who preferred to concentrate on other issues, particularly the issue of the vote. Yet, says O'Neill, since the masses of women were married, or wanted to be, the only way that equality between the sexes could have been achieved was through a "revolution in domestic life," a revolution that was never at all attempted.

The parallels are obvious. The two largest factions of the present women's movement are married professionals, who concentrate most heavily on issues of professional employment, and young middle-class single women, who agitate strongly against marriage or motherhood or both. To a great degree both approaches make sense. After a period of the greatest oversell of domesticity in American history (it worked—women in their prime childbearing years in the 1950s and early '60s may well go down in the history books as the most fecund group of females in the twentieth century), it is time that the very real disadvantages of domestic life were recognized and that other avenues were made more possible. It is also time that staying single and/or childless was seen as a legitimate, often wise path to follow, particularly for the career-bound, not something ever to have to apologize about. The articles in this book by Caroline Bird and Betty Rollin pursue these points at length. Still, as Ms. Rollin points out, "No matter what anyone says, motherhood isn't about to go out like a blown bulb . . . Only the [Motherhood] Myth must go out, and now it seems to be dimming." And that goes for the romantic myth of marriage as well.

In fact, although a hundred headlines would have us believe that no one wants to get married anymore except homosexuals and renegade priests, with the nuns just beginning to be heard from, the reality is that a record number of couples went to the altar in the past few years, many for the second or third time, with the result that the highest proportion of American adults in our history are currently married. Not to mention all those living together unmarried, very often in name only.

As for the near future, if there is any discernible change in the statistical wind, it appears to be for young, college-educated women to delay getting married until they are closer to twenty-five or older (perhaps living with their potential mate and others first) and, to the relief of the population experts, to want smaller families than did their prolific 1950s' counterparts. With smaller families, with more education for women, with longer lives, hopefully with new attitudes about sex roles, the need for more opportunities for women will grow.

Yet, contrary to the fascinating palaver about the imminent death of the family, there is no evidence that more than a small proportion of American women (and they, as always, will be predominantly the most educated and career-motivated of women who can afford to go it alone) and an even smaller proportion of men (and they, as always, will be predominantly the poorest of men who can't afford to assume additional financial responsibilities) will forego family life entirely. In both cases, if our current sex-role system would change—if a woman could more easily combine a career and family, if a man could count on the equal and shared income of his wife—then even these relatively small numbers of people who never marry might decrease. (At the least, their decision would be truly a choice, not another virtue made out of necessity.)

For even members of communes, chief rejectors of the kinship model, so one would assume, seem to have an insistent need to divide into pairs and to call their total living groups "families" (although, as Rosabeth Kanter shows, these families are often the most fragile of all). Add to these the quite serious desires among at least some homosexuals and Catholic clergy for the right to be married, and the yearnings of most people for some form of family life, official or not, foreverafter or for three years after, seems almost universal. Why, in the age of the swinger, amid rampant divorce and disillusionment, amid overpopulation and safe and easy copulation, should this still be so?

Is it only that most of us have been conditioned—what we now so quaintly call socialized—to want a family? Or is it that economically our society makes other ways of life impossible to afford? Or, along with the burdens, particularly for women, are there some actual benefits in marriage and children that most people want to preserve?

With no pretense to scientific proof, it seems evident that in different degrees for different people in different stages of their life, all these factors apply. We have been conditioned. Our occupational and child-care and housing and tax patterns, based once again on the male-breadwinner mystique, make life intensely difficult for all but the most affluent women who try to carry on alone. (Read Gail Sheehy for an updated look at the life of the gay divorcee, the one with children.) And, at the same time, along with the injustices, there are—or at least can be —satisfactions in family life (the "roots" Simone Weil believed we all long for, the link to the past and the future, the promise of love, stability, call these what you will) that in our society are hard to sustain elsewhere and that consequently, despite the high risk of divorce, most people, women as well as men, still don't want to do without.

There are, of course, satisfactions in a career that many people don't want to do without, either. And naturally only women have ever had to choose between the two. Middle-class men have always taken it for granted that they could have both a family life and a rewarding career and, thanks to the male-designed sex-role system, they have usually been right. The striking thing one finds in the profiles of the most successful men is that they invariably marry very young (although again, as Jan Dizard shows, these marriages are often unhappy). In contrast, the striking thing about the most successful women is how many marry very late or not at all. Many felt forced to make that choice.

Highly achievement-oriented, vividly aware of how women have been trapped by their family roles, today's feminists urge others to rip the domestic curtains from their eyes and pursue a challenging career. In this respect they find themselves at heavy odds with the counterculture, whose main contribution perhaps has been to point up the repressive side of the old get-ahead work ethic. In each case the nature of the protest comes out of the nature of the problem. Counterculture men—often the biggest male chauvinists of them all, according to several contributors—have had to resist the great pressures on middle-class men (and most of the counterculture is middle-class) to devote their whole lives to a career and making money. Women in the movement have had to resist the great pressures on them to devote their whole lives to a husband and children and to forgo any self-advancement at all.

But the substitution of one half of a loaf for another is not necessarily the way to get the most nourishment. If to counter-act the glorification of domesticity women have to recommence the glorification of work, I'm not sure how much progress has been made. In any case, the majority of women, who now work mainly out of necessity, simply won't settle for it. In discussing the "deep disillusionment of kibbutz women who discarded their traditional roles only to find that the fulfillment they expected did not materialize," Menachem Gerson in this book issues what might be a profound warning:

> Women's striving was toward identification with men, toward an equality that . . . set forth male qualities and activities as the model for both sexes. This distortion of the concept of sex equality has occurred in the early stages of other women's-emancipation movements. There is little doubt that this period in kibbutz development was tinged with an unconscious postulate of male supremacy. . . . [It] left kibbutz women with a hidden distrust of women's-liberation slogans, and . . . planted the seeds of their later disillusionment.

In a different vein, Alice Abarbanel writes:

> Women . . . must have the choice not to have a child. That is happening a lot and is really necessary. I hope, however, that women don't stop at the *not*-being-a-biological-mother state. If women are merely "not-mothers," then we stay in our old cycles

by doing the opposite. . . . What we need is a new definition of motherhood.

Which is to say, by implication, a new definition of fatherhood as well. Which is to say, by implication, the end of our male-breadwinner, female-homemaker model.

II

When I first started to plan this book I mainly wanted to explore how women in different economic and marital straits are affected differently by the family roles society demands we play —how we are damned (and benefited) in different ways whether we go along or we don't. But in the course of reading more and listening more I began to feel that to focus in this book on the woman's role alone was to leave out too large a piece of the family puzzle.

For it is not only that women are systematically held back by the American family model, although that is true and of paramount importance. It is not only that children are often treated as possessions to be taught the old sex-role stereotypes, although that is true and of paramount importance. It is also true, I believe, that the assumption of a male-breadwinner society—and the social policies and occupational structure and sexist attitudes that flow from that assumption—ends up determining the lives of everyone within a family, whether a male breadwinner is present or not, whether one is living by the rules in suburbia or trying to break them on a commune.

More than any other factor, and to a degree further than found in most other industrial countries (which often provide some form of children's allowance and medical care) the health and welfare of an American family is determined by the basic fact of who the head of the household is and how well he is doing in the labor market; and if the head isn't male, thanks to our male-breadwinner policies you can usually be sure she isn't doing very well. Find out who the head of an American household is and you will be able to predict the kind of medical attention the children will receive from the day they are conceived, the neighborhoods they will grow up in, the schools they will and won't be able to attend, and, perhaps most important, the vision of the future—the possibilities and impossibilities—that will grow before their eyes.

How can two children coming from different family backgrounds be given an equal chance in life? That has been the debate of the ages, and since we live in what was meant to be a democracy and not an aristocracy it supposedly is still a political question of the first order. And now to that question women are adding: How can two children coming from two different *genders* be given an equal chance in life? The answers most commonly relied on in both cases are education and employment, two solutions that can never work for more than an exceptional handful so long as our schools and labor market continue to reflect the class bias, race bias and sex bias of society in general. But until recently the issue that has almost never been posed in the fight against inequality is the inequality that begins in the family by virtue of the male-breadwinner system itself.

Yet, as I think this book will show, whether one is mainly concerned with changing family roles, or decreasing women's economic dependency on men, or providing quality child care, or advancing children's rights, or attaining racial equality, or helping the old, or humanizing community life, or redistributing the dollar, the male-breadwinner model (and what it does to those who conform and those who don't) is at the heart of so many of our problems.

I think you will see this clearly in Part One of this book, where there is a personal look at the lives of mothers, fathers and children in widely different economic and marital situations. Their problems are dramatically different, as is to be expected, but you may also see a common thread: a pervasive note of frustration felt by men as well as by women about the boundaries of their lives. Whether because the man is literally away or because his work keeps him jumpy and preoccupied, there is a tendency for American children, affluent and poor, to be increasingly underfathered and therefore for women to have to take on ever larger slices of the parental work load. What comes through for me in Part One is that many men are also unhappy with this present state of family affairs. And this for a moment makes me believe that the possibilities for change may be greater than I originally thought.

Then, in Part Two, the book gets more theoretical and explores what some of these changes might be: they are both personal and political, like the women's movement itself. They concern, naturally, child care and equal work opportunities, but more basically they entail an overthrow of our sex-role system and a reordering of the meaning of motherhood, fatherhood, work, community and "success" itself. And at this point what loudly comes through is how far there is to go.

For even couples like Alice Abarbanel and her husband, and David Steinberg and his wife—who, as you will see, are struggling to break out of their sex-role conditioning and completely share the parenting and breadwinning tasks—are utterly dependent on our male-designed occupational structure to make their equality possible. And if poverty ever flies in the window, the new equality may have to walk out the door. For most people it simply isn't possible for the husband to stay home half time and divide the child care in two. As it is, most wives are already forced to work to help keep the family afloat. This, after all, is a country where, according to the federal government, it now costs somewhere between $80,000 and $150,000 to rear two children and put them through college. Personal attempts from family to family at breaking down sex roles are crucial, but they will be far from enough to bring about equality for all.

Throughout history the future of the family has been bitterly debated—some always sure it was about to die out, some always sure it would stay just the same—while the family itself in a hundred variations has continued to change and alter to meet the needs of—what else?—the "economy." From agricultural to industrial to post-industrial. From rural to urban to suburban.

Once, in the days of close-knit crowded, extended families, came a literature extolling the virtues of individuality, privacy, the lonely search for self. Today, from young and old in our small, travel-light, middle-class families, we hear about the need for community, for an escape from loneliness. From our poor and working-class families we find we are miles behind other countries in terms of infant mortality rates, maternal and child health, provisions for day care, children's allowances, pensions to the old. While politicians carry on about the sanctity of the American family, we learn, as Urie Bronfenbrenner puts it, that in the scale of national priorities our children and families really come last. After freeways. After pork subsidies. After the billions spent on munitions in the name of national defense.

It is now time, many contributors to this book have the temerity to suggest, to reverse the usual procedure. It is time to *change the economy* to meet the needs of American families. It is time to change our job structure and work schedules (through measures such as those suggested by Jessie Bernard) so that family sex roles can finally be discarded. It is time to change our housing patterns (see Platt, Burgess, Hochschild) so that cooperative forms of living are possible for those who want and need them. It is time to provide all children with the care they need, within and outside of the home, and make it economically possible for both sexes to do so. It is time to give all women a chance for self-fulfillment and a choice of ways to define it. It is time for the "revolution in domestic life" that William O'Neill spoke of. It is time to stop debating the future of the family and start creating it.

PART ONE

MEMBERS OF TODAY'S FAMILY

Mothers

Occupation: Mother

by ANNE RICHARDSON ROIPHE

Novelist and essayist, Anne Richardson Roiphe is the author of *Digging Out,
Up the Sandbox!*—from which this piece is taken—and a third novel, recently
published, *Long Division.*

After the children's nap, I repeated the morning's chores in
an abbreviated fashion. I took chicken out of the freezer com-
partment for dinner. I smoothed the bed. I changed the baby
and I yelled at Elizabeth for pulling the petals off my white
geranium, its blossom now picked and scabby, tilting to one
side. It sits on the windowsill next to a cellophane bag of half-
consumed chocolate cookies, looking, I suppose, as if it belongs
to us. Suddenly I am in a hurry to get out of the apartment. The
brick wall behind the kitchen window lets in no light. The
dishes in the sink seem unbearable and the spilled orange juice
on the counter surface seems a defacement, like obscenities
scrawled in lipstick on public monuments. The early-June heat
and the garbage, not entirely contained within the aluminum
can, combine in a terrible odor.

We rush out the door, barely remembering pail and shovel,
money for ice cream. In the dark hallway at first I feel relieved.
It's cooler, the dampness and draft are stored in the green-
painted cement walls and as in a cave there is the chill of objects untouched by sun or open air—a sense of bats and mice
and snakes that hide, cool under the rocks. I hold Elizabeth
close, and ring again and again for the elevator, which lumbers
its way up to the sixth floor. The door slides open, and then before I can insert the stroller, the gray steel slabs move quickly
shut and we jump back. The unthinking machine, responding to
another call, would chop our hands off, decapitate the children,
and crush us in its unrelenting need to obey an electronic im-

pulse. Slowly it creeps to the tenth floor. I watch the numbers light on the plaque above the door. I ring again and it stops in its descent. A woman, a vertical neighbor, holds the proper button as I maneuver the stroller, Elizabeth and myself inside. She releases the button; the door groans and shuts. We stare at the panel of lights telling us of our slow progress downward, as if a message were being sent and only with total concentration can we decipher the code. At last the first floor. The lady holds the "Open" button as I lead Elizabeth and the baby out. We hurry through the yellow lobby.

At last out in the sunshine. Hit by the sudden heat and light, Peter cries and pulls at his thin hair. The motion of the carriage soothes him and we cross Broadway, quiet in the early afternoon. A truck is delivering rolls to a bakery down the block, a few children are jumping rope outside the laundry, and the dwarf lady who lives in our building is hurrying across the street, her shopping bag filled, her fat legs bare and her feet encased in their usual heavy orthopedic shoes. . . .

I push the carriage into the park; my dress is stained with perspiration. The heat muffles the street sounds, and the green leaves and the grass seem so pleasant, I am glad to be here in the park. There are other mothers in the playground. It's still early and many benches are free. A child runs to the concrete fountain and by leaning with all his weight against a metal button embedded in the grainy cement produces a trickle of cool water that bubbles erratically above the metal spout. He gets his shirt all wet trying to position his mouth correctly and finally gets down, walks to his mother's side. She talks to the mother on the bench next to her about a badminton club in Brooklyn where she and her husband happily release their accumulated aggressions. I look around at the pull toys, the hoop and the roller skates that lie just beneath the bench next to mine. They have in themselves, these objects of commercial greed, mass-produced wonder and childhood lust, a curious beauty in

the shade beneath the bench, like shells on the shore, emptied
of their inner life.

I pick up my baby and hold him on my lap. He looks up at
my face, his fingers exploring my mouth, digging at my nose.
What stays on, what comes off—I can see him wondering. I
could starve him—or leave him behind me, dropping him on the
cement, crying in the park till the police come and assign him
some nameless future. But he has nothing to fear because, despite an angry thought or two, we are connected deeply and
permanently. And with each feeding, each soothing, each moment we live together, I grow into him. My spirit oozes out, I
feel myself contracting and him expanding, and the ties between us solidify. And I am almost his possession. Elizabeth's
too. My selfish purposes are also served, as the children make
for me a universe, with a design and a rhythm and a function.
And instead of being, as I was before I conceived a child, a bit
of dark matter orbiting aimlessly, brooding on my own molecu-
lar disintegration, I am now a proper part of ordinary society.

I think of Paul in the library now, probably in one of the
study cubicles, with its desk piled with documents on the Spanish Civil War. He said he was looking for testimony, reports
from the original members of the Abraham Lincoln Brigade. I
know the way his hair hangs across his face when he reads, the
way he chews on his fingernails and screws up his eyes when
he detects dishonesty or distortion in his text. I wish somehow I
could be with him—the days seem so long when he's absorbed
that way, as if I didn't matter, as if the children were peripheral
noise, as if his scholarship and theories were food sufficient. And
then I get sad, because nothing I have ever read or done,
nothing I will ever learn or speculate about, can replace being
near him. I would put anything down to go for a short walk
with him. There is a terrible inequality of love in that, and I am
so reduced. I am like the heroine bound and gagged by the villain, lying on the railroad tracks waiting for her rescuer. He
comes, releases her, kissing the tears away. Only he leaves, this

hero with many interests, and the villain returns, and the scene must be repeated over and over. The metaphor is melodramatic. Actually, Paul and I exist in a more ordinary way. We live, not like explorers, not like Lewis and Clark charting the wilds of the Northwest, more like land surveyors blocking out lots for a new housing project or a county shopping center. The possibilities for raw adventure under such circumstances are limited.

Two students walk by, peering between the playground bars. They still feel about public events as if they could mold them like the clay that used to yield beneath their fingers in art classes in elementary-school afternoon programs. They go to the barricades, hair flying, jaws set, to reform a system whose basic injustices are beyond reach, hidden and perpetual. They list grievances of representation, scholarships, draft, university alliances with military matters, and they shake the ground on which they stamp their feet, and their catcalls are reported in the press, and the drama around here is great. And above them and below them, the web stays. The fabric vibrates like a trampoline, bouncing us in somersaults we execute with more or less grace. And the same words are said by different people over and over. The students move on to look at other interesting sights in the park.

If I were younger, I would join the student revolutionaries. If Paul were just a few years younger, he would have had his head bashed in on the principle of student power. As it is, Elizabeth needs a daily bath and other things, and the baby must have what the books call consistent mothering or his small soul will warp and bend in strange directions, and he might decide it's not worth growing and reverse the process, curl himself in fetal position and look only inward, refusing food until life itself is extinguished. And so with my hands, when I touch him and wipe the cereal from his face and the b.m. from his bottom, I make life again each day, like Penelope weaving a shroud, never to be complete till Ulysses returns. I wonder, if I were Penelope, if I should not have smuggled myself aboard the ship originally headed for Troy. Or if perhaps, even now, I should not accept the hot kisses of some impatient suitor who would rape me on the hills and carry me off to a different city where the language itself would be unknown to me.

I'm no Penelope, no romantic heroine or creature of historical importance. I'm just Margaret Reynolds, wife and mother, not yet thirty . . . too old for an identity crisis and yet not past the age of uncertainty. . . . I grew up like all the other ordinary field flowers on an ordinary hill in a nice suburb, and my daddy was a nice accountant-daddy who counted the money in counting houses of several corporations conveniently located in nearby Newark, and I had a dog of no particular breed and a mother who played cards with her lady friends in the afternoon and solitaire alone on the couch waiting for my father to come home in the evening. The only distinguished thing that happened to me was that my father had a coronary in his office when I was twelve and died very quickly, to the shock of his partners and his small family. I was left with a perfectly unchanged life, because my daddy had been prudent, but I developed a concern over questions that didn't unduly trouble my playmates and friends. When I went to Barnard and found I was a garden-variety girl . . . I became comfortable in my surroundings and vowed I would live in the city the rest of my life . . . crossing the river back only on such occasions as last Sunday, when we were supposed to go to my mother's in New Jersey. . . .

An aunt's birthday was to be celebrated on the lawn. My mother had hired a caterer, and little tables with candy-striped cloths and pink carnations were going to be scattered over the grass. Paul never complains about this sort of event, taking the gruesome exposure to my family in his stride. I, for my part, cringe under the glaring eyes of relatives who stare at me as though I were some abnormality. They compare my state in life with that of their own children, and they gloatingly tell sad stories of my promising youth. My mother winces because my shoes or clothes are wrong, my hair unwashed, or Elizabeth's dress too short. Across the George Washington Bridge there is a world of disapproval, a native tribe whose customs are inviolable, and defectors, members who have snuck off to the bush, are—if apprehended—shown no mercy. We would have gone, nevertheless, to my aunt's birthday party, but the night before had sapped us of all our strength and we spent the day in bathrobes, with the shades pulled down, reading and rereading the fine print in the Sunday *Times*.

On the way home from the park I stopped in at Woolworth's. Elizabeth loves the five-and-dime, the hamsters turning on their wheels in tiny cages, the goldfish swimming in tanks along the far wall, the rack of dog chains and cat trays, the birdseed and the sickly parakeets all dazzling in their unspoken promise of possession. Elizabeth also likes the ribbon rack, the nail-polish counter, and the rows of plastic dolls and birthday-party paper hats and plates. I am always tempted by such a display. I fight the urge to fill my basket with safety pins, and cotton balls, and hair bows and colored aprons and rainhats, and up and down the rows I prowl—with ten dollars I could almost gratify all the longings I suddenly have, but that would be immoral. Beyond the expense, it would be improper. I am an American Puritan, and no sentence in the stockades would be long enough to ever expiate all my sins. I settled on two chocolate brownies and a package of rubber pants, and I bought Elizabeth a little box of crayons and a coloring book with outlined pictures of elephants and tigers.

When we got home, I rested for a moment in the stuffed armchair Paul's father had given us as a wedding present. It came from the parlor of his house in Stockbridge and had become our favorite possession. We had driven down in a borrowed station wagon, and the chair had been shoved in the back on end, like a great sea turtle overturned. We had sat next to each other on the front seat and I had felt a kind of exhilaration, as if the chair were our homestead and signaled the beginning of the plowing and the fencing of the land. I touched him, rubbed against him, hindered his driving, fondled the hair on the back of his neck, and I was so hot and moist and charged with irrepressible willfulness that somewhere in northern Connecticut he was forced to pull the car off the highway, onto a more personal back road with trees arching overhead, a farm in the distance, and a diner half a mile beyond. There in the dark we lay in the back of the station wagon, zigzagging our bodies around the immovable chair. Then we had greasy grilled-cheese sandwiches in the diner. I fell asleep the last part of the trip. He was whistling a Bach aria and I knew he was pleased.

When I got up from the chair, I undressed the baby and bathed him in the tub. I powdered him and put on his flannel nightgown, unpressed but clean. He and I were talking to each other, the mass of happy sounds probably preferable to speech and all the concomitant woe that comes with long sentences and exchanged opinions. I had left Elizabeth in the living room playing with her crayons and her new book. As soon as I had the baby settled, I called her for her bath. I helped her undress and splashed the water for her and soaped the park dirt off. I looked at her small body, a vagina so smooth and hidden, the tiny clitoris still white, like a marble statue, so unlike my hairy mound, so unlike my full labia and the pulsating, discharging, odorous, membranous opening, scarred by two episiotomies (a slight scar—I needed a magnifying mirror to notice it). If I looked very closely I could see the soft blond fuzz on Elizabeth's mound that would one day grow thick and bushy, covering the oozy changes that would go on below. I felt sad somehow that we couldn't preserve the sculptured perfection of our own immature genitals. I washed behind her ears and we talked about the rather sticky subject of baby lambs and lamb chops, one of her favorite foods. Different animals eat each other up, that's just the way it is, I said. And I saw reflected on her young face the same moral shock, the unbelieving righteousness, that had gripped my mother when years ago I had explained that no one in my college dormitory was a virgin, no exceptions at all. I was gleeful in that revelation to my mother, but I felt embarrassed by Elizabeth's stare, and somehow compromised by my indifference to the fate of baby lambs.

Paul came home. I heard the thud of the briefcase and felt the quickening of my mind, a kind of lightening as in the last weeks of pregnancy when the baby slips down and it's suddenly easier to breathe, a relief. I rushed to the mirror and patted my hair and tucked the errant strands into the proper clip. I looked for my powder but couldn't find it, probably having left it in the kitchen in the morning. He had worked hard; his eyes had that dazed look of a man returning from a long trip. He admired Elizabeth's new coloring book and held the baby while I prepared the children's supper. He wandered about the apartment picking up toys that had scattered, a comb that had fallen under the bed. He likes things to be in better order than I seem to be able to keep them. I know what there is to be done and still I have trouble.

Eat, eliminate, prepare food, clean up, shop, throw out the garbage, a routine clear as a geometric form, a linear pattern that seems almost graceful in its simplicity. Despite computers and digit telephone numbers, nuclear fission, my life hardly differs from that of an Indian squaw settled in a tepee on the same Manhattan land centuries ago. Pick, clean, prepare, throw out, dig a hole, bury the waste—she was my sister. She would understand why there should be one day of total fast each week.

The disaster started innocently enough, after the children were in bed and I was starting to heat the chicken for us. Paul was collecting his notes for tomorrow's work in the library when he found a page of neatly written quotes from Robespierre attacking the ambitions of Danton. The page had been done months ago and held for probable use in his chapter on the French revolutionaries. Diabolical madmen all, was what he was saying. The page had been thickly crayoned on in heavy bold purple and green strokes. Elizabeth had made circles, aimless lines, a possible stick figure with frizzy hair that sprawled across the bottom of the page. Most of the words themselves, collected from many sources, were now obliterated by thick crayon. It must have happened while I was bathing the baby.

He turned pale, and I knew at that second how the following hours would go. His lips formed quickly into a thin line and his eyes went dead. "You let this happen. You let her destroy my work paper. You just casually without a thought allowed her to crayon on my paper. You might just as well· give her a paint-brush, let her do the walls. Or a scissors. Why not give her the rest of my manuscript to make paper dolls?" And he turned his back, controlling a terrible stream of invective. He threw him-self down in our armchair, a thick wall of fury blocking my ac-cess. And although I tried not to let it happen, I felt myself crumble, my adult, womanly, maternal self dissolve before a cloud of childhood guilt, of vases broken, milk spilled at the table, arithmetic homework not handed in, misspelled words, messy bureau drawers, grape-juice stains on party dresses—a sense of abandonment, aloneness, a need for my bed, my pillow, sanctuary, a place where under the covers my hands could rub on my own body till, somewhat eased, I could fitfully sleep, forgetting the furies I had aroused. In numbness I finished the dishes, and when I looked at him again he was sitting rigid in the chair, as if the outer edges of his body were the silent streets just beyond the bombed-out area of the city. Those buildings whose foundations were rocked by the nearby blast seemed to hold themselves taut so they too will not turn to rubble, mean-ingless formless piles of chipped and broken stone. So he sat in the chair and glared at me. He didn't speak, and I didn't dare. I knew ultimately this issue would end. I reassured myself with thoughts of other early-morning reconciliations, and it was true, I was careless, I did allow the children to strew the apartment with the litter of their activities. I had permitted milk stains to blotch the rug, I had myself burned a cigarette hole in the couch cover. There were odds and ends of possessions all out of order, in irregular and unmanageable places. The chores each day, if I faced their demands, were overwhelming, and only by laxity, a certain bohemian looseness, was I able to keep us all together. Sometimes I wanted my mother and her maid to come and take care of it all. I fairly screamed out for home, for the days when the ultimate mess was undreamed of and marriage seemed a game of picking out a trousseau and addressing thank-you notes to relatives for lovely presents that came wrapped in tissue paper that someone else threw out.

At last Paul got up and without a word left the apartment; martyred, he slammed the door behind him, and when I stood at the bedroom window I could see him walking down Broadway. I could see fatigue in his posture. Where would he go without me—to an art movie at the Thalia, a double feature of grade-D Westerns at Loew's, a Spanish love story in an uptown movie house? Would he go to a bar, or the park; would he call a friend and hike across the George Washington Bridge? Other more lurid images I pushed away. I could only follow his back till it disappeared from view, and I knew all the while he was regretting the day he met me.

I went in to check on Elizabeth. She was quiet and eager for privacy or sleep, as if she needed refuge from the electricity he and I had discharged. I pulled the armchair—our armchair—over to the window. I tried to read Anthony Trollope—perhaps the boils of English society, gently lanced, would soothe me.

Slowly, with skillful hand, the picture built of lovely estates and gracious characters beset with the problems of ordinary English life. My restlessness grew. I needed a more violent story, one of my own century. I picked up a paperback copy of a biography of Christine Jorgensen, the man who had been changed to a woman by clever surgery—courtesy of modern Denmark. The story started with the little boy surprised in the act of trying on his mother's brassiere and panties. I couldn't concentrate. Someday maybe they would make a pill, no nasty operation necessary, and everyone could choose a sexual identity and perhaps switch back and forth at different stages of life. If I was angry with my husband, I could spite him the ultimate spite and change my sex so that he could no longer claim my passive attending love. I would not be waiting at the window while he stalked out into the night. But then I thought about it more graphically. To have that incredible member grafted on, swelling and shrinking and hanging about, dangling between my legs—how would I walk or sit? And then I would have to give up all the pleasures that I was so used to—lying outstretched on the bed with my womb silent, unfelt, but expecting, reacting, infinite in its possibilities. How could I possibly give up my body and myself, waiting for things to enter me, to travel up and down dark areas, and split and divide? The caves of my own personal labyrinth could be explored endlessly. I decided to wait for Paul and not be so very angry with him.

I saw the drugstore close and the owner pull his iron gate across the windows filled with bubble bath, lipsticks, hairbrushes and inviting pictures of sultry girls sporting cosmetics that I always finally bought, only to be disappointed in their effect. I watched the crowds move up and down the street: the students, male and female, arms about each other, sandals, long hair, Indian prints and tinted glasses—a style of life that fairly shouted of psychedelic secrets and rejected station wagons and homes in the country. I watched, leaning out the window on my elbows, too high to clearly make out faces, but low enough to feel the surge, the rhythm of the girls in their Afro haircuts, men in dashikis, Puerto Rican women bulging in satin dresses, the smell of sex. I was suspended above the street like a smiling Humpty-Dumpty Macy's Day balloon, as if the strings to my shape were being held by some small men down below. I wanted to deflate, to be down there, pouring from the subway, out of the movie, stopping to stare, to eat pizza and ice-cream cones, to wander in the glare of the lights.

Many hours later the avenue became quiet, an addict or two walking in slow motion, each slipping through his private fog. There was an old man exercising a dog of indiscriminate origin. The fire engines break the quiet with their shrieking sirens. A half hour later they come quietly back down the other side of Broadway. I am eager one day to see something with rich red flames burn all the way to the ground.

Later still. I am not able to sleep alone. I wait by the window.

The bar on the corner releases its last boisterous patrons, who flow onto the middle of the street; with drunken bravado they shout at the occasionally passing cars. Time is no longer contained within the numbers of the clock. I am orbiting. Many years or moments may be passing. I am adrift with other lifeless matter in the solar system, and simultaneously I am listening for a sound at the front door.

At last the bell rings. He had left without his keys. He comes over to me, pale and tired, his eyes like pages in last winter's magazine left in the waiting room of a dentist. "I went to see a Betty Grable movie," he said. "You would have liked it." The anger was gone, and with his return I again felt myself complete, no longer a discarded fragment or a bit of peeling from the old paint. I was a whole, excavated treasure, an amphora waiting to be filled. We went immediately to bed, the important thing no longer the crayoned paper or his desertion, or my long night of waiting. It was now just the touch of each other, familiar and tender, exciting without being frightening. Suddenly as we slipped together I remembered I had not, not expecting him, not planning for the evening to end this way, I had not put in my diaphragm, and it was sitting on a shelf in the medicine chest where it served me not at all. I thought of saying something, of stopping us, and then decided, or perhaps more accurately gave up making a decision, and relaxed into a love that would last uninterrupted by other pressures for a short while.

We did not go out to New Jersey. I called my mother and told her Elizabeth had a cold. (A lie is a wish, I read somewhere: do I so punish Elizabeth for her crayoning on history notes?) All morning I poured coffee down us to fight the fatigue of too much feeling. Tomorrow things will be back to normal.

"Working-Class Mothers May Not Have Much, But There's a Lot of Us!"

by MYRNA WOOD

The following discussion took place between Myrna Wood, a member of the women's-liberation movement in New York, and a woman who came from an economically depressed rural area. These two women met through a community organizing project. Their friendship formed, in fact, a women's-liberation group of two, and their discussions over the years have affected not only their consciousness as women but also the growth of their politics in general.

You came from a rural mining area. . . . Would you like to go back?

No. I wouldn't like to go back now, because I'm married to a laborer and the mines aren't really working. There is also a very large steel plant in the town, and it's not working, either. It's bought out by a big company. None of the men of the town are employed, and haven't been for a number of years.

Your family broke up, didn't they?

My father left my mother. I think they were separated long before he left.

What do you think that did to her?

My mother? Well, you have to understand that this is a very, very small town, and when my father left it was with another woman from that same town. They live in a house about a mile from my mother, and, you know, my mother's pride is hurt, she's very bitter. She started drinking, . . . she doesn't drink all the time, but the frustration builds up until finally she just sits down and gets a couple of bottles and gets stoned right out of her mind, and then she goes along for a couple of more months.

Her whole life left her when your father left?

Right, because my mother never did anything except everything my father wanted done. She lived her whole life for him.

He said supper at four o'clock and that's when it was there, on the table and waiting. And he said this is where we'll go on Monday night and that's what they did on Monday night. But it was always what he said and what he wanted. My mother never did anything on her own and she never had even a dime to spend without his OK.

How did you leave that small town?

I left there because I became pregnant. I had left home, doing housework, and my mother found out I was pregnant and she broke the news to my father, and he was going to kill me. She quieted him down and calmed him—took care of that end of it. Really why I left was because I was pregnant and we were fighting so much. And he used to beat me up and he used to beat my brothers and sisters up, too. I was scared, and so I left. My mother asked me to come home and we talked about it and she cried a lot and she cut her fruitcake—I'll never forget that, because my mother never cuts her fruitcake before Christmas Day. This was about two weeks before and she cut a piece, and I really felt bad. Because I had hurt her. But then I found that it wasn't her so much as what if the neighbors found out. That's what she was worrying about more than that I might have to go through something really difficult because I was young—I was only fifteen.

So they sent you away to the big city?

Yes. I really think, to be fair with my mother, that she was hoping that if I got away I might be able to gain some of the things that she never could, 'cause I know those are things that my mother always dreamed of doing. Like getting out of that town and seeing places that she had never seen.

What about you then, when you were young and got to the big city—did you want to do something besides get married?

Yeah, I think I would have— I don't know, though—I was

pretty young and pretty lonely and scared all the time. I had lost my baby and I had really wanted it—like that was the first thing that I ever had that was really mine and that I could really love. And it was a pretty bad experience. It took me a long, long time to get over that.

I think that maybe if I had never met anyone who wanted to marry me it wouldn't have bothered me that much, because I was happy working. I had a fairly good job I really liked, and it was really a surprise to me that I could do it. I found that when they trained me for something I learned it fairly quickly and I enjoyed it. And that surprised me. 'Cause my father was always telling me what a stupid bitch I was. And I really think down deep I believed it, you know? Still do. So when you find that you can do something it really comes as a surprise, and I'm not being boastful—I was really amazed that I could do it.

But you did get married?

Yes. I really, really looked up to him, when we were first married, I didn't think he could do anything wrong. I worshiped him, and that's very bad in marriage. Because I found out that he was human after all, and I had to learn to live with him. And it isn't too bad, living with a human being.

Back in those years what did you think of birth control?

I didn't know anything about it. Obviously. We didn't have the pill, and the only other thing I had ever tried after the first baby was a diaphragm. But I'm allergic to the rubber and it's the same with a condom, so I couldn't use them.

What do you think of it now that you have two teenage children?

Well, I have two children who are old enough to either get pregnant or cause someone to become pregnant, and I think they should know and that's why they've been told. I would like my daughter to be in the position that if she is going with someone she should have birth-control pills. I'm a firm believer in that, because I'm thirty-three years old and I'm not stupid enough to think that she's never going to do anything before she's married. And I don't ever want her to have to go through an experience like I did.

Do you think most women are dissatisfied in some way with their lives?

Right—even the ones who say, "Oh, those crazy women's-liberation groups—aw, those women are nuts," and stuff like this. I think I would be safe in saying that half the women in the world are not even aware of the fact that they're downtrodden or put upon or whatever the hell way you want to put it. They are not aware of it because they never stop to think of it, because their mothers were like that and their grandmothers, and all the women they know are like that, and so if they know twenty women and they have a bit of an edge on those twenty women they think they've got it made. This is the whole damn thing.

What does your husband think of women's liberation?

Scares him to death. But at the same time he listens and we talk about a lot of things and he always ends up saying things like "Well, I don't care if you get liberated. You can get liberated all you want, but I'm always the boss around here." But I think he really is scared.

He was saying to me that he thought men were as oppressed as women, if not more oppressed than they.

That's true and you will find, just in our own acquaintance-ship, a few couples where the wife is really very dominant. We know this couple where this guy doesn't have one minute to himself or nothing that he can call his own, there is nothing in his life. And his wife continuously bitches at him. Why does she bitch at him? Because she's so damn frustrated with the way she has to live. But she is very unhappy and so she takes it out on her husband. He *is* oppressed! I know that he feels this way because he is a workingman, and he can't find jobs suitable to raise his children like they should be—and he works twelve hours a day, six days a week. There are a million men just like him in the world. Well, goddammit, they're not liberated, either. This is what we're fighting for, isn't it? Equal pay, equal time, equal rights.

So she's doing the same thing to him that most men do to women?

Right, and if she can't get what she wants any other way, by bitching, by crying, by fighting, then she uses sex, it's very simple. And eventually he's the kind of man that gives in to her. And my husband looks at this guy and says, "That poor bugger, talk about oppressed, that poor bugger needs to be liberated." What I would like to make him see is that they both need something better.

And it's like my own husband, who is laid off right now and that's why I'm working. He would rather I didn't work and prefers to have me home. He knows that I've got seven children and the house to run and that's enough. He knows that there's a lot of other things that I like to do, like this for instance, and I don't have time for it, and yet if I wasn't working, I still probably couldn't do them, because I couldn't afford to. Because it does take money for babysitters to go to meetings, and if you get involved in things it does take a certain amount of time. And it just is not available. . . . And what happens then is that I get so worried and involved in these problems at home, that I couldn't do anything and function properly in any group anyway. It really makes it hard. But then I also realize that the only way that we're going to get out of it is if we get together and do something about it. So no matter how little time and money you have you're going to have to do it eventually, anyway.

Most women would find it very difficult to get out of the house to work in the movement or to even go to meetings one or two nights a week.

Yes, they would. Probably three fourths of those women couldn't: they have children, they can't leave, there's no money —it's just not possible.

And they might have problems with their husbands, too.

This is true. And I think this is part of what women's liberation is going to have to do; like it's not the university men, because I think they know—or maybe they don't really know, I don't know what I'm talking about here—but the ordinary workingmen have their weird ideas about women's liberation, like the women are going to rise up and beat hell out of them or something. They're really scared. I mean, how many women are going to stand up and fight their husbands night and day for something? It makes it a really bad home to live in and you don't want to be fighting with your husband, because most women love their husbands. And would like to more so if they could. But they get so damn frustrated with the way they have to live that they can't.

So what's really got to be done is that these men have to be educated in what the hell we're fighting for, because what we're fighting for is really for their betterment, too. I mean, hell, if I can go out and do a job and make the same money that a man would make doing the same job, well, I'd be making double the money I'm making now, so, dammit, I'd only have to work two days a week to make what I'm making right now, and I could have three days at home. So I'm bettering my family. If he could understand that I'm fighting for better working conditions, better pay, better jobs for women, that's to his advantage.

I don't think that you can get a really good women's-liberation movement without somehow or other involving men, because in this kind of family, let's face it, if I want to get involved in something that's going to take a day, or two days, or two nights a week, who is going to babysit? Well, my husband. He has got to believe in what I'm doing or he's not going to spend all that time babysitting. If I argue with him and he says, "Oh, go," then what's going to happen, he's going to be miserable and who is going to pay for it? The kids.

And you.

Right, and I'm not going to go, because I don't want that kind of situation at home. But I also find—I don't know about other husbands, but with mine if I sit down and talk to him and listen to what he's saying, sooner or later you find out what the fear is. Then, if you can discuss it and make him understand how you feel and point out what it is that you're trying to do, nine times out of ten he can see. Not always. But a lot of the time he can see where you're right. Or he might say, "Well, all right, if it means that much to you, I don't go along with it, but go ahead."

What does he think of your working?

Well, I don't really know. Because he never wanted me to work, ever. But this winter when he's been unemployed—well, I said, "It's better if I work, because we're not going to survive the winter if I don't." And I got a chance to get this job and I really like it—and in that I'm really lucky, because a lot of women are doing work that they don't like to do, and I'm getting fairly good pay, so therefore I don't mind going to work.

There's a big change from the way your husband felt about your working in the past.

Right, even two years ago he wouldn't even hear of it. But I also know that if I kept on working in the summer and if we were having trouble with all the children being at home, he'd probably get upset and he'd want me to quit.

How much do you make?

I make $1.55 an hour, and for a salesgirl that's not bad, around here it's usually $1.30 an hour.

You and I are exactly the same age and have similar backgrounds. What would you say accounts for the difference in our lives?

Number one, seven kids. Makes a big difference.

You had the seven children and I didn't. I got divorced.

Something that was strongly put into us when we were growing up was that once you got married you stayed that way. You never got out of it. During the years when things were *really* bad and maybe I had lots of reason to get divorced or leave or just give it up, that attitude was still there—you stayed, no matter what. And I stayed. Besides, by the time I got to thinking, well, to hell with it, maybe I would leave, I'd already had four children, and what was I going to do with them? And in no way did I want to leave my children. And really now, after sixteen years, I don't really want to leave my husband either. We don't agree on a lot of things, sometimes I feel him to be unreasonable, and sometimes I feel that he's domineering, but like I said before, I had to learn to live with a human being. Well, he's doing the same thing. And all in all, I can't think of anybody else I'd sooner live with. Besides, sixteen years makes a lot of ties. Although at times I'd like to be away, maybe when my kids are all grown up I'll be able to go more, but—how can I explain it—I don't ever want to be really free of him all the time.

What do you think of the women's-liberation movement?

Well, you may not like what I say, but I think right now that the women's-liberation movement isn't doing a whole hell of a lot to help me. And when I say me, I mean my kind of people. Although I really think it would be a great thing that if I got pregnant I could go and ask for an abortion, I don't think that's the most important thing in my life right now. I know it's an important part of it. Although I think it would be a really great thing to be able to come in and say to my husband, "Sorry, I'm going away for the weekend," and demand my freedom, that's not the most important thing. And I think that the women's-liberation movement could be a really great group.

What is the most important thing?

Well, those things are important because they're all tied in together, but they are not the whole thing. I think that women's liberation has got to be the kind of group that is willing to go out and educate the husbands and men. And it's got to be involving people like me and the things that are really important to us. Like if we've *got* to work, we need a job where we can earn a decent salary. Women who are living alone should be able to support their own families. A woman who would like to have a child and is not married should have some kind of way that she could support that child as well as if it had a father, because that's half the stigma of an illegitimate child, isn't it, the fact that it's not going to have the same advantages as a child with a father. Why? It should have.

Most of the people in the women's movement now are unmarried and young.

And this is one thing that's wrong with the women's movement. Women's liberation cannot possibly be for just unmarried women, it can't be just for university women, it can't just be for white women, it has got to be for every woman. Every woman has got to be involved. And you've got to have a meeting where you can listen to what I want to beef about, because these are the things that are wrong with my life. These are the things that I want to be damn well liberated from. You want to listen to the lady down the street and the woman from the university, because her beefs are legitimate, too, but you can't liberate one group of women. It isn't going to work. And I know that you really believe in women's liberation, but the article that was written by what's-his-name, Tiger [Lionel Tiger, author of *Men in Groups*] well, maybe he had a point there.

He says that men can band together.

He says that men have the ability to band together and that women don't have it. Well, OK, when are we going to prove him wrong? Because we haven't proved him wrong. We know damn well that he is wrong, but if you're going to liberate only one type of woman, then you're doing exactly what he's saying. Why can't the female doctor come together in the same group with the female nurse, along with the female teacher, along with the female housewife, or unmarried mother, or a black woman, or a yellow woman or that red Indian? They're all females. And if you don't do it you haven't got anything. Because I'll tell you, I would probably be safe in saying that a whole lot more than half of the women in the world are not university-educated women.

I was thinking, when you said men have banded together you were referring to unions, and men do have experience because they work, while women are usually in their kitchens.

That's right, they needed to get together. And you'll find, too, that if you look at men and women as groups you'll find that men as a group—when they go out in the evening, they sit around and talk about things, they might even fight. But at least they're standing on an issue somewhere, even if it's a stupid issue and means nothing. Like who is the strongest. They've done this right down through the generations.

So what do women do, they get together over coffee, and what do they do—they talk about the one that isn't there. And about their husbands and what dirty deals they got and about their kids and how worried they are about them, and everybody tries to outdo everybody else on the best housekeeping and the best cooking and getting their laundry out the whitest and the earliest because these are the things that have always been the most important to women. Until recently. And I'm wrong there, too, because even as far as the early part of this century, women were concerned about other things, because we had the suffragettes, let's face it.

Women are really put down—they've been put down so damn long that we don't really think that we can do anything. It's like me when I got a job that I really never thought I could do. It's the same thing. They're made to think that the only thing they know how to do is to look after the home and children, and most women think that they can't even think anything halfway worth bothering about. When, really, if you sit down and get women to talking about things besides their kids or problems with their husband, they can say some really great things and they don't even know they're saying them. If you just stop and listen, and then you have to make them aware of the fact that, Christ, you thought this up all by yourself, you're saying it— because they don't realize that they have a mind.

What would you say the future of our present movement would depend on?

Well, that's a foregone conclusion—it depends on getting all the women involved. Not just single women or young women. I don't think that women's liberation is going to do a whole lot for me, because we don't have time. I'm thirty-three years old, by the time there is any great change made, let's face it, it's too late for me for a lot of things that can't be changed. But I'd like to think that if I worked for it, it would mean a big change for my daughters. And I also feel that if I can get thinking this way and other women can get thinking this way, then they can talk to their daughters, so they are going to have a whole different outlook and it's going to be a whole lot easier for them. Not only that, but they can do the same thing with their sons, which is really important. That means that women's liberation in the next generation isn't going to have to go around educating all these husbands.

Do you think that we could have a time when we would not need the family system as we have it now?

Yeah, probably, it's going to have to change. If I knew as much and looked at things the same way when I was seventeen as I do now, I might never have gotten married, and yet I really wanted children. This is a change in family life right there. No woman with several children can hold down two steady jobs indefinitely—sooner or later your body is going to give out. You can't do it. A man is physically stronger than a woman, and he couldn't do it. So there is going to have to be some kind of change there or women are never going to be able to do what they'd like to do. And yet I couldn't picture my life without children. Even if I went back now with the same knowledge, I think I'd still like to have children. And you can't have both the way it is now. I know how tired you can get. And I have a husband and children who help a lot. But there are a lot of women who don't have that. If I was alone with those children and also had to work it could be a really bad situation. So if you want all these things, obviously the family situation has to change.

To refer back to Mr. Tiger, a lot of people say that women do not have close relationships with each other. They are always in competition, as they were trained to be. But I notice that you always have friends that you help with their problems, either financial or personal, and they help you in return. Therefore, couldn't you imagine women's-liberation groups beginning on that level, as housewives and friends around the block—for instance, get together and discuss their problems in a more formal way than just having coffee in the morning?

Sure they could, there is no reason why they couldn't. I might go to one place and the woman has certain problems and she needs someone to talk to about them—she's alone with children. And so if I'm sympathetic and she knows I won't say anything she'll talk to me about them. If I can help I do, and then I might go to the next house and she might have certain problems and it's the same thing over again. But the woman in the first house doesn't want the woman in the second house to know that she has any problems, and vice versa. I don't know why they're that way.

They think their problems are unique and something to be embarrassed about.

Right, they're embarrassed about the fact that they're in a fix. For instance, one woman on our block has no husband, her husband deserted her. That woman has never really gotten over it, like my mother, and it's not "what the neighbors think" and it isn't really hurt pride—I think it's the fact that she didn't make it as a woman. That really bothers her, you see. Deep down inside, that really bothers her, because she couldn't hang on to her man. It's really stupid. She's forever saying, "I was a really good wife, always lived my whole life for him, and then what thanks do I get—he's gone." Which goes to prove that men don't always want that, I guess.

I don't believe that. Naturally, if my husband walked out on me, I'd want to find out why. But it's like a man saying the only reason his wife would ever leave him is for another man. My husband thinks that way. The only reason I'd ever leave him is for another man—why? Because it's an ego-booster. And women are the same way. They haven't really made it as a woman if they don't have a baby or if they can't hold on to their man. It's stupid, but it's so.

But when women talk to each other, they find out that others have the same problems.

Of course. There are two ladies on our block who live side by side. They were both left with children and no money, and they are trying to solve these problems in different ways. But the damn problem is the same. And all it takes is for one person outside to hear both stories and to say, "Do you know, the same happened to her?" The next step is to get them together. And we all get to discussing it. Hell, I can tell you about a few times my husband left me, too. We can discuss this. It may not seem very important, but it's a beginning. The next thing you know you've got a meeting, and the next thing you know you've got a liberation group.

I'd like to see a really good women's-liberation movement.

I'd like to see women getting together and working together and not patronizing one another. I know what I feel women's liberation should be to me, but I find it difficult to find how to put it into words. But I really feel that it's going to have to involve all women. Right from the top to the bottom, you've got to get them all. And I think you've got to start with the biggest group available, and that's the ones at the bottom. And if you do that, the rest will follow, maybe.

Let's face it, we may not have much, but there's a lot of us!

Divorced Mothers as a Political Force

by GAIL SHEEHY

Gail Sheehy is a contributing editor to *New York* magazine and writes frequently for many other magazines as well. She is the author of *Lovesounds,* a novel about the breakup of a marriage, and *Speed Is of the Essence,* a collection of her articles.

When you step off the bus on New York's West Ninety-fifth Street after six, your footfalls echo in the canyon of divorced mothers. Mitchell-Lama houses rise like brick mountains in every direction. The streets are deserted. The babysitters have gone. The working moms have come home to their hurry-up children. Up they go twenty stories into these subsidized houses for scrambling-to-be-middle-incomers, safe from human contact, soundly trapped in adult detention homes. Now is the hour for the phone to ring in the canyon of divorced mothers. For the voice of the office hero to offer, "I'm in the neighborhood, how about I come up for an intimate drink?" The answer is simple. "What happens in this apartment at seven is we all eat peanut butter sandwiches and watch *I Dream of Jeannie.*"

This is a political issue?

One recent evening in the canyon five women met to make it so by launching a brand-new battle for NOW (National Organization for Women) in behalf of single, divorced and separated mothers. They were doing a dry run as panelists for NOW's May 4 speakout entitled "Is Mother's Day a Meaningless Hypocrisy?" From there will proceed active support for bills before the state legislature—one to permit full deduction for the cost of child care as ordinary business expense, another to prohibit discrimination in housing because of marital status. Still being formulated are proposals to eliminate required information about age, marital status and dependents from employment applications; to expand centers for child care and aid-to-youth (teenage) care, and to enforce court support orders. Finally there is the hope of establishing vocational-rehabilitation centers. NOW is suggesting the state borrow back some of the $883,583 in funds presently supporting conciliation centers—a piety which came in with the new divorce law and has proved less than effective.

Our panelists came to rehearsal on the bus to save cab fare for their sitters. Five single mothers over thirty with three master's degrees among them, their hands prominently veined and conspicuously ringless, their faces attractive but with no moist expectancies left in the eyes, their bodies stylishly pantsed but steadily depreciating in the flesh market. Invisible people until now—though they have on their side some very heavy statistics:

One American family in ten is now headed by a woman.

Eight million children under the age of eighteen are being cared for by single women.

The median income of these families with eight million children headed by women is $4,000. Compare this with the median family income of $11,600 for families headed by men.

Only 9 percent of families headed by women in 1969 had incomes over $10,000.

After the liberalization of the divorce law, New York State's 14,454 divorces in 1968 leaped in 1969 to 26,462.

On the national level, total families increased by 14 percent in the last decade, while female-headed families multiplied by 24 percent.

What the statistics don't tell is that most of these women come out of that vast, forgotten era of pre-pill, pre-lib, pre-career, pre-commune, pre–Masters and Johnson marriage for love. Their attitudes have changed, but one unalterable fact about their lives hasn't—the presence of children to support.

"Single mothers are our most oppressed members," says Jackie

Ceballos, the new president of NOW, who claims to know because she is a single mother herself. "The real power of the movement will be coming from this group." But why silent for so long? Single mothers have also been the most scared group, says Jackie Ceballos, and once having tiptoed through two years of torment in therapy sessions, they want to forget.

Another unspoken reason is that NOW drew most of its former spokeswomen from young singles, safely married professionals and lesbians. None of these were particularly interested in the problems of divorce and child support. In fact, much of the early writing from all quarters of the movement offered men relief from alimony, as a tradeoff in the argument that women's lib would bring liberation to men too. Many potential members turned off NOW, believing it supported the abolition of alimony. Definitely not, says the new leadership, until something better such as marriage insurance is worked out. Let us not forget the mature woman without skills whose husband renews his life at forty with the help of his nubile secretary.

Our five gay divorcees begin talking out their problems in order of importance. "Most men assume what heads the list is sex," says Louise, an original member of Parents Without Partners. "The men you work with think they'll do you a favor and come home with you. If you don't respond, you have trouble on the job." The truth is, no woman has trouble getting sex if she wants it. The single mother's list begins with basics: money, child care, housing, job.

Right off the bat this discussion departs from most women's-lib raps. Age holds the upper hand. For a husband, the years between twenty-five and thirty-five are crucial in taking him over the middle-management hump. The same period for wives is peak child-rearing time. As the latest U.S. Labor Department report notes, "Among women heads of family between the ages of 25 to 45—presumably the prime candidates for training and employment—nearly half have three children or more."

There is a ceiling on the number of years a woman can trade on the pure flesh market, as no one knows better than these single mothers.

Did I say gay divorcees? Most of them work to provide a separate bedroom for their children.

"We're all living on top of our kids," offers Verna as problem number one. On the salary of a college instructor she is trying to survive in the city with two sons. The natural comeback is, Why did you get a divorce? "The big myth," says Verna, "is that we are shrews who rejected our men. The truth usually is . . . we were dying." Verna's husband was an alcoholic. For a year after the divorce she went to sleep at nine, when the kids did. The morning after her first date, the ladies of the suburbs expressed shock. Verna moved to Manhattan, driven out because she was ousted from her babysitting pool.

The next problem is the cost of getting out of the apartment to look for a job. Child care is not considered an "ordinary and necessary business expense" by the Internal Revenue Service. Under a special exemption category, divorced, deserted and separated women can deduct only $600 for care of one dependent, $900 for two dependents or more. Real-life working mothers pay anywhere from $1,000 to $5,000 for the sitters who are the cornerstone of their feeble independence. Furthermore, it's a rare tax attorney who knows that the $6,000 income ceiling on deductions for child care *does not* apply to divorced women (only married women).

"The solutions society offers us are all dependency solutions," says Kay, whose private life is now occupied with study of the legislative system. "Everyone pushes you to remain a child and remarry. It's too expensive for the state to think about finding jobs and financing retraining programs for single mothers."

Louise, a mature parent, knows the hoax of remarriage only too well. "Any man with a head on his shoulders is not about to marry a woman with several children who is looking for a meal ticket. Why should he take on the burden of expense dumped by the real father?"

Next problem: lying to get the job. Jane, the hostess, introduces herself as the editor of a small magazine and secret head of the household of four. Personnel interviewers used to say, "Three children—why aren't you home taking care of them!" Jane learned to fake it; she admits to only one child (not even her new and easily frightened boy friend knows). "Employers don't give a damn about the kids, they only care whether I'm going to be absent."

The myth abroad here is that America cares deeply for her children. But the move is on in New York to repeal the abortion law, rectify the welfare mess by throwing ADC [Aid to Dependent Children] mothers off the rolls first, and retract Medicaid payments for abortions to those who only recently gave up coat hangers. And now State Assemblyman Albert Blumenthal, a reform Democrat, is sponsoring a bill which would repeal alimony.

"The same folks who brought you My Lai are bringing you the slow death of American children," concludes Verna.

The rest of our panelists' problems roll out in sequence—lack of space, lack of sleep, the horror of losing their looks prematurely, the long wait for children to grow up so they can invite a man to dinner again without their sons asking, "Are you going to stay overnight?"

Hostess Jane looks around at the faces in her apartment, eight years after her divorce, and voices the unspeakable doubts. Her husband was a doctor. She put away a Phi Beta Kappa key to put him through medical school. Don't work, he said, and she had three babies instead. Take another sleeping pill, he said, until she became literally addicted to marriage. When pills stopped working, Jane's husband comforted her with needles full of barbiturates. "One day between four and eight, I sobered up long enough to get out." But how could she divorce a *doctor?* her mother demanded—"Happy schmappy, the man is supporting you!"

Tonight Jane's son is asleep in the dining alcove. He is teenaged, and his feet hang over the cot. Her two daughters are cramped into the small bedroom. She, Jane, is thirty-six years old with certain truths to face. Her blond mane is a little wheatier, and where there was a perfect size eight filling her hot pants, the thighs are now turning to porridge. Jane knows that she will never, not remotely, make a living to touch her ex-husband's $40,000-a-year medical practice.

"After eight miserable years I have one loan from Household Finance, one from Tenafly Finance, a lawsuit from Gimbels and two hundred dollars a month alimony—which the state may be about to take away." She wonders if Mother was right.

"No!" chorus the panelists. "You'd be just another drunk wife in the suburbs," says Louise. "At least you have the dignity of independence," reminds Kay. And then someone wonders aloud how it would be to look forward, on the way home from a hard day at the office, to someone waiting dinner and ready to rub one's feet.

"Don't you sometimes wish you had a wife?"

Mother Courage and Her Children

by JUANITA SIMPSON, interviewed by TODD GITLIN
and NANCI HOLLANDER

One of the founders of SDS and a long-time activist in radical movements, Todd Gitlin writes widely on political issues. Nanci Hollander is also an activist; her photographs have appeared in underground magazines and newspapers.

Courage has learned nothing from disasters that befall her.
—BERTOLT BRECHT

Juanita Simpson and her four sons—David, Carl, Michael, and Joe—are some of uptown Chicago's many Indians. Actually she is half American Indian: her father was East Indian—"they are the original Indians, you know; old Indians"—and she tries to fuse her two Indian backgrounds in a single identity. Because she fails, she finds herself not so much an Indian as simply a resident of Clifton Avenue. Though dark skin brings her and her sons some dark looks, they are as much at home in race-spotted Uptown as they would be anywhere. "How are you?" you ask. "Oh, just here."

Her husband was killed in a hunting accident five years ago; she is on welfare. Michael is mentally retarded—at age twelve he is still in the third grade of the public school. Carl is a junior in high school. He paints surrealist visions. He and Private First Class David share an intellectuality and an interest in science usually attributed only to the children of the middle classes.

Mrs. Simpson—no one ever uses her first name—is illiterate in English. She is very religious, something of a mystic, though her thoughts are on this world, not the next. Harking apocalyptically to Masonry, ESP, and yoga, she remains a realist.

She will do what is right for her children at any cost; she is Mother Courage.

It is no honor to have to be on relief or Aid to Dependent Children. It's no disgrace, but it's not no honor. It does something to you, something that I can't explain very deep. It makes you feel like you've lost all your rights. You have no right to vote —you feel that way. You feel that you have nothing to look forward to. You are walking around dead in mind, you can't even think straight. The category they put you in, you don't feel human any more. After they get through talking to you you feel just so low like you're just smaller than a little animal. There just isn't any foundation in it. You're not getting anywheres. You're going farther back instead of ahead. And sometimes it just seems impossible to buy food and pay rent, buy clothes. And to look decent and to *live* decent and to *be* decent you have a pretty rough time in this world. 'Course, it pays off in the long run, because you want to be decent, but *because* you want to be decent and respectable the big guy thinks you are a fool. They think you have no right to try to go forward, because you are on some kind of relief or Aid to Dependent Children. It keeps the kids in a bad frame of mind when they aren't living under nice conditions. They don't allow you to have a television. If you got a television you got to sell it. If you got a new radio or anything in the house new, maybe it doesn't cost over ten or fifteen dollars, they want to know how did you buy it.

So you have to live as poor as you can, what else can you do? You don't have the money to do nothing with. Half the time we don't have enough chairs in the house. Now, as it is, to sit on we got, I think, three chairs in the kitchen, because we got burned out and lost everything we had. We got a table in there that the welfare gave us; the legs is broke on it, they need fixing. That's the way they give it to us. Supposed to be one hundred thirty dollars' worth of furniture and it's nothing but junk. Got a bed in there, it's about to fall apart. And I mean, well, living under those conditions, it's just hard for me to explain to you—I'm trying the best I can. When you leave home you hate to come back. It's just that depressing.

And many times you know people you would like to invite

to your house but you don't want to invite them because you figure, well, our house doesn't look as good as theirs, or probably the Social Service might come in and want to know, "Well, who are these people visiting you?" If they sit down at your table and you give them a cup of coffee and the caseworker comes by, they want to know, "Is this person contributing any finance toward your family? And where does this person live and where does this person work?" And you just don't have no rights as a citizen when you get on this here assistance that they give you. It's very nerveracking. It keeps you under a mental strain. You go to bed nervous, you get up nervous. You want to do better, but you don't have anything to go upon to do better.

Then they'll offer you some kind of a little job that doesn't pay no more than maybe seventy-five cents an hour, working probably five days a week. And if you have a family of four children or five children, you cannot support those children on that type of money and pay rent and buy food and clothes for 'em and send 'em to school looking as decent as any other children that are decent-looking going to school. Well, if you don't accept that type of job that they give you, many times they cut your help off, which is your assistance, or they hold your check up. And I mean you just aren't making any progress. You're just at a standstill.

They take away all your decency. If you have a grandmother that's dead, they will ask you all of the details on her background. And she can't do you no good, because she's dead and buried. And your grandfather's dead—they will ask you about him. He can't do you no good, he's dead and buried. They ask you your whole life's history. They almost ask you why were you born.

My oldest boy, he went in the service. When we got burned out he was very much disturbed. We was sleeping on floors at some friends of ours. He got hisself together one day and he made up his mind on the spur of the moment. He said, "I want you to sign these papers. I'm going into the Army. I'm sick of being on this here kind of thing they call aid. It's embarrassing to be on this. When I go to seek employment, when they find out how old I am, they say I'm not old enough for full-time work. I have to do part-time work after school. If I get a job and work," he says, "part time it isn't enough to do any good. And the minute the Social Service finds out you are working part time they will deduct that off of your check." So my son, who is seventeen years old, says, "I'm going in the service, I'm going in the Army. They can take their little help and keep it."

Now, those are the words he told me: "I'll be able to finish my education in there and I'll get a wonderful training. I'll at least know that I'll be eating at least three meals a day. I don't know what kind of meals they'll be, but they'll at least be meals."

Now that he is in the service, this caseworker thinks that he should send his allotment home to me. And he doesn't get that much money. When he gets out of the service he's planning on getting married. Now this caseworker wants him to give me his allotment so that they can deduct that off my budget. Which I wouldn't be able to live off of that small amount that he would send me home.

So then I informed the caseworker when he first went in, that he was in the service. Well, now, Mrs. Morelli, she's a very fine caseworker, she didn't take him off of the check. So just before Christmas another caseworker comes out to the house, a new one, a young lad. He says to me, "Mrs. Simpson," he says, "we forgot to take your son off of your budget. Now I will have to deduct seventy-four dollars off of your check in the month of January. So what you do, your son was allowed thirty-two dollars," he says. "So you take the thirty-two dollars, since your son is not here anyhow, and," he says, "save it till the month of January. And you won't be so short when we take this big lump off of your check."

I says, "Well, can't you take part of it now and part another time?"

He says, "No, the record's made out already and sent in." You know he knows, he's a caseworker. He is supposed to know. Sure he knows. I says OK.

How can you save? What can you save and how can you save? Well, it's fair for them to take him off the budget. He's not living here with me to receive that money. But I reported it to the first social worker. If you be decent with 'em, you see what happens, huh?

So I mean it's very disgusting really when you think of it all. And there's no future. I mean it does something to the youngster's mind. And the majority of the youngsters, it makes almost criminals out of 'em because the conditions they are living under. Most of the majority of people that are on relief, Aid to Dependent Children—their children, they don't have the privileges that other people's children have, because most of the time they don't have necessary food, and without necessary food, without eating proper, children cannot sit in the classroom in the school and study properly. They can't think as clear as other children that have those things.

Some families, they have mother and father. The father works and he makes a good salary and he is able to buy the necessary foods that they require for children to give the necessary vitamins and calcium. People on relief, they eat a lot of starches. They'll eat rice maybe two, three days in succession, probably cereals, oatmeal, and a lot of potatoes. Well, to be frank with you, they really need meat every day, not once or twice a week. So if they don't get those necessary things they become weak. The majority of children, that's why they keep getting sicker and sicker, because they don't have the proper foods, and not enough vitamins like meat, vegetables. A family that has four children, they have to live off of a dollar a day, approximately thirty cents for each meal. That isn't sufficient for children; children need milk every day. But you're lucky if they get one glass of milk a day, and this is very true. Like now my son came in from school and he asked me in the kitchen, "Ma, do we have any milk in the refrigerator?" I had very little in there. He would not drink it. He said, "Leave it for the little ones, because it's not enough to go around for all of 'em."

They're very much worried and concerned about those other

people that are hungry and starving over in other countries, and many of the people right here in this country are eating out of garbage cans. I have saw this with my own two eyes. I don't see too much about where they're trying to solve the problem here.

Alternate-Culture Mirror America

by MARGARITA DONNELLY

Margarita Donnelly is a feminist, a mother, and a writer of poems and what she terms "prose-pieces," such as the one that follows.

Oh, it was beautiful to be the earth mother. It was middle America in the year 1966 and the crossroads were Haight and Ashbury and many of us women were pregnant . . . what else can you expect with free love . . . we were the Sweet Lorraines and Lady Madonnas and for nine months it was groovier than hell.

We walked the streets like queens . . . the world was at our feet . . . our minds and bodies pregnant with the wisdom of life and love . . . the sacred vessels of our men's desires, the harbingers of the new world to come. We would bring forth new life . . . the new generation and love would come into its own. I became a poem hanging on the beauty of love and the poetry of words words words . . . music was around us, everywhere . . . it was around us and in our beings. We were new and different and undaunted. Oh great middle mirror America . . . it was around us but not touching us.

So it went our world along its separate (?) course . . . symbolically independent . . . but the summer of love came and with it the babies . . . reality strode heavy into our lives . . . babies in all their full bloom with wild cries that didn't fit earth mother and Lady Madonna images. Our hip brothers forgot us . . . it's hard to be a queen after childbirth.

Bodies refuse their previous refinements . . . they make demands on any woman . . . so does the child. Most of the brothers skipped out . . . it didn't matter . . . we were strong and undaunted still. Love would suffice . . . our lives were independent . . . we did not need what our mothers had—security—material comfort—fathers for our children . . . we were a new culture . . . no ties or binds on anyone . . . but then the babies began to grow as they do . . . the men came and went . . . the scenes came and went . . . the summer of love wore its way out . . . the winter that followed became a horror of great middle mirror America . . . so some of us began to move . . . many of the sisters married their love brothers in ceremonies of their own in the woods and hills of great America . . . with simple love rites and our hippie love children at our feet . . . . we moved away to make new lives in the unknown places of our great land . . . but everywhere we went reality strode heavy into our lives . . . the men kept walking out . . . the children kept growing.

The enchantment wore off—our relationships deteriorated—the communes could not survive on leathercraft, bead stringing, and love—none of it was pure enough—true enough—no trip was "right" enough—the men kept splitting—the children kept growing—we kept finding ourselves alone with the children—children of the men who made our world. Flower children—suddenly defoliated.

Six years later those children stare at us finding lives defined by the only image that stands by them—their mothers' . . . women who have, in time, grown strong . . . who finally are rising . . . Standing up from years in the kitchens and nurseries of mirror America—undaunted and strong—still in contact with our feelings, we rise with wings at last—wings of rage and pity and freedom . . . crying tears with feelings that are still in contact with the earth and stars . . . but Powerful with the blood of our bodies and the sweat of our labors. We find our true alliances with our mothers and all our sisters—the wave is building, growing, gathering strength . . . our wild children grow strong with us . . . great middle mirror America lies exposed . . . our fathers and our flower children's fathers—two images blended into one reflection in the looking glass of alternate America.

Motherhood: Who Needs It?

by BETTY ROLLIN

Betty Rollin wrote this article (© Cowles Communications, Inc.) shortly before the demise of Look magazine, where she was a contributing editor.

Motherhood is in trouble, and it ought to be. A rude question is long overdue: Who needs it? The answer used to be (1) society and (2) women. But now, with the impending horrors of overpopulation, society desperately doesn't need it. And women don't need it, either. Thanks to the Motherhood Myth— the idea that having babies is something that all normal women instinctively want and need and will enjoy doing—they just *think* they do.

The notion that the maternal wish and the activity of mothering are instinctive or biologically predestined is baloney. Try asking most sociologists, psychologists, psychoanalysts, biologists—many of whom are mothers—about motherhood being instinctive; it's like asking department-store presidents if their Santa Clauses are real. "Motherhood—instinctive?" shouts distinguished sociologist-author Dr. Jessie Bernard. "Biological destiny? Forget biology! If it were biology, people would die from not doing it."

"Women don't need to be mothers any more than they need spaghetti," says Dr. Richard Rabkin, a New York psychiatrist. "But if you're in a world where everyone is eating spaghetti, thinking they need it and want it, you will think so, too. Romance has really contaminated science. So-called instincts have to do with stimulation. They are not things that well up inside of you."

"When a woman says with feeling that she craved her baby from within, she is putting into biological language what is psychological," says University of Michigan psychoanalyst and motherhood-researcher Dr. Frederick Wyatt. "There are no instincts," says Dr. William Goode, president-elect of the American Sociological Association. "There are reflexes, like eye-blinking, and drives, like sex. There is no innate drive for children. Otherwise, the enormous cultural pressures that there are to reproduce wouldn't exist. There are no cultural pressures to sell you on getting your hand out of the fire."

There are, to be sure, biologists and others who go on about biological destiny—that is, the innate or instinctive goal of motherhood. (At the turn of the century, even good old capitalism was explained by a theorist as "the *instinct* of acquisitiveness.") And many psychoanalysts still hold the Freudian view that women feel so rotten about not having a penis that they are necessarily propelled into the child-wish to replace the missing organ. Psychoanalysts also make much of the psychological need to repeat what one's parent of the same sex has done. Since every woman has a mother, it is considered normal to wish to imitate one's mother by being a mother.

There is, surely, a wish to pass on love if one has received it, but to insist women must pass it on in the same way is like insisting that every man whose father is a gardener has to be a gardener. One dissenting psychoanalyst says simply, "There is a wish to comply with one's biology, yes, but we needn't and sometimes we shouldn't." (Interestingly, the woman who has been the greatest contributor to child therapy and who has probably given more to children than anyone alive is Dr. Anna Freud, Freud's magnificent daughter, who is not a mother.)

Anyway, what an expert cast of hundreds is telling us is, simply, that biological *possibility* and desire are not the same as biological *need*. Women have childbearing equipment. For them to choose not to use the equipment is no more blocking what is instinctive than it is for a man who, muscles or no, chooses not to be a weightlifter.

So much for the wish. What about the "instinctive" *activity* of mothering? One animal study shows that when a young member of a species is put in a cage, say, with an older member of the same species, the latter will act in a protective, "maternal" way. But that goes for both males and females who have been "mothered" themselves. And studies indicate that a human baby will also respond to whoever is around playing mother—even if it's father. Margaret Mead and many others frequently point out that mothering can be a fine occupation, if you want it, for either sex. Another experiment with monkeys who were brought up without mothers found them lacking in maternal behavior toward their own offspring, and a similar study showed that monkeys brought up without other monkeys of the opposite sex had no interest in mating—all of which suggests that both mothering and mating behavior are learned, not instinctual. And, to turn the cart (or the baby carriage) around, baby ducks who lovingly followed their mothers seemed, in the mother's absence, to just as lovingly follow wooden ducks or even vacuum cleaners.

If motherhood isn't instinctive, when and why, then, was the Motherhood Myth born? Until recently, the entire question of maternal motivation was academic. Sex, like it or not, meant babies. Not that there haven't always been a lot of interesting contraceptive tries. But until the creation of the diaphragm in the 1880s, the birth of babies was largely unavoidable. And, generally speaking, nobody really seemed to mind. For one thing, people tend to be sort of good sports about what seems to be inevitable. For another, in the past, the population needed beefing up. Mortality rates were high, and agricultural cultures, particularly, have always needed children to help out. So because it "just happened" and because it was needed, motherhood was assumed to be innate.

Originally, it was the word of God that got the ball rolling with "Be fruitful and multiply," a practical suggestion, since the only people around then were Adam and Eve. But in no time, supermoralists like St. Augustine changed the tone of the message: "Intercourse, even with one's legitimate wife, is unlawful and wicked where the conception of the offspring is prevented," he, we assume, thundered. And the Roman Catholic position was thus cemented. So then and now procreation took on a curious value among people who viewed (and view) the pleasures of sex as sinful. One could partake in the sinful pleasure but feel vindicated by the ensuing birth. Motherhood cleaned up sex. Also, it cleaned up women, who have always been considered somewhat evil, because of Eve's transgression (". . . but the woman was deceived and became a transgressor. Yet woman will be saved through bearing children . . . ," I Timothy 2:14–15), and somewhat dirty because of menstruation.

And so, based on need, inevitability and pragmatic fantasy—the Myth worked, from society's point of view—the Myth grew like corn in Kansas. And society reinforced it with both laws and propaganda—laws that made woman a chattel, denied her education and personal mobility, and madonna propaganda that said she was beautiful and wonderful doing it and it was all beautiful and wonderful to do. (One rarely sees a madonna washing dishes.)

In fact, the Myth persisted—breaking some kind of record for long-lasting fallacies—until something like yesterday. For as the truth about the Myth trickled in—as women's rights increased, as women gradually got the message that it was certainly possible for them to do most things that men did, that they live longer, that their brains were not tinier—then, finally when the really big news rolled in, that they could choose whether or not to be mothers, what happened? The Motherhood Myth soared higher than ever. As Betty Friedan made oh-so-clear in *The Feminine Mystique*, the 1940s and '50s produced a group of ladies who not only had babies as if they were going out of style (maybe they were) but, as never before, turned motherhood into a cult. First, they wallowed in the aesthetics of it all —natural childbirth and nursing became maternal musts. Like heavy-bellied ostriches, they grounded their heads in the sands of motherhood, coming up for air only to say how utterly happy and fulfilled they were. But, as Mrs. Friedan says only too plainly, they weren't. The Myth galloped on, moreover, long after making babies had turned from practical asset to liability for both individual parents and society. With the average cost of a middle-class child figured conservatively at thirty thousand dollars (not including college), any parent knows that the only people who benefit economically from children are manufacturers of consumer goods. Hence all those gooey motherhood commercials. And the Myth gathered momentum long after sheer numbers, while not yet extinguishing us, made us intensely uncomfortable. Almost all of our societal problems, from minor discomforts like traffic to major ones like hunger, the population people keep reminding us, have to do with there being too many people. And who suffers most? The kids who have been so mindlessly brought into the world, that's who. They are the ones who have to cope with all of the difficult and dehumanizing conditions brought on by overpopulation. They are the ones who have to cope with the psychological nausea of feeling unneeded by society. That's not the only reason for drugs, but, surely, it's a leading contender.

Unfortunately, the population curbers are tripped up by a romantic, stubborn, ideological hurdle. How can birth-control programs really be effective as long as the concept of glorious motherhood remains unchanged? (Even poor old Planned Parenthood has to euphemize—why not Planned Unparenthood?) Particularly among the poor, motherhood is one of the few inherently positive institutions that are accessible. As Berkeley demographer Judith Blake points out, "Poverty-oriented birth control programs do not make sense as a welfare measure . . . as long as existing pronatalist policies . . . encourage mating, pregnancy and the care, support and rearing of children." Or, she might have added, as long as the less-than-idyllic child-rearing part of motherhood remains "in small print."

Sure, motherhood gets dumped on sometimes: Philip Wylie's Momism got going in the '40s and Philip Roth's *Portnoy's Complaint* did its best to turn rancid the chicken-soup concept of Jewish motherhood. But these are viewed as the sour cries of a black humorist here, a malcontent there. Everyone shudders, laughs, but it's like the mouse-and-elephant joke. Still, the Myth persists. When a Brooklyn woman was indicted recently on charges of manslaughter and negligent homicide—eleven children died in a fire in a building she owned and criminally neglected—her lawyer sputtered, "But my client, Mrs. Breslow, is a mother, a grandmother and a great-grandmother!"

Most remarkably, the Motherhood Myth persists in the face of the most overwhelming maternal unhappiness and incompetence. If reproduction were merely superfluous and expensive, if the experience were as rich and rewarding as the cliché would have us believe, if it were a predominantly joyous trip for everyone riding—mother, father, child—then the going everybody-should-have-two-children plan would suffice. Certainly there are a lot of joyous mothers, and their children and (sometimes, not necessarily) their husbands reflect their joy. But a lot of evidence suggests that for more women than anyone wants to admit motherhood can be miserable. ("If it weren't," says one psychiatrist wryly, "the world wouldn't be in the mess it's in.")

There is a remarkable statistical finding from a recent study of Dr. Bernard's, comparing the mental illness and unhappiness of married mothers and single women. The latter group, it turned out, was both markedly less sick and overtly more happy. Of course, it's not easy to measure slippery attitudes like happiness. "Many women have achieved a kind of reconciliation—a conformity," says Dr. Bernard, "that they interpret as happiness. Since feminine happiness is supposed to lie in devoting one's life to one's husband and children, they do that; so *ipso facto*, they assume they are happy. And for many women, untrained for independence and 'processed' for motherhood, they find their state far preferable to the alternatives, which don't really exist." Also, unhappy mothers are often loath to admit it. For one thing, if in society's view not to be a mother is to be a freak, not to be a *blissful* mother is to be a witch. Besides, unlike a disappointing marriage, disappointing motherhood cannot be terminated by divorce. Of course, none of that stops such a woman from expressing her dissatisfaction in a variety of ways. Again, it is not only she who suffers but her husband and children as well. Enter the harridan housewife, the carping shrew. The realities of motherhood can turn women into terrible people. And, judging from the fifty thousand cases of child abuse in the United States each year, some are worse than terrible.

In some cases, the unpleasing realities of motherhood begin even before the beginning. In *Her Infinite Variety*, Morton Hunt describes young married women pregnant for the first time as "very likely to be frightened and depressed, masking these feelings in order not to be considered contemptible. The arrival of pregnancy interrupts a pleasant dream of motherhood and awakens them to the realization that they have too little money, or not enough space, or unresolved marital problems . . ."

The following are random quotes from interviews with some mothers in Ann Arbor, Michigan, who described themselves as reasonably happy. They all had positive things to say about their children, although when asked about the best moment of their day they *all* confessed it was when the children were in bed. Here is the rest:

"Suddenly I had to devote myself to the child totally. I was under the illusion that the baby was going to fit into my life, and I found that I had to switch my life and my schedule to fit *him*. You think, 'I'm in love, I'll get married, and we'll have a baby.' First there's two, then three, it's simple and romantic. You don't even think about the work."

"You never get away from the responsibility. Even when you leave the children with a sitter, you are not out from under the pressure of the responsibility."

"I hate ironing their pants and doing their underwear, and they never put their clothes in the laundry basket. . . . As they get older, they make less demands on your time because they're in school, but the demands are greater in forming their values. . . . Best moments of the day are when all the children are in bed. . . . The worst time of day is 4 P.M., when you have to get dinner started, the kids are tired, hungry and crabby—everybody wants to talk to you about *their* day . . . your day is only half over."

"Once a mother, the responsibility and concern for my children became so encompassing. . . . It took a great deal of will to keep up other parts of my personality. . . . To me, motherhood gets harder as they get older, because you have less control. . . . In an abstract sense, I'd have several. . . . In the non-abstract, I would not have any."

"I had anticipated that the baby would sleep and eat, sleep and eat. Instead, the experience was overwhelming. I really had not thought particularly about what motherhood would mean in a realistic sense. I want to do other things, like to become involved in things that are worthwhile—I don't mean women's clubs—but I don't have the physical energy to go out in the evenings. I feel like I'm missing something . . . the experience of being somewhere with people and having them talking about something—something that's going on in the world."

Every grown-up person expects to pay a price for his pleasures, but seldom is the price as vast as the one endured "however happily" by most mothers. We have mentioned the literal cost factor. But what does that mean? For middle-class American women, it means a life style with severe and usually unimagined limitations; i.e., life in the suburbs, because who can afford three bedrooms in the city? And what do suburbs mean? For women, suburbs mean other women and children and leftover peanut-butter sandwiches and car pools and seldom-seen husbands. Even the Feminine Mystiqueniks—the housewives who finally admitted that their lives behind brooms (OK, electric brooms) were driving them crazy—were loath to trace their predicament to their children. But it is simply a fact that a childless married woman has no child-work and little housework. She can live in a city, or, if she still chooses the suburbs or the country, she can leave on the commuter train with her husband if she wants to. Even the most ardent job-seeking mother will find little in the way of great opportunities in Scarsdale. Besides, by the time she wakes up, she usually lacks both the preparation for the outside world and the self-confidence to get it. You will say there are plenty of city-dwelling working mothers. But most of those women do additional-funds-for-the-family kind of work, not the interesting career kind that takes plugging during "childbearing years."

Nor is it a bed of petunias for the mother who does make it professionally. Says writer-critic Marya Mannes:

> If the creative woman has children, she must pay for this indulgence with a long burden of guilt, for her life will be split three ways between them and her husband and her work. . . . No woman with any heart can compose a paragraph when her child is in trouble. . . . The creative woman has no wife to protect her from intrusion. A man at his desk in a room with closed door is a man at work. A woman at a desk in any room is available.

Speaking of jobs, do remember that mothering, salary or not, is a job. Even those who can afford nursies to handle the nitty-gritty still need to put out emotionally. "Well-cared-for" neurotic rich kids are not exactly unknown in our society. One of the more absurd aspects of the Myth is the underlying assumption that since most women are biologically equipped to bear children, they are psychologically, mentally, emotionally and technically equipped (or interested) to rear them. Never mind happiness. To assume that such an exacting, consuming and important task is something almost all women are equipped to do is far more dangerous and ridiculous than assuming that everyone with vocal cords should seek a career in the opera.

A major expectation of the Myth is that children make a not-so-hot marriage hotter, and a hot marriage hotter still. Yet almost every available study indicates that childless marriages are far happier. One of the biggest, of 850 couples, was conducted by Dr. Harold Feldman of Cornell University, who states his finding in no uncertain terms: "Those couples with children had a significantly lower level of marital satisfaction than did those without children." Some of the reasons are obvious. Even the most adorable children make for additional demands, complications and hardships in the lives of even the most loving parents. If a woman feels disappointed and trapped in her mother role, it is bound to affect her marriage in any number of ways: she may take out her frustrations directly on her husband, or she may count on him too heavily for what she feels she is missing in her daily life.

". . . You begin to grow away from your husband," says one of the Michigan ladies. "He's working on his career and you're working on your family. But you both must gear your lives to the children. You do things the children enjoy, more than things you might enjoy." More subtle and possibly more serious is what motherhood may do to a woman's sexuality. Even when the stork flies in, sexuality flies out. Both in the emotional minds of some women *and* in the minds of their husbands, when a woman becomes a mother she stops being a woman. It's not only that motherhood may destroy her physical attractiveness, but its madonna concept may destroy her feelings of sexuality.

And what of the payoff? Usually, even the most self-sacrificing maternal self-sacrificers expect a little something back. Gratified parents are not unknown to the Western world, but there are probably at least just as many who feel, to put it crudely, short-changed. The experiment mentioned earlier where the baby ducks followed vacuum cleaners instead of their mothers indicates that what passes for love from baby to mother is merely a rudimentary kind of object attachment. Without necessarily feeling like a Hoover, a lot of women become disheartened because babies and children not only are not interesting to talk to (not everyone thrills at the wonders of da-da-ma-ma talk) but are generally not emphathetic, considerate people. Even the nicest children are not capable of empathy, surely a major ingredient of love, until they are much older. Sometimes they're never capable of it. Dr. Wyatt says that often, in later years particularly, when most of the "returns" are in, it is the "good mother" who suffers most of all. It is then she must face a reality: the child, the appendage with her genes, is not an appendage but a separate person. What's more, he or she may be a separate person who doesn't even like her— or whom she doesn't really like.

So if the music is lousy, how come everyone's dancing? Because the motherhood minuet is taught free from birth, and whether or not she has rhythm or likes the music every woman is expected to do it. Indeed, she wants to do it. Little girls start learning what to want—and what to be—when they are still in their cribs. Dr. Miriam Keiffer, a young social psychologist at Bensalem, the experimental college of Fordham University, points to studies showing that "at six months of age, mothers are already treating their baby girls and boys quite differently. For instance, mothers have been found to touch, comfort, and talk to their females more. If these differences can be found at such an early stage, it's not surprising that the end product is as different as it is. What is surprising is that men and women are, in so many ways, similar." Some people point to the way little girls play with dolls as proof of their "innate motherliness." But remember, little girls are *given* dolls. When Margaret Mead presented some dolls to New Guinea children, it was the boys, not the girls, who wanted to play with them, which they did by crooning lullabies and rocking them in the most maternal fashion.

By the time they reach adolescence, most girls, unconsciously or not, have learned enough about role definition to qualify for a master's degree. In general, the lesson has been that no matter what kind of career thoughts one may entertain, one must, first and foremost, be a wife and mother. A girl's mother is usually her first teacher. As Dr. Goode says, "A woman is not only taught by society to have a child; she is taught to have a child who will have a child." A woman who has hung her life on the Motherhood Myth will almost always reinforce her young married daughter's early training by pushing for grandchildren. Prospective grandmothers are not the only ones. Husbands too can be effective sellers. After all, they have the Fatherhood Myth to cope with. A married man is supposed to have children. Often, particularly among Latins, children are a sign of potency. They help him assure the world—and himself—that he is the big man he is supposed to be. Plus, children give him both immortality (whatever that means) and possibly the chance to become "more" in his lifetime through the accomplishments of his children, particularly his son. (Sometimes it's important, however, for the son to do better, but not too much better.)

Friends too can be counted on as myth-pushers. Naturally one wants to do what one's friends do. One study, by the way, found an absolute correlation between a woman's fertility and that of her three closest friends. The negative sell comes into play here, too. We have seen what the concept of nonmother means (cold, selfish, unwomanly, abnormal). In practice, particularly in the suburbs, it can mean, simply, exclusion—both from child-centered activities (that is, most activities) and from child-centered conversations (that is, most conversations). It can also mean being the butt of a lot of unfunny jokes. ("Whaddya waiting for? An immaculate conception? Ha ha.") Worst of all, it can mean being an object of pity.

In case she has escaped all of those pressures (that is, if she was brought up in a cave), a young married woman often wants a baby just so that she'll (1) have something to do (motherhood is better than clerk-typist, which is often the only kind of job she can get, since little more has been expected of her and, besides, her boss also expects her to leave and be a mother), (2) have something to hug and possess, to be needed by and have power over, and (3) have something to be—e.g., a baby's mother. Motherhood affords an instant identity. First, through wifehood, you are somebody's wife; then you are somebody's mother. Both give not only identity and activity, but status and stardom of a kind. During pregnancy a woman can look forward to the kind of attention and pampering she may not ever have gotten or may never otherwise get. Some women consider birth the biggest accomplishment of their lives, which may be interpreted as saying not much for the rest of their lives. As

Dr. Goode says, "It's like the gambler who may know the roulette wheel is crooked, but it's the only game in town." Also, with motherhood, the feeling of accomplishment is immediate. It is really much faster and easier to make a baby than to paint a painting or write a book or get to the point of accomplishment in a job. It is also easier in a way to shift focus from self-development to child development—particularly since, for women, self-development is considered selfish. Even unwed mothers may achieve a feeling of this kind. (As we have seen, little thought is given to the aftermath.) And, again, since so many women are underdeveloped as people, they feel that, besides children, they have little else to give—to themselves, their husbands, to their world.

You may ask why, then, when the realities do start pouring in, does a woman want to have a second, third, even fourth child? OK: (1) Just because reality is pouring in doesn't mean she wants to face it. A new baby can help bring back some of the old illusions. Says psychoanalyst Dr. Natalie Shainess, "She may view each successive child as a knight in armor that will rescue her from being a 'bad/unhappy mother.'" (2) Next on the horror list to having no children is having one. It suffices to say that the only child not only is OK but even has a high rate of exceptionality. (3) Both parents usually want at least one child of each sex. The husband, for reasons discussed earlier, probably wants a son. (4) The more children one has, the more of an excuse one has not to develop in any other way.

What's the point? A world without children? Of course not. Nothing could be worse or more unlikely. No matter what anyone says, motherhood isn't about to go out like a blown bulb, and who says it should? Only the Myth must go out, and now it seems to be dimming.

The younger-generation females who have been reared on the Myth have not rejected it totally, but at least they recognize that it can be more loving to children not to have them. And at least they speak of adopting children instead of bearing them. Moreover, since the new nonbreeders are "less hung up" on ownership, they seem to recognize that if you dig loving children, you don't necessarily have to own one. The end of the Motherhood Myth might make available more loving women (and men!) for those children who already exist.

When motherhood is no longer culturally compulsory, there will, certainly, be less of it. Women are now beginning to think and do more about development of self, of their individual resources. Far from being selfish, such development is probably our only hope. That means more alternatives for women. And more alternatives mean more selective, better, happier motherhood—and childhood and husbandhood (or manhood) and peoplehood. It is not a question of whether or not children are sweet and marvelous to have and rear; the question is, even if that's so, whether or not one wants to pay the price for it. It doesn't make sense anymore to pretend that women need babies, when what they really need is themselves. If God were still speaking to us in a voice we could hear, even He would probably say, "Be fruitful. Don't multiply."

Fathers

Questions to a Father

by ROCHELLE JOFFE

Rochelle Joffe is eleven years old, lives in Philadelphia, and attends the
Solomon Schechter Day School.

I once asked my father
What really is a cat?
And all he said was
"Please hand me my hat."

I once asked my father
What really is a goat?
And all he said was
"Please hand me my coat."

I once asked my father
How do you spell achoo?
All he said was, "God bless you!"

And then I asked my father
Are you going someplace?
And I could tell he was mad
By the expression on his face.

So take my advice
And don't ask your father
Because you know
He'll think you're a great big bother.

My Father

by MADELINE BELKIN

Madeline Belkin is a member of the Up from Under collective, which publishes a women's-liberation magazine. With Deborah Babcox, she edited *Liberation Now!,* an anthology published by Dell. She is currently at work on an oral history of her family. This interview is with her father.

Could you tell us about your family and where you were raised?

I was born in the Ukraine, the black-soil region. Roughly, it's a little north of the Black Sea. My mother came from a farm family and my father was the son of a rabbi. My father was a craftsman, a woodcarver. He found it difficult to make his living beyond what was known as the Jewish Pale. The Pale was the area Jews lived in, and beyond which we were not supposed to go, live, settle, or try to make a living. Soon after his marriage my father left for the United States. It took him ten years to save up enough money to finally send for our family. By the time we were able to leave there had been a war, revolution, counterrevolution, eight years of constant turmoil. One of my brothers died of starvation, my only sister died, and my mother lost her hearing after a long illness. For the most part I lived with my two brothers in children's homes, and I remember mainly being always hungry and very sick. When I dreamed of going to America, which was all the time, I used to dream I would get there by curling up on the inside of a wagon wheel and just rolling across the country. I guess as a kid I never thought about how that wheel would go over oceans!

What did you think of this country when you finally got here?

I was disillusioned. We disembarked at the docks in Brooklyn and we were already citizens, because of my father's being here. I got into a cab, all the time looking at my father. I hadn't seen him for ten years. When he left I was only one year old. I noticed his hands were hard, he really worked hard for a living. The picture I used to look at of him which we had on the bureau showed him with wavy black hair, a celluloid collar, very young. When I saw him that first day in New York, he was getting gray and I knew immediately his life wasn't easy. Well, we headed right for the Lower East Side and it was all dirty, dingy and crowded—different than the farm we had come from. But I wasn't really looking at the houses, I kept staring at the people, because I had always imagined Americans would look like something else, like gods. Instead, the people I saw were just people, tired, hungry people. The pace seemed faster, and the traffic confused me. It just wasn't anything like what I expected to find in the new country, because by comparison, since the Ukraine was over a thousand years old, I expected to find brand-new things in this new country. But it wasn't so.

What kind of work did your father do in this country?
He was a house painter—a house painter who died one day in a fire on his job.

What kind of work have you done?
Not counting odd jobs, like the days during the Depression, when I worked around the country at lumber camps and so on, for the greatest part of my life I've been a house painter.

How far did you go in school?
I completed high school.

Did your parents want you to work?
Yes, as soon as possible. My first job was in a grocery while I was going to school. I delivered breakfasts in the morning, went to school, came back, and went back to work. It did affect my schoolwork, but I felt obligated to help out. I never objected to it, but I didn't like it.

Did you ever think you would want to be a professional when you grew up?

No, not especially. That was really beyond my reach. In those days it was generally accepted that a workingman's son would follow his path. It's very seldom that anybody ever rose above their class and broke the barrier, so to speak.

You're still a house painter now. How do you feel about your work?

It's a means to a livelihood. But don't get me wrong, see, I have dignity in my work. My work is not demeaning. There's nothing wrong with a man doing hard work for his money. It's dignified. I don't feel I have any obligations to society, in the sense that I'm not taking anything from anybody else, I'm just a workingman with all the responsibilities that go along with that. I take pride in my work.

If you had a choice, what kind of job would you like?

Truthfully, I'd rather do something else. I'd like to have time—time to write, read maybe, travel.

Did you ever have any feeling about being referred to as "the brawn" or "the little people"?

I've never felt that people who work for a living are little. After all, we create all the wealth we have in this country. No, I've never felt I was a lower class. In my book, I'm with the people. I do bitterly resent it when people call us "little," and I don't think there's any truth in it. But if you understand what's behind it, it makes sense. See, if you have to exploit a man's labor, you have to make sure he feels small enough so that he'll keep in his place.

What were your school influences?

In school [laugh] they couldn't care less! I wasn't channeled into anything. I just showed up every day because I was still of school age, and although I was an exceptional student I was never encouraged to do anything with it. Nobody ever spoke to me. In spite of the fact that I was outstanding and was a member of the art club, I was never led to believe I should take any of this seriously.

Do you think there was any difference in the way boys were treated in schools and in the family, as compared with girls?

It's hard for me to say, since I went to an all-boys school and there were only sons in my family. Generally speaking, we all felt poor more than anything else, and I can't say I really noticed a difference, outside of biological differences.

Did you ever help with the housework?

Occasionally, yes.

Did you ever feel that was your responsibility?

I always felt I should do it, but very often I was just too tired after a day's work. I'm out of the house at five-thirty in the morning, you see.

Do you think there's a difference between the working class and the middle class?

Yes. It's been my observation that the middle class has played a role in my time as the shock troops between us and the struggle for power. They're right on top of us all the time, holding us down. We threaten them. If you look back in history it's been so in every country where the middle class achieved power —they have either failed or sold out the people who work for a living.

Why do you think so many people from the working class want to forget their class origins?

It's hard to say how many of them really feel that way. But those that do, I imagine, have an illusion about what makes a satisfactory life, what real happiness means. I don't think many of them have found a solution, and this explains, to a large extent, the desperation of all those middle-class children. Rightfully, I think, they are rejecting their parents' values because they see the hypocrisy of it. For instance they were taught "fair play," but you wouldn't call what happened in My Lai fair play. For working people, some have the illusion that by serving the masters, they become masters.

Why do you suppose workers have racist attitudes?

I think it's largely economic. Also, it's a social disease. You see, anybody who feels he's at the lowest level—and our society daily tells the workingman he's nothing—will always look for a scapegoat. When you believe you're nothing, you always have to find a guy who's worse off than yourself. You can say, "He earns less money than me, he's less skilled than me, less smart, therefore he's inferior." So you get all kinds of hate, chauvinism, racism, you name it.

Would you want a change in roles, if you had a choice, in marriage?

I would have wished that we could have shared responsibilities more evenly. It's a real burden to devote your life totally to hard labor in order to pay bills. You never seem to really get anything out of it. And it would help to have the wife bring some money in, and by the same token then the man could do some housework and get to know his children better. I think that would get much better results.

Do you think it will be hard for men to change?

Realistically, I'm afraid so. Until such time as men achieve a more aware attitude of the society we live in and see how it dehumanizes us, there can't be a change. Men have been conditioned to think that the woman does the chores in the house, has the children, and the man is to go out and break his back to keep the home going. It's very difficult to break that kind of tradition. Call it a tradition, because it doesn't make any sense from any other standpoint.

Do you think the man benefits as the family exists now?

No. This division between the sexes worsens our conditions, because the responsibilities are not evenly shared and it keeps us stunted in many ways. A woman would grow outside the house, and the man would probably learn a lot if he spent more time in the house.

If a man is at work, how does this affect his relationship with his children?

That depends largely on the kind of work he does, how old the children are. But there is a definite void, a strain. Maybe it would help to have child-care agencies, programs designed outside the school for children. See, if a man works for a living you're away eight, ten, twelve hours a day. As much as he'd like to be with his children, sometimes he can't. Under this system, many women can't find work because they're not sufficiently trained or educated. So centers would relieve the burden from the women. I think men could contribute things which are lacking in the home like—well, I don't know, I haven't really thought about it, but I think a man doesn't have to be a buddy, he can just be an instructor.

Why can't he be a buddy?

Because there's such a difference in age. But I just don't think men have to be buddy-buddy. I think boys and girls could learn things from men, maybe men would be better at giving instructions in sex so that children don't have to find out in the streets.

How did you learn about sex?

In the street.

What was your biggest shock when you married?

I wasn't shocked at all, I was prepared for it. I think it was good. Our biggest problems were always economic. And then there's always an adjustment to each other.

If a son or daughter were arrested, whom would you turn to for help?

I would like to get a good lawyer.

Can you afford to pay a good lawyer?

No, not really, but I'd try. There's really a difference if you have money. Rich people don't usually get into the same difficulties poor people do, because they pay their way through and their kids get out. If a poor boy gets picked up on a narcotics charge, he's in much greater difficulty than a governor's son.

What do you think love is?

Love . . . it's a feeling you have toward people. It's such a wide thing it's hard to put your finger on it. I guess it's just a special feeling you have for people.

Are you afraid of women?

No! [Laugh]

Do you like women?

Yes, I think women are warm and gentle. More so than men. Women have a sense of justice. It's a proven fact, women will rise against injustice quicker than men. Perhaps it's because she's closest to children and she identifies all children as being her own.

What do you think about emotions, about men crying?

Well, if a man has good reason to cry, why not? It depends on the individual. I've seen women who can be just as cruel as men can be. Inside, I guess I'm emotional. Not outwardly. I only get emotional when I have a very good reason. I think showing emotions all the time is a waste of energy. You have to save your energy for when you really need it.

Do you think housewives should be paid by the state for their labor?

That's not a bad idea.

How did you feel your children's lives would differ from yours?

I thought it would be slightly better for them. You always hope for a better life, but you shouldn't achieve it by depriving other people. I couldn't take from other people to make it good for my own.

If you had your life to do over again, what would you change?

Well, I'm not sure at this point. This may shock you, but I don't think I would have come to this country. I've worked very hard here, but it's always like being on a treadmill that keeps going backward.

What did you think of the work your mother did and the work your father did? Were they equal?

My father was a workhorse, and he wouldn't have known what else to do with himself if he tried. He had a deep sense of responsibility which made it impossible for him to do anything else. My mother was a very tidy woman who tried to keep our home looking nice. I don't remember her ever complaining about housework. I guess in many ways it was good for her to be together with the family for the first time. But I do remember that she had lots of activities outside the home. I couldn't say, though, that either my mother's or my father's work was more valuable than the other.

What do you think of "woman's work"?

How does that saying go? "Women's work is never done!" Seriously, it's been my observation that women could contribute much more talent and energy than they're allowed to. A lot of this talent goes to waste because of misconceptions, because of the nature of our society, and because the establishment wants it so.

Do you feel badly that your wife was left with the main burden of raising your children and taking care of the house?

Well, I don't want to get dramatic about it, but really I

shared responsibilities in more ways than one. I feel I guided my children so that they'd have no misconceptions about where they came from, where they were heading, what to expect.

But what about housework?

[Laugh] There goes the old housework thing. OK, OK, maybe I don't do enough, but I really didn't have any choice about it.

Do you think men have more options than women?

Today, no. You may really disagree with me, but I think men are more exploited. We're more useful to the establishment. It's no secret that much of the muscle to build our dams and cities, pave our streets, work in sewers, all the bull work, is manpower. In that sense, just in brute labor, we're more exploited. It's the men who end up in their wars as cannon fodder. A man, a workingman I should say, is physically abused all his life. I'm sure you can give me arguments on the woman's side, but I'm just telling you my side. After all, all the basket cases in V.A. hospitals are men. Lots of men were killed building this country, lives used and thrown away by the bosses. And I never saw a woman with arms and legs shot off going begging. Men, workingmen particularly, are the most expendable people in this society. Just think of the diseases people get from the work they do. Most painters, myself included, have totally rotten lungs. And when you're too old to work, then what? Welfare, I guess. I tell you, we're on a backward treadmill.

Confusions of a Middle-Class Husband

by S. M. MILLER

Professor of sociology and education at New York University, S. M. Miller most recently co-authored *The Future of Inequality* with Pamela Roby.

When I was in my twenties, I would try to convince marriage-oriented women to become involved with me by predicting, on the basis of experience, that within six months of such involvement they would very likely be getting married—though not to me—because the association with me seemed to drive women to marriage. In my forties, I find that young women's work association with me seems to correlate highly with their movement into women's liberation. Irrespective of whether proximity to me induces a liberation spirit or whether this spirit could possibly be due to larger cultural forces, my female co-workers have led me to think much more of late about sexism, and to review my own experiences over the decades within that framework.

Two interchanges with my colleagues particularly struck me. One wrote me a strong note asking why I was not publicly active in fighting sexism if I thought that I was so good on the question. I was somewhat stung by this passionate indictment, and in cool, clear, parsimonious prose replied that I did not consider myself to be very good on the sex issue, but that, looking around at most men of my own and perhaps younger ages, I was constantly surprised to find myself much better in my attitudes and behavior than they, though not good enough, etc.

But a nagging vision persisted despite my measured rejoinder. True, my wife worked, and always had worked, and I pushed her to do more professional writing, to establish herself solidly in her professional life; true, I had played a major role in bringing up our children, especially when they were young and my wife was going to school; true, in arguments with friends I had always taken pro-liberation positions. For decades I had argued against the then fashionable *Kinder-Küche* motif of suburban existence and had counseled students against it. I advised husbands whose wives were diffusely unhappy that they should drive their talented and educated, if unsure, spouses into work, for staying home all day and taking care of a household made for a malcontentment that was compounded by social disapproval of the expression of unhappiness in mothering and wifing. Yes, all that was true. But how different was the present pattern of my own family life from that of a family with a more obviously backward husband than I?

Another female colleague, more disposed to be kindly toward me, told me, when I questioned a particular emphasis of women's liberation, that I did not realize how backward young men now in their twenties and thirties were: they had been brought up in the suburban sadness in which their mothers played the required "good mother-wife" role, in which their sisters and their dates accepted the necessity of catering to men in order to make a "good catch." She went on to say that these men had not been confronted on sexist issues (this conversation preceded the media's elevating women's liberation to celebrity status); indeed, they were largely unaware that there might be some injustice in the present ordering of the world.

My experience, I replied, had been different. In the left-wing ambience of New York City in the '40s and '50s, "male supremacy" and "male chauvinism" were frequently discussed. True, my male friends and I discussed the issues with our female friends and then often proceeded to exploit them, but a dexterous awareness we did have. (But I add, in order to avoid a reassuring self-debasement, that we did encourage our women friends and wives to think and to develop themselves; and I even believe that I was less exploitative than most.)

Yet I am dogged by the feeling expressed in the notion "If you're so smart, how come you're not rich?" Where is the egalitarian family life one would reasonably expect from my sophistication about women's issues and my personal experience with them in my younger manhood?

WAY BACK WHEN

I have never had an intellectual problem with sexism. One reason may well have been the women who surrounded me as a child—my father's mother, my mother, and two considerably older sisters—although I know it sometimes goes quite the other way. My father slept, and my mother dominated—partly out of force of character and partly, one sister informed me fairly recently, because of the occupational and other failures of my father. He had tried to make it in America—and could not. His was the immigrant's rags-to-rags story. He started as a factory worker, and became a small businessman, only to be wiped out by the 1921 depression. He worked again as a machine operator, and then started a dress store, where he did the alterations and my mother was chief saleswoman. Again his enterprise was rewarded by a depression—this time, that of the 1930s. He went back to working at a machine in the lowest-paid part of the garment industry, where he stayed until he retired in his early seventies. From the depression days on, my mother worked as a saleslady. I was a "latchkey kid" from an early age, warming up the meals that were left for me by my mother.

My mother was very smart and witty, and so was my older sister. They were obviously intellectually well-endowed, although not well-educated. My mother had a few years of formal schooling; my sister just managed to graduate from high school. (I think I developed my repugnance for credentialism because I recognized that these were two very smart though not well-educated women.)

From this experience, I grew up regarding women as competent and capable of making family and economic decisions. (By contrast, my mother disliked cooking; and it was a shock to me when I began to eat away from home to discover what a bad cook she was.) Women worked and ran things well. On the other hand, there was a notion that people frowned on women's working, so we tried to hide the fact that my mother worked. I think I felt both ashamed that my mother worked and irritated that "society" thought that it was wrong for women to work, especially when their incomes were needed.

Furthermore, sexism was, in principle, alien to the egalitarian and participatory circles in which my closest friends and I were passionately involved. We were out of step with the intellectual climate of the '40s and '50s because of our egalitarian, populist, anti-elitist spirit. We criticized Stalinist democratic centralism and American celebration-style pluralist democracy because of their inadequate attention to equality and participation for all. We could no more subscribe to intellectual rationalizations of a low status for females than we could condone the miseries of oppression and deprivation among other parts of the population.

A third reason I see myself as intellectually escaping sexism has more manifest emotional roots. Looking back, I don't believe that I could have accepted a woman who would center her life completely on me and devote herself to making me happy. (Children were not part of my purview.) At one level, the intellectual: how could one individual be worthy of such dedication by another? At a deeper and, I suspect now, more significant level, I rejected or stayed away from easily giving or male-centered women because I did not consider myself worthy of another person's total devotion or capable of evoking the sentiments that would sustain it beyond the initial impulse. Furthermore, such devotion would demand an emotional response that I possibly could not make. In short, I did not think so well of myself that I could live with (overwhelming) devotion. As a consequence, I was usually involved with young women with strong career goals who were seeking their identity through work, not through family. They were my intellectual equals, if not superiors.

Thus I had a good beginning, it seems to me, for having a

marriage that did not embody sexist currents. But I don't see that my current life is very different from that of men who espoused or expounded more sexist values. Years ago a good friend told me that I had the reputation among the wives in our circle of being "an excellent husband"; and he said, "You know, that's not a good thing." I now have the feeling that families that openly embrace both bourgeois and sexist values don't live very differently from us. I sense that we are engaged in a "lapsed egalitarianism," still believing in our earlier commitments and concerns about equality, but having drifted from the faith in our daily life.

WHAT HAPPENED?

Probably the most important factor in accounting for the direction we took was our amazing naïveté about the impact of having children—a naïveté, incidentally, that I see today having a similarly devastating effect on many young parents. We just had no idea how much time and emotion children captured, how they simply changed a couple's lives, even when the wife's working made it possible, as it did in our case, to afford a housekeeper.

The early years of child rearing were very difficult. Our first son was superactive and did not sleep through the night. We were both exhausted. My wife insisted that I not leave everything to her; she fought with me to get me to participate in the care of our son and apartment. I took the 2 A.M. and 6 A.M. feedings and changings, for our ideology would not allow me just to help out occasionally: I had to "share," "really participate," in the whole thing. I resented that degree of involvement; it seemed to interfere terribly with the work I desperately wanted to achieve in. Indeed, I have always felt put upon because of that experience of many months.

To make matters worse, I did not know of other work-oriented husbands who were as involved as I with their children.

True, I realized that my sons and I had become much attached to each other and that a lovely new element had entered my life; but I resented the time and exhaustion, particularly since I was struggling to find my way in my work. I did not consider myself productive and was in the middle of struggling to clarify my perspective. I looked at the problem largely in terms of the pressure of my job, which required a lot of effort, and, more importantly, in terms of my personality and my inability to work effectively. Although I wrote memoranda with great ease, I wasn't writing professional articles and books.

In restrospect, I think that it was the influence of the McCarthy and Eisenhower years that was more significant in my lack of development. My outlook and interests were not what social science and society were responding to. That changed later, and I was able to savor in the '60s that infrequent exhilaration of having my professional work and citizen concerns merge and of gaining both a social-science and a popular audience and constituency. But I did not know in the 1950s that this would unfold, and I felt resentment.

What I experienced was that, unlike my friends, I was working hard to make things easier for my wife, and I did not see rewards. Yes, she told me she appreciated my effort; but my activities were never enough, my sharing was never full, in the sense that I equally planned and took the initiative in the care of child and house. She was tired, too, and irritated by child care; and, in turn, I was irritated by what seemed to be her absorption in taking care of the children.

And there were always those male friends who did so little, compared with me. I could, and did, tell myself that at some point along the line they would be paying heavy "dues" for their current neglect of their wives' plight, but it was small balm at the time. I wondered if I was not rationalizing my irritation by an intellectualizing metaphor about how one pays prices sooner or later and by a plaintively reassuring injunction never to envy anyone else, for who knew what lurked behind the façade of family equanimity?

Things were further complicated by another factor—less typical of today's young marrieds: my incomplete early socialization as a family member. For example, since as an adolescent and pre-adolescent I had eaten meals by myself, I had developed the habit of reading while eating. (Indeed, I am a compulsive reader, a "print nut"; if there is nothing around to read, I will study the labels on ketchup bottles.) The result was that marriage required a resocialization: I had to learn to talk to someone at mealtimes, and not to turn inward to my own thoughts or to the New York *Times*.

Of course, the reading is only the personal tip of the iceberg of a larger problem of not closing myself to others and becoming inaccessible because of stress or intellectual absorption. I am now, again, in a conscious period of trying to make myself more accessible emotionally to my family, but it is a struggle. For example, when we vacation, I spend the first few days devouring three to four mysteries a day—"decompressing" I call it —hardly talking to anyone. And, of course, when I am at a deadline, or caught in my inability to work out an idea, or just unable to get to work (there are few other conditions for me than these three), I am rather inaccessible, to say the least. I work against this tendency, but don't do notably well. While I do the mundane tasks of the household, psychologically I am often not much there. I think that I am winning the struggle against withdrawal, but what is a giant step to the battler may appear as a wiggle of progress to the beholder.

My wife has accommodated to my dislike of fixing things and "wasting time" on such things—not great matters in themselves, but symptomatic of the process of my disengagement from the burdens of home and family.

From a narrow perspective, I have useful incompetences protecting me from diversions of my energy and focus. I don't like to fix things and don't do them well (or soon). In my youth, in my proletarian near-idealization, I felt Arthur Miller was right when he had Willy Loman say that a man isn't a man unless he can do things with his hands. So I tried adult-education shop courses and the like for a brief time. I went in a klutz and came out a klutz. Now, in a spirit of reactive arrogance or greater self-pride, I boldly assert the counterposition that I believe in the division of labor and prefer to pay for specialized labor. I do little around the house—and that usually long delayed. Since skilled labor is hard to get at any price, things are undone, or my wife does them; but my principle of specialization (for me) remains unimpaired.

Similarly, I have been relieved of the task of paying bills. With my usual speed and my disdain for trivia, I did this job very rapidly and made mistakes. Now my wife spends time doing this task. It is easier, in her view, for her to do it than to keep after me to do a competent job. Failure is its own reward: I have escaped another task. Of course, I have been after my wife to have a part-time secretary and bookkeeper and have located several people for her. But she resists, as they do not provide enough help to make it worthwhile. The result is that my personnel efforts reduce my feelings of guilt when she spends evenings writing checks. After all, I did try to get her out of that function. But I am still irritated by her doing the checks—for that act is another indication that she is failing me by not showing our true equality by spending more time on her professional writing and research.

I guess what dismays me and makes me see my marriage and family as unfortunately typically upper-middle-class collegial, pseudo-egalitarian American—especially in light of my own continuing commitment to an egalitarian, participatory ethos—is that I assume no responsibility for major household tasks and family activities. True, my wife has always worked at her profession (she is a physician), even when our sons were only some weeks old. True, I help in many ways and feel responsible for her having time to work at her professional interests. But I do partial, limited things to free her to do her work. I don't do the basic thinking about the planning of meals and housekeeping, or the situation of the children. Sure, I will wash dishes and "spend time" with the children; I will often do the shopping, cook, make beds, "share" the burden of most household tasks; but that is not the same thing as direct and primary responsibility for planning and managing a household and meeting the day-to-day needs of children.

It is not that I object in principle to housekeeping and child rearing. I don't find such work demeaning or unmasculine—just a drain of my time, which could be devoted to other, "more rewarding" things. (Just as I don't like to shop for clothes for myself, even though I like clothes.) My energies are poised to help me work on my professional-political concerns, and I resist "wasting time" on other pursuits, even those basic to managing a day-to-day existence.

The more crucial issue, I now think, is not my specific omissions and commissions, but the atmosphere that I create. My wife does not expect much of me, which frees me for work and lessens the strain I produce when I feel blocked from working. Even our sons have always largely respected my efforts to work, feeling much freerer to interrupt their mother at her work. The years have been less happy than they would have been if I had been more involved and attentive and my wife had not lowered her ambitions.

Outstanding academically from an early age, a "poor girl" scholarship winner to a prestige college and medical school, excelling in her beginning professional work, my wife expected, and was expected, to do great things. But with children, she immediately reduced her goals. Of course, medical schools don't pay much attention to faculty members who are part-time or female, and the combination of the two almost guarantees offhand treatment.

She is now realizing fuller professional development. I have always felt guilty about her not achieving more, so I have nagged her to publish, though I have not provided the circumstances and climate that would make serious work much easier. I have had the benefit of feeling relieved that I was "motivating" her by my emphasis on her doing more, but I have not suffered the demands on my time and emotions that making more useful time available to her would have required. In the long run, I have undoubtedly lost more by limited involvement, because she has been distressed by the obstacles to her professional work. But the long run is hard to consider when today's saved and protected time helps meet a deadline.

SOME LESSONS

What are the lessons of this saga of a well-meaning male?

One is that equality or communality is not won once and for all, but must continually be striven for. Backsliding and easy accommodation to the male (because it is less troublesome) are likely to occur unless there is, at least occasionally, effort to bring about or maintain true communality rather than peaceful adjustment.

From this it follows that women must struggle for equality—that it will not easily be won or rewon. (A male is not likely to bestow it—in more than surface ways. Some women are arguing that it is not worth the effort to have equality with men in close personal relations and that they should not bother with men, but equality and communality among women will not be automatic, either.) The struggle does not necessarily mean nastiness, but it does require the perceptiveness and willingness to engage issues not only of prejudice and discrimination but also of subtle practices requiring female accommodation to males.

I know that the point I am about to make is often misused, and will open me to much criticism; but let me try to make it. A third lesson is that the bringing up of children must be changed, and that many women are lagging in this respect, although present day-care concerns suggest a possible change. For all of male reluctance, resistance and avoidance, many women, particularly when they have young children, end up structuring life so that it is difficult to achieve a partner relationship. Indeed, the concentration on, nay, absorption with, children makes even a low-level decent relationship, let alone an egalitarian one, difficult. Yes, I realize that the subordinate group is never the main source of difficulty, that men make women embrace the mother-housemother syndrome; but cultural and personal history are involved as well as direct or more covert husbandly pressure and unwillingness to be a full partner. Overinvolvement with children may operate to discourage many husbands from full participation because they do not accept the ideology of close attention to children.

I am *not* saying that the problem is with women, but that this part of the problem shouldn't be ignored. Even for the young parents it is important to have some measure of agreement on the mode, the style of child care. This is difficult to realize before actually becoming parents. Perhaps it will not be an issue for those in their twenties who may have a different and more relaxed attitude toward children. (And, of course, many no longer feel unfulfilled if they do not have children.) For some, yes; but I doubt if that will be true of most relatively "straight" parents. What is needed is a reconsideration of what is required in parenthood and in running a household.

Let me consider the household care first. The easy notion that in the right atmosphere housework is not so bad seems wrong to me. A lot of jobs can be stomached, treated as routine; that is the best one can say of them—that they are manageable, "doable." But they are not exciting, stimulating or satisfying except to the extent that they are completed or "accomplished," i.e., gotten rid of for the moment. This is especially so when one's other interests are high, for then these tasks become highly competitive with other ways of using one's time and thus are dissatisfying. Housework can be a full-time job if it is not guarded against. Some agreement on a minimum, satisfactory level of household care and some efficiency and sharing in performing it are important for a couple.

I have mentioned, verbally at least, the desirability of "salutary neglect" (before Moynihan, incidentally). But it has been difficult for my generation, whose adolescence and early twenties were stirred by Freud and who have wallowed in the guilt of parental omniscience and ethnic parental concern, to erase the sense of responsibility and guilt for how our children develop. What if one's son doesn't graduate from college or becomes a bomb-thrower or a homosexual—isn't it the parents' fault? When a son or daughter is eighteen or twenty, it seems easier to deny the responsibility, since so many youths are also in troubled times that it is difficult to talk of Freudian acting-out rather than of a generational change in consciousness. But at earlier ages it is much more difficult to shake the feeling of responsibility for how a child is developing. Obviously I don't advocate callous neglect; but some less constraining and demanding views of parenthood—and probably some additional institutional aids like day care—are needed.

The problem is not always in the mothers' attitudes. Some studies show that working-class women are very interested in working, but that their husbands feel that it is important to the children for their mothers to be home. The issue is not so much that the mother or father is lagging but how to move toward new views on child development and new institutions to further these views.

But all these "implications" are minor, except for the importance of struggle. *What strikes me as the crucial concern, at least for the occupationally striving family, is the male involvement in work, success and striving.* This is the pressure that often molds the family. Accommodation to it is frequently the measure of being a "good wife"—moving when the male's "future" requires it, regulating activities so that the male is free to concentrate on his work or business. It isn't sexism or prejudice against women that is at work here—although they are contributing factors—but the compulsive concentration upon the objective of achievement and the relegating of other activities to secondary concern. Egalitarian relationships cannot survive if people are not somewhat equally involved with each other and if the major commitment is to things outside the relationship that inevitably intrude upon it.

So long as success or achievement burns bright for the male, it is going to be difficult to change drastically the situation of the family and the woman.

However, although I am strongly of the mind that success drives should be banked and other more humanitarian urges encouraged, I don't accept that all of the drive for success or achievement is pernicious or undesirable. This drive is exciting, and can be fulfilling. But it is a great danger to be avoided when it becomes all-embracing or when the success is without a content that is both personally and socially satisfying or beneficial.

To do interesting and useful things, to feel a sense of accomplishment, should be made easier. As in military strategy, a "sufficient level" of achievement rather than a "maximum level" of security or position should be sought. Being "number one" should not be the goal; rather, high competence should be enough for both men and women. I have seen many talented people blighted in their work by "number-one-ism" when they probably would have done outstanding and useful work by adopting high competence-performance criteria.

If women accept "success" to the same extent and in the same way that many men do, the problems will be enormous. If women simply adopt the "number-one-ism" that dominates the workplace, the drive for achievement will probably lead them into the same narrowing and unpromising obsessions that destroy many men.

A more egalitarian society in terms of the distribution of income and social respect would, of course, make it easier to escape "number-one-ism." But, meanwhile, we shall have to struggle with the values that surround us and corrode true equality in the home.

Finally, men have to feel some gain in the growing equality in their relationship with women. Over the long run there may well be greater satisfaction for males in egalitarian relationships, but in the short run the tensions and demands may not lead to enjoyment and satisfaction. Some short-term gains for males will be important in speeding up the road to equality. But such gains are not easily or automatically forthcoming. That is why I made the first points about the inevitability of struggle. Successful struggle requires modes of living and relationships to which the male can accommodate without total loss, which is hard to achieve without women's falling back again to accommodating to men.

I recognize that I concentrate upon the upper middle class and upon the experience of one male. I don't think either is the world—I really don't. But I do perceive that some of my experiences and interpretations are not solipsist pieces of life, that with things changing, others are experiencing similar shocks and stresses. I wonder whether the egalitarian changes I see in some young families will mean permanent changes, or "lapsed egalitarianism" once again. My hope is that the future will be different.

Weekend Father

by CHARLES HOWE

San Francisco journalist and novelist, Charles Howe is the author of *Valley of Fire*. He is currently at work on a novel about newspapermen entitled *Fool's Errand,* from which the following excerpt is taken.

When the time came on Saturday morning to pick up his son and spend the weekend with him, Baker arrived in a borrowed Volkswagen bus loaded with a hundred dollars' worth of camping equipment he had bought the day before. Although he had been shepherding his money carefully since he had moved into the furnished room a month earlier, buying the big sleeping bag, the pots and pans and the gasoline stove had been a pleasure.

He had spent all afternoon on Market Street, pricing camping equipment; unfolding tricky jackknives and pulling zippers back and forth on various bags.

"My son and I are going out in the woods," Baker told a clerk who was impatient to wait on another customer.

"Is this the first time?" the clerk asked absently.

"No. We used to do it a lot."

That had spoiled it. He paid for the equipment quickly and shrugged off the clerk's offer to help carry it to his car.

She was out in the garden with a spade, hoeing at weeds, when he arrived. She looked a little tired and very alone and for a moment he thought of spending an hour or so helping her, doing a task he had never enjoyed when they lived together.

"He's been waiting for you ever since you called Thursday night," she said. "He misses you so much."

Baker nodded. "Did you get the check I mailed? Are you hurting for money?"

She shook her head. "We're fine."

The screen door banged open and his son ran out. He carried one of Baker's old briefcases and he was neatly dressed, as if for church. He hit Baker hard, dropping the briefcase and clutching him around the knees.

"Oh, Daddy, I didn't see you for a long time. Were you sick?"

He grabbed his son, lifted him to his chest and smelled of all the good things that are a child.

"Hey, Jimmy . . . little boy . . ." While they held each other she started hoeing again.

"Where are we going, Daddy?"

"We're going camping and we're going to catch some fish," Baker said. He knew nothing about fishing, had never fished before. "And we're going to pan for some gold in the river and sleep out under the stars, like the old trappers do, and maybe I'll teach you to talk to the bears."

"Daddy knows how to talk to the bears," Jimmy told his mother.

"I know," she said.

"The Indians taught him. One time we went out at night and he told the bears to guard us while we were sleeping so that the wolves wouldn't get us." The boy thought for a moment. "Were you with us, Mommy? Were we married then?"

"Yes. Be a good boy and do what your father tells you." The hoe began to rise and fall again. "Have a good time," she said. "And drive carefully."

They headed north, toward Grass Valley and a little ghost town at the fork of the Yuba River called Washington. Baker and his wife had camped there for years running, even before his son was born. One had to pack in for a quarter of a mile down a rocky ravine to get to the beach at the fork of the river, and this was one of the reasons Baker liked the place.

Because of the long walk it would be deserted; the transistorized married couples with their transistorized portable television sets were not up to the hike. They would be miles upstream, at a campground, and Baker had no desire to talk to them—to talk to anyone except his son.

They stopped once, outside Sacramento, to buy some salmon eggs and a six-pack of beer. Instinctively, Jimmy placed his hand in Baker's as they crossed the street.

"Carry me, Daddy?"

"You're getting too big for that. How old are you these days?"

"I'll be six pretty soon. In November, I think."

"What month is it now?"

"Saturday!"

They reached the little town shortly after noon, and by one o'clock they had brought down all of their equipment. Baker laid the sleeping bag out near the bend in the river after clearing the ground beneath it. Then he cached the six-pack in the water, covering it with rocks.

"That's so it will be cold when I want a beer," he told Jimmy. It was hot, and both father and son stripped down to their shorts.

"Are we going to catch a fish, Daddy?"

"Sure." Baker assembled the fishing pole. It was a cheap affair with an unfamiliar reel. Almost an hour later, as he and his son sat on a rock, he finally got the hang of casting the line. He was bored with the pole; there seemed to be no fish in the river, and for a moment he toyed with the notion of going back to camp and reading a paperback book. But downstream Jimmy saw a fisherman wearing rubber boots and carrying what looked like expensive tackle. The man caught a fish as they watched.

"Daddy, why aren't we catching any fish? That man did."

"Maybe he's got a secret thing on his hook," Baker said, handing Jimmy the pole.

"Can we get that secret thing?"

"The store's all out of them, son." Baker remembered seeing a trout farm miles back with a sign: "Fish All You Want for $5 —We Guarantee a Fish." He thought that on the way home he and Jimmy would stop off, but he wasn't sure whether he wanted the fish for his son or as a kind of show trophy.

After a while they gave up fishing and tried panning for gold. A century earlier the stream had been alive with gold and there were still signs of hydraulic mining; divots dug into the sides of surrounding cliffs.

Baker had brought a phial of simulated gold dust of the sort sold to tourists in little gift shops. And while Jimmy worked the pan, he salted it with the glittering bits of metal.

"Gold, Daddy! I've got some gold!" The child poked at the stuff with his finger. "What is gold?"

"It's metal, like iron. Only because there isn't much of it—because it's scarce—it's worth a lot of money."

"How much money?"

"Oh, enough for some candy at the store."

When dusk came they walked a mile down the road to a little country store and his son ordered some candy. Baker winked at the old man and covertly put a dollar behind the counter while Jimmy handed him a bit of paper with the fake gold wrapped inside.

"You hit a bonanza?" the old man asked.

"Daddy and I found some gold."

On the way back, Baker carried Jimmy on his shoulders. It was almost dark now; one could hear crickets and sounds of the river. Baker walked easily; he had not thought of the impending divorce for hours and the boy was light on his back.

He made dinner after priming the Coleman stove: hamburgers, beans, bread and butter, and Kool-Aid made from the water from the Yuba. Then they cleaned their plates with the fine sand from the bottom of the river and Jimmy dried them with paper towels while Baker cleaned the gasoline stove. When they had finished, it was completely dark. Baker looked at his watch: it was only seven o'clock.

He undressed Jimmy down to his underpants and a tee shirt and helped him climb inside the bag.

"Will you sleep with me tonight, Daddy?"

"Sure. I'm just going to make some coffee first and then smoke a cigarette and read for a while."

Jimmy sighed. "I wish you would sleep with me all of the time."

Baker lit a cigarette and shivered, though the night was warm.

"Smoking is bad for you, Daddy. Mama said it was bad and that was why you cough."

He put the cigarette out, although he badly wanted to finish it. "You won't smoke, will you, Jimmy?"

"No. I've kicked the habit. I saw that on teevee."

He found himself holding his son's head, running his fingers through his hair.

"Daddy, will there always be a war?"

"Why?"

"I just wondered. There is always a war on television."

Baker felt a remote anger. It was always the television, the fucking television, running for hours like an unattended water hose that gradually soaks a good lawn into muck. And now he wasn't around to offer an alternative.

"No, son. Most of those wars you see are movies. There is a war in Vietnam, but I think it will be over soon. And a war isn't going to come here."

"Our soldiers kill people in Vietnam, Daddy."

It was like a child who has just heard the word "nigger" and wants to know what it means, Baker thought. You have to tell them Custer was a fool sooner or later, but you hope it will be much later.

"That's what a war is all about," Baker said. "And that's why it's bad to send young people off to fight."

"You were in a war and you got blowed up by a mine one time. Mommy said so." Jimmy thought for a moment. "Did you kill people, Daddy?"

Baker trembled. "Yes. A long time ago in Korea."

"Would you do it again?"

"Never for all the money in the world. I was a boy then and I didn't know any better. But you'll know better, won't you?"

"I won't be a soldier. You'll take care of me, Daddy. If the policemen come to get me when I won't go to be a soldier, will you be there to take care of me?"

"You won't have to go and be a soldier," Baker said, wondering how many weekend fathers all over the country were being asked questions, knowing their answers would be lame as his. They don't write a manual for part-time fathers, he thought; they don't tell you what the answers should be.

"Some soldiers kill little children, Daddy. The man said so on the television."

"*Jesus!*" Baker yelled. Jimmy twitched in fright. "I'm sorry, son. I'm truly sorry."

"Are you mad at me, Daddy?"

He embraced his son, "Oh, no . . . I'm not mad at you. . . . I want you to grow up and be better than I am, and I'm not around enough to help you . . ."

There were a thousand things he wanted to tell Jimmy, but he felt like a mute come to confession. He wanted to tell him he was frightened about a future that began when he left home: a future of furnished rooms and living on the cheap to support two households.

He wanted to ask forgiveness because in his own way now he was being a better father than he had been when he was living at home. He remembered nights months back when Jimmy would ask, "Read to me, Daddy? Tell me a story?" and his face burned as he recalled how he had fobbed the child off: "Daddy's tired, I'll do it—tomorrow."

He wanted to tell his son that nobody had been wrong—that he and his wife had just burned out and she had been smart enough to realize it.

That he was worried that Jimmy would grow up and gradually become estranged until Baker became, at last, a kind of comic-relief Uncle Louie who showed up at Christmas and on birthdays with a load of gifts: a dimly remembered cliché.

The child sighed. "When will you not be mad at Mommy?"

"I'm not mad, son. But maybe . . . maybe we won't live together anymore even though we both love you. Maybe someday I'll get a house someplace and you could live with me for a while."

"And could we get a dog named Spot?"

"Sure, we'll get a dog named Spot and we'll have a house and it'll have a secret garden out in the back and a fort you and your friends can play in."

He began talking faster and for several minutes he was telling his son of visions he once had, as a child Jimmy's age, thirty years ago in Arizona, when he too had longed for his father to hold him and kiss him.

". . . and we'll go looking for the Lost Dutchman Mine and then maybe we'll go down to Dixieland, where they play ragtime. And then we could go to Mexico . . ."

"Daddy, why are you crying?"

"Because I love you so much." He wiped at his face and then turned the gasoline lantern off, so that he could be in the dark.

"If you get another wife will I still be your little boy?"

"You'll always be my little boy."

Fathers Without Children: A Study of Streetcorner Men

by ELLIOT LIEBOW

Elliot Liebow is chief of the Center for Studies of Metropolitan Problems at the National Institute of Mental Health.

"Streetcorner Men" is Mr. Liebow's term for two dozen black men "who share a corner in Washington's Second Precinct as a base of operations," whom Mr. Liebow studies in his book Tally's Corner, *from which this article is drawn. "These men are unskilled construction workers, casual day laborers, menial workers in retailing or in the service trades, or are unemployed. They range in age from the early twenties to the middle forties."*

In the springtime, on a Sunday afternoon, Richard's four-year-old son lay seriously ill in Ward E of Children's Hospital. He and the other twelve children in the ward, almost all from low-income Negro families, were being visited by some twenty-five relatives and friends. Not a single man was among the visitors.

The men had their reasons. Some had separated from their wives and children and did not know their children were hospitalized. Others knew but couldn't or wouldn't make it. Richard had intended going, but something came up, he would probably go tomorrow, and anyway he never did like being in a hospital, not even to visit someone else.

But whether the fathers were living with their children or not, the result was the same: there were no men visiting the children in Ward E. This absence of the father is one of the chief characteristics of the streetcorner father–child relationship.

The relationship, however, is not the same for all streetcorner fathers, nor does a given relationship necessarily remain constant over time. Some fathers are not always "absent" and some are less "absent" than others. Moreover, the same father may have relationships of different intensity with his different children at the same time. The spectrum of father–child relationships is a broad one, ranging from complete ignorance of the child's existence to continuous, day-by-day contact between father and child. The emotional content of the relationships ranges from what, to the outside observer, may seem on the father's part callous indifference or worse all the way to hinted private intimacies whose intensity can only be guessed at.

Leaving aside, for the present, the emotional and affective content, father–child relationships can be grossly sorted out and located along a spectrum based upon the father's willingness to acknowledge paternity, his willingness to acknowledge responsibility for and to provide financial support, and the frequency and duration of contact. At the low end of the spectrum are those relationships in which the children are born of casual, short-term, even single-encounter unions; at the high end are legitimate children of married parents, all of whom live in the same household. Since the majority of streetcorner men do not live in the same households as their children, the majority of father–child relationships appear at the low and low-middle bands of the spectrum. The number falls off quickly as one approaches the other end.

At the low end of the spectrum there may be no father–child relationship at all. In some cases, the father may not know he is the father of the child; in others, even the mother may not know who the father is. Here too, at the low end, are those fathers who acknowledge possible or actual paternity but who have had no subsequent contact with mother or child. Such seems to be the case with many of the men who, while still in their teens, had a baby "back home." Thus, Richard recalls that, before his marriage to Shirley, a girl told him he was the father of her child. He did nothing about it and neither did she "because there was nothing she could do." Richard subsequently saw the mother and child on the street during a visit back home but did not speak to them. His sheepish laugh seemed a mixture of masculine pride and guilty embarrassment as he admitted that the child looked startlingly like himself.

Somewhat further along the spectrum are the relationships of Wesley and Earl with their children. Each has a child "back home" in the Carolinas and each acknowledges his paternity. Wesley has visited his home town and has seen the mother of his child once or twice since the birth of the baby. Wesley and the child's mother are on friendly terms, but Wesley gives her nothing and she asks for nothing. Earl's child also lives with its mother, but Earl and the mother have remained fond of one another. Earl sees her regularly and sometimes sees the child too, on those two or three times a year he goes back home. If he has spare cash, he leaves it with her for the baby.

In the middle range of the spectrum are the father–child relationships of those once-married men who, though separated from their wives and children, remain accessible to them. These men admit to a financial responsibility for their children, provide emergency and sometimes routine financial support, and are more or less informed about their children's general well-being. Contacts between the men and their separated families are almost always initiated by the mothers, usually for the purpose of getting money for the children. Sea Cat's wife calls him on the telephone in his rooming house to tell him when she is coming. Sometimes she brings one or both of their children, sometimes not. Stoopy's wife does not usually call. She comes on Saturday mornings, brings the two children along and stays for an hour or two.

Relationships in this middle range are by no means limited to legitimate children. Tally is the father of Bess's eighteen-month-old son. For a time, at least, their relationship was indistinguishable from Sea Cat's and Stoopy's relationships with their wives and children. On Tally's payday, Bess would sometimes call the Carry-out shop and ask that Tally be told she would be there that evening. Tally would meet her on the corner, pay her taxi-cab fare, then give her five or ten dollars for a doctor, a pair of shoes, or other extra expenses for the child.

In those few cases where the child is cared for by the father's mother or other members of his family, the father–child relationship seems to be closer than when the child is with the mother or members of her family. Such a child regularly carries the father's family name. The father provides at least partial financial support. He is often informed of the child's special needs and general well-being, and, even where they are separated by great distances, father and child see each other one or more times during the year. Sweets, for example, has a child "back home." The child is being raised by Sweets's mother. Occasional letters are exchanged during the course of the year, and there are birthday cards and gifts for the child. Sweets manages to get down there for one or two weekends a year, and during the summer his mother and his child come to spend a week or two with him in Washington. Tonk's relationship with his seven-year-old daughter, also "back home" where she is raised by Tonk's mother, is an even stronger one. They exchange letters and gifts and, at school's end, she comes to spend the whole summer with him. Stanton's daughter lives with his "sister" only two blocks from where Stanton lives. The daughter remains his financial responsibility and, depending on circumstances or need, she moves in with him occasionally for short periods of time.

At the high end of the spectrum are those relationships where father and child are regular members of the same household. In such cases, even when the father and mother are not formally married to one another, there is no question but that the child carries the father's family name. Whether his wife is working or not, and unlike the men who are separated from their children, the father who is living with his children is, in his own eyes and in the eyes of those around him, charged with the day-to-day support of his wife and children. Father and child, as members of the same household, are in more or less continuous contact.

Looking at the spectrum as a whole, the modal father–child relationship for these streetcorner men seems to be one in which the father is separated from the child, acknowledges his paternity, admits to financial responsibility, but provides financial support irregularly, if at all, and then only on demand or request. His contacts with the child are infrequent, irregular, and of short (minutes or hours) duration.

When we look away from these more formal aspects of father–child relationships and turn to their quality and texture, a seeming paradox emerges. The men who do not live with their own children seem to express more affection for their children and treat them more tenderly than those who do live with them. Moreover, the men are frequently more affectionate toward other men's children than toward their own.

Fathers who live with their children, for example, seem to take no pleasure in their children and give them little of their time and attention. They seldom mention their children in casual conversation and are never seen sitting or playing with them on the steps or in the street. The fathers do not take their children to tag along while they lounge on the streetcorner or in the Carry-out, nor do they, as they see other fathers in the neighborhood do, promenade with them on Easter Sunday or take them for walks on any other Sunday or holiday. When the father walks into the home the child may not even look up from what he is doing, and the father, for his part, takes no more notice than he receives. If their eyes happen to catch one another's glances, father and child seem to look without seeing until one or the other looks elsewhere.

Perhaps this routine absence of warmth and affection accounts for the way in which an offhand gesture by the father can suddenly deepen the relationship for the child, for however brief a time. John casually distributed some change among his six children. His wife Lorena describes what happened: "He give Buddy and the others a dime. You'd think Jesus had laid something on them. They went all around the neighborhood bragging their daddy give them a dime. I give them nickels and dimes all day long and they don't think anything about it. But John, he can give them a dime and they act like he gave them the whole world."

Since father and child are seldom together outside the home, it is in the home that casual gestures bespeaking paternal warmth and tenderness are most likely to occur. Leroy and two friends are in Leroy's house passing the time. Leroy sits on the bed and absent-mindedly strokes the head of his small son lying next to him. In Richard's house, Richard distractedly rolls a ball or marble back and forth across the floor to his four-year-old son, at the same time going on with his drinking and talking; or he casually beckons to his son to come stand between his knees and, with one hand around the child's waist, the other around a can of beer, he goes on talking.

The easy manner with which the fathers manage these intimacies suggests that they have occurred before. But the child does not manage them casually. He is excited by these intimacies, and the clear delight he takes from them suggests that he assigns to them a special quality and that they are by no means routine. Indeed, physical contact between father and son seems generally to be infrequent. When it does take place, it is just as likely to be a slap as a caress.

Compared with fathers who live with their children, separated fathers who remain in touch with their children speak about them more often and show them more warmth when father and child are together. For separated fathers, the short, intermittent contacts with their children are occasions for public display of parental tenderness and affection. When Bess brought the baby along on her money-collecting visits to the Carry-out, she and Tally would sometimes remain on the corner with Tally holding the baby in his arms, cooing at or nuzzling the baby as he and Bess talked. On a Saturday morning, after a visit from his wife, Stoopy stands on the corner with three other men, watching his wife disappear down the street with their two school-age children on either side of her. "There goes my heart," says Stoopy. "Those two kids, they're my heart." The other men nod understandingly. They would have felt and said the same thing had they been in his place.

These are fathers whose children are raised by the mothers. Even closer to his child is the father whose child is raised by the father's mother or members of his family. For him too the child is "my heart," "my life," or "the apple of my eye." Parental pride and affection are even more in public evidence when father and child are together. When Tonk's daughter arrives for her summer stay, Tonk walks around holding her hand, almost parading, stopping here and there to let bystanders testify that they didn't know Tonk had such a pretty girl, such a smart girl, or a girl who has grown so much so quickly. No, Sweets won't be at the Carry-out tomorrow afternoon, he has to take his daughter shopping for some clothes. He swears he didn't recognize her when his mother first walked up with her. It hadn't even been a year and he almost didn't know his own kid. If she hadn't called him "Daddy" he would still not have known, that's how big she got. And (with pride) she wants to be with him all the time she's here, go everywhere he goes.

But after the brief visit is over, each goes back to his own life, his own world, in which the other plays so small a part that he may be forgotten for long stretches of time. "Out of sight, out of mind" is not far off the mark at all for any of these separated father–child relationships.

There are many ways to explain this paradox in which fathers who live with their children appear to be less warm, tender and affectionate in their face-to-face relationships with their children than separated fathers. The most obvious, perhaps, is that the separated father, like the proverbial doting grandfather or favorite uncle, not charged with the day-to-day responsibility for the child, with the routine rearing and disciplining and support of the child, can afford to be attentive and effusive. Since his meetings with the child are widely spaced, he comes to them fresh and rested; since the meetings are brief, he can give freely of himself, secure in the knowledge he will soon go back to his own child-free routine.

No doubt, factors such as these are at work here and do account, in part, for the differences between fathers living with and those not living with their children. But one of the most striking things about the relationship between the streetcorner men and children is that the closest of all relationships are those where the men do live with the children, where they have accepted day-to-day responsibility for the children, but where they have done so on a voluntary basis, that is, where the children are not their own.

Not all streetcorner men who took on the role of stepfather or adoptive father were able or even attempted to establish a warm personal relationship with the children they were living with, but some of them were better able to achieve and sustain such relationships than any of the biological fathers. Thus, Robert, who had been living with Siserene and her four children for a year and a half, had become, in that time, a primary source of aid and comfort to the children. When they fell or were hit or had an object of value taken from them, they ran to Robert if he was there. He comforted them, laughed with them, and arbitrated their disputes. He painted pictures for them, made plywood cutouts of the Seven Dwarfs for them, and brought home storybooks.

Before and after Leroy and Charlene had their own child, Leroy looked after Charlene's little sisters and brother to such an extent that both their mother and the children themselves came to rely on him. Together with Calvin, a frail and ailing forty-year-old alcoholic and homosexual who looked after the children in exchange for a place to live, Leroy bathed the children, braided the girls' hair, washed their clothes at "the Bendix" (laundromat), played with them, and on their birthdays went shoplifting to get them gifts.

Even more than to Leroy, the children were attached to Calvin. When he could summon the courage, Calvin often interceded on their behalf when their mother was dealing out punishment. There was little that Calvin did not do for the children. He played with them during the day when they were well and stayed up with them at night when they were sick. During one period, when he had resolved to stop his homosexual practices (he had been married and a father), he resumed them only on those occasions when there was no food or money in the house and only long enough to "turn a trick" and get food for the children. When this did not work he raided the Safeway, despite his terror of still another jail sentence. He was proud of the part he played in their lives, and he played it so well that the children took his love and support for granted.

It would seem, then, that differences in father–child relationships do not depend so much on whether the man is in continuous as against intermittent or occasional contact with the child but on whether the man voluntarily assumes the role of father or has it thrust upon him.

The streetcorner man who lives with his wife and children is under legal and social constraints to provide for them, to be a husband to his wife and a father to his children. The chances are, however, that he is failing to provide for them, and failure in this primary function contaminates his performance as father in other respects as well. The more demonstrative and accepting he is of his children, the greater is his public and private commitment to the duties and responsibilities of fatherhood; and the greater his commitment, the greater and sharper his failure as the provider and head of the family. To soften this failure, and to lessen the damage to his public and self-esteem, he pushes the children away from him, saying, in effect, "I'm not even trying to be your father, so now I can't be blamed for failing to accomplish what I'm not trying to do."

For the father separated from his children, there is no longer the social obligation to be their chief support. His performance as father is no longer an issue. His failure is an accomplished fact. But now that he is relatively free of the obligations of fatherhood, he can, in his intermittent contacts with his children, by giving money for their support and by being solicitous and affectionate with them, enjoy a modest success as father in precisely those same areas in which he is an established failure.

The Paradox of the American Father

by MYRON BRENTON

Myron Brenton is a social science writer whose articles have appeared in most of the major national magazines.

"What about the father? As far as his biological role is concerned, he might as well be treated as a drone. His task is to impregnate the female and then to disappear," wrote the great anthropologist Bronislaw Malinowski. The contemporary American father isn't being looked on as a drone, of course, but the atmosphere surrounding him is oddly jeering or contemptuous. So lacking in essential dignity has Dad become (except on Father's Day, when his presence makes a healthy impact on the gross national product) that he's tailor-made for the sneer approach. Whatever his shortcomings and however much he may have fooled himself about his power, the patriarchal father of fifty or a hundred years ago at least didn't have to sit by and watch the mass media amuse themselves at his expense. Nor, one suspects, would he have permitted such a thing to happen.

For one thing, he wasn't exposed to the denigrating magazine cartoons prevalent during the past several decades. *Playboy*'s "Love, Death and the Hubby Image" surveyed the cartoon scene as it reflects the contemporary father image and found the American male lampooned in dozens of cartoons in magazines. Author William Iversen concluded that "examples of such down-with-Daddy husband razzing are so numerous that it would take no more than a few minutes to fully document a charge of pictorial sadism, verbal castration or symbolic patricide."

THE BIOLOGICAL MYTH

The father's status as a vestigial figure derives from some popular and, in part, debatable interpretations of biology. These interpretations are based on one unquestionable fact: The father impregnates, but the mother conceives. She's the one who has the fundamental biological connection with the child. Fatherhood, it has been emphasized by Margaret Mead and others, is a "social invention" learned "somewhere at the dawn of history"—society's way of providing protection for mother and child. Some behavioral scientists—Dr. Josselyn for one— challenge the view that, as she put it, "the role of fatherhood is a psychologically foreign one, artificially imposed by the culture for the survival of the race." Nevertheless, the fact remains that in any popular comparison between the roles of mothering and fathering, the latter—being far less based on biological ties— seems relatively unimportant.

One may ask whether the mothering role does indeed find its wellspring entirely in conception and parturition or whether learning plays a more significant part than is popularly granted. Is woman born with a full array of maternal feelings which grow and mature in conjunction with her physical maturation? Or do these feelings take on shape and form during the process of enculturation?

She isn't *automatically* a mother, with all the subtleties and complexities of attitude and action the word implies. All these she learns from her culture, absorbing its particular ways of motherliness. The learning process doesn't begin the moment that the rabbit test shows positive; it doesn't begin when the pubertal breasts first ripen and the menstrual flow initially starts. It begins, as the result of countless cultural clues, much farther back, from infancy on. As Morton Hunt observed, a human mother, unlike an animal mother, must *"learn* how to be kind and loving, and how to want and to care for a child."

Here, then, is a crucial point to consider in this exploration of fatherhood: When we view the maternal role in the context of a learning process, the dichotomy between it and the paternal role becomes far less striking. *Both* mothers and fathers are—and must be—culturally prepared for their child-rearing functions. The differences between motherhood and fatherhood become even less striking when we consider the relative ease with which women can suppress their mothering tendencies—can, in effect, learn *not* to want children or at least not a sizable number of them. The alacrity with which women latch onto each new advance in contraceptives specifically designed for them shows that the maternal drive (if there is any such thing) isn't so powerful that nonmaternal wishes can't supersede it.

MISSING: THE CONCEPT OF FATHERHOOD

Seen in the light of learned maternal behavior, American males are on the whole woefully short-changed when it comes to learning and being encouraged to learn their paternal roles. Preparation for motherhood is a cumulative experience. It starts in very early childhood and is progressively reinforced until the girl actually becomes a mother. By comparison, men are clearly disadvantaged in their preparation for fatherhood. Since their potential for the paternal role isn't structured by a biological framework, boys ought to be made especially cognizant of the multifarious parental responses they'll be called on to exhibit one day. Instead, they see—in their own homes—that fatherhood either assumes narrow dimensions or is more or less irrelevant. They don't get the feel of fatherhood the way a girl gets it for motherhood. The result is that, as psychoanalyst Bruno Bettelheim has said, "Only very occasionally, for boys, is fatherhood added like an afterthought as part of their self-image as mature men."

No wonder fatherhood so often and so quickly bores a man. No wonder a research study into what pre-adolescent (eight-to-eleven-year-old) boys consider the appropriate images for themselves and for girls shows enormous differences in orientation. These boys think girls must stay close to home; keep clean; play more quietly and gently than boys; are prone to cry when scared or hurt; and are afraid to venture to hazardous places like rooftops and empty lots. Girls play with dolls; fuss over babies; talk about clothes; need to learn cooking, sewing and child care—but it's considered much less important for them than for boys to learn such things as spelling and arithmetic.

The fact that the girls would become mothers someday was implicit throughout. Contrast this with the way that the same boys viewed their own roles. Only in the most indirect fashion did they acknowledge their own potentialities for fatherhood—and then only in terms of the breadwinning (protective) role. Boys "have to be able to fight in case a bully comes along; they have to be athletic; they have to be able to run fast; they must be able to play rough games; they need to know how to play many games—curb-ball, baseball, basketball, football; they need to be smart; they need to be able to take care of themselves." They should also know all of the things girls don't know—how to climb, make a fire, carry things. Furthermore, "they should have more ability than girls; they need to know how to stay out of trouble; they need to know arithmetic and spelling more than girls do."

One wonders how a boy building up a mosaic of stereotypes like these (suitably laced with male chauvinism) will grow into a man able to handle the various paternal challenges, big and little, that come along to test his mettle as a father and a male. How, for instance, will the father handle the first major crisis —the birth of his first child? Unprepared for the new demands that will be made on them, lacking readiness for the new roles they'll be called on to play, many fathers face the prospect of parenthood with real foreboding and genuine feelings of inadequacy.

The insecurity such a man feels is heightened by the fact that he's suddenly shoved out of the favored position in the family as his wife necessarily identifies much more closely with the needs of the new baby than with his. He may then withdraw psychically or become a submissive, loving, but easily manipulated third party to the symbiotic mother–child dyad.

How, being relatively unprepared for the fathering role, will he handle the close attachment that his young sons are likely to develop for their mothers? Freud postulated the existence of an Oedipus complex, stating that each boy, from the age of (roughly) three to seven, passes through a difficult phase in which he views his father as a rival for his mother's affections. In Freud's terms, it's the crucial phase in the formulation of the boy's masculine identity. There's considerable skepticism among a portion of the psychological community about the reality of the Oedipus complex as an innate phenomenon. Anthropological data denies its existence in many other cultures. But there can be no doubt that in our society a triangle situation often does develop between the boy, the mother who gives him so much attention and provides for so many of his needs, and the father. Frequently the father considers himself—or is made to consider himself—extraneous to this close relationship between the two others and withdraws even further from the fathering role. Alternatively, he meets the boy's hostility and moodiness toward him with his own hostility and moodiness. Either way, a lack of balance is created in the family. The boy misses a male figure whom he can respect and identify with and who will help him grow out of this phase.

To an extent, of course, a mother sensitive to the situation can compensate for a father who absents himself physically or psychically. She can maintain his identity in the home, his presence and importance, as it were, by the way she refers to him in front of the children when he isn't there. But if she herself feels cheated by his absence—as is sooner or later likely to happen—the tensions that build up aren't going to predispose her to refer to him affirmatively. On the contrary, consciously or unconsciously, she's apt in time to denigrate him and tear down his image.

How will the unprepared father handle the feelings of rivalry likely to come when his son is a teenager anxious to display his own burgeoning masculinity? The boy may be a source of pride —but also a threat. By his very presence he tells the father, "Your strength can't go on forever. I'm here challenging you." Some competition may be inevitable, and on the boy's part it

may be a healthy aspect of growing up. If the father feels inadequate as a parent or as a male, he's likely to show ambivalence:
urging the youngster to do well, but trying to crush his ego at
the same time. Many fathers are "thrown" by a son's first request for the use of the family car or for a bigger allowance for
dating purposes or by other manifestations of approaching manhood. The Crestwood Heights study of suburbia showed fathers
becoming pals with their sons as a "cultural ideal" because the
community's "concept of time makes ageing and the looming
prospect of the termination of the career a very real threat to
the man; the prospect can be softened by playing down the
actual gap in years between father and son."

How will the man who has little concept of the fathering role
handle his relationship to his daughter—a relationship presenting its own delicate problems? To his daughter, the father represents, so to speak, the first man in her life. He's largely responsible for the way she forms her general attitude toward
men. If he is fearful of women and shows it either by retreating
into passivity, by using brutal authoritarianism, or by insisting
that the females in his family adhere to rigidly patriarchal patterns, she soon senses it. It doesn't take her long to discover that
—directly or via the manipulative approach—her mother is the
real, the only strength in the family. Her images of masculinity
and femininity, of the male–female relationship, develop accordingly.

How is the father going to handle the most difficult and crucial job—that of giving his children the materials they need to
fashion a coherent, mature, meaningful set of personal values
for themselves? How is he going to provide them with the
guidelines that will help them recognize the differences between freedom and license, assertiveness and anarchy, self-
worth and self-seeking? This is the crux of the matter, the area
of his paternal functioning in which his failure to exercise sufficient authority and initiative shows the most blatantly deleterious results. That he *is* failing is hardly surprising.

THE BREADWINNER

When sociologist Helena Lopata of Roosevelt University queried more than six hundred women in the Chicago area to find out how they viewed their roles in life, in order of importance, she discovered that they considered themselves mothers first of all. When she asked them to do the same for their husbands, their replies were an even greater revelation. Did these women—suburban wives in their thirties with a family income between $6,000 and $10,000, urban wives with a median age of forty-nine and a family income from $5,000 to more than $16,000—see their mates primarily as husbands? As fathers? Or as breadwinners? The answer, startling though it is, isn't difficult to guess. Nearly 65 percent of the wives in both groups stated unequivocally that the most important role of the man of the family is, in their eyes, his breadwinning one. Father came in second; husband, a poor third.

These statistics lend themselves to a very plausible explanation. Since the American male bases his masculine identity so narrowly on the breadwinning role, since it occupies—both psychically and physically—the central position in his life, his wife naturally is inclined to see him in the same utilitarian way. If one leaves aside the implications this has for the emotional relationship between husband and wife, the fact is that by depending so heavily on his breadwinning role to validate his sense of himself as a man, instead of also letting his roles as husband, father, and citizen of the community count as validating sources, the American male treads on psychically dangerous ground. It's always dangerous to put all of one's psychic eggs into one basket.

This is not to deny the meaning and importance of work in a person's life. Ideally, work is an outlet for creative energy, a way of channeling aggression, a tie with reality, and what Erik H. Erikson has called the backbone of identity formation. What is suggested here is this: (1) The other roles a man plays in life may also be very valuable in these respects; (2) present-day working conditions seldom permit fulfillment of the traditional psychological aims of work to any significant degree; and (3) a narrow concentration of work in terms of his identity does not allow the male enough scope and flexibility to deal with the complexities of the times.

Not surprisingly, the man who adjusts least well to retirement is the one who identifies himself—as a man—most closely with the breadwinning role. Conversely, the man who adjusts best is the one whose psychic investments have throughout the years been multidimensional; according to Donald Super:

> The physician-artist finds it easy to keep on painting, for he took up painting in the first place because of his interests; medical and artistic interests have been shown to tend to go together. Indulging these interests is purely avocational; it contributes nothing to his status as a physician; it brings him no fame or fees, merely satisfaction and friends. On the other hand, the executive does not find it easy to keep up his golf, his yachting or his cards, for he took these up originally not so much out of interest in the activities themselves as for the associations they would bring him. Mixing with the right people at the club brings clients, customers, contracts, and the right people are glad to mix with him for the same reasons. Once the business motivation is removed the association no longer has the same mutual appeal, and the activity itself loses point. There are exceptions, of course; businessmen have real friendships, as well as friendships of convenience, and some businessmen like golf, yachting or cards for their own sakes. But these *are* probably the exceptions.

If avocations help the male adjust to retirement, it stands to reason that a flexible view of what it is that constitutes masculinity, a fundamentally equalitarian approach to marriage, will also help enormously. The husband who doesn't look at himself or his wife in terms of roles, who's not demasculinized by doing the dishes or by having a working wife or by showing tenderness and love—the man who in his conception of himself finds genuine rewards in being a successful husband and father, as well as breadwinner—is hardly going to feel, after he retires, that he doesn't belong at home.

EQUALITY, FLEXIBILITY AND FAMILY HAPPINESS

The traditional psychiatrists and sociologists don't quite see it like this. They don't approve of the loose-knit equalitarian marriage. Their way is to pigeonhole men and women into neat categories. They envision the ideal family, from the mental-health viewpoint, operating on the basis of clear-cut role differentiation. The man is the instrumental or task leader, the breadwinner, the authority figure, the one who gets things done, the parent who offers conditional love. The woman is the emotional or expressive-integrative leader, the one who keeps house and raises the children, the one solely responsible for binding the family's psychic wounds, the parent who offers unconditional love.

Such an inflexible division of roles rides roughshod over any individual characteristics. Task division is sharp—people know exactly what their roles are and no mistake about it—but focus on the uniqueness of individual personality is very blurred.

Moreover, in today's world, it isn't even really functional. It isn't functional because, the way the American pattern is going —especially in terms of ecological shifts—the American family absolutely needs strong, flexible men *and* strong, flexible women to get things done.

Studies at the University of Southern California, Dr. James Peterson's bailiwick, show that when marriages have a strict division of roles in the traditional pattern—that is, when the husband is solely the task leader, the wife solely the expressive leader—the family as a functioning unit ceases to function. He explains:

Unless there's an interpenetration of roles, the whole thing doesn't work—that is, if the wife cannot play the instrumental role, can't do the tasks that previously the man would insist on doing, the family breaks down. But likewise, if the husband is not an expressive leader, emotional leader, and gives his wife these things, the family breaks down . . .

To be sure, society may insist that a man who responds emotionally enough to give this kind of leadership has a considerable feminine component in his personality. It may insist on a whole sequence of elaborate rules and standards for what constitutes appropriate masculine and feminine response, for the most part erroneously and arbitrarily connecting them to innate sex-linked traits. But to the extent to which such elaborations require demonstration as proof of sexual identity, to this extent many individuals will suppress portions of their personalities, or they will try to conform to the rules and standards but feel insecure because not all aspects of themselves really fit in with what is expected.

However, gaining a feeling of security about one's sexual identity doesn't really require such heavy reliance on any superficial or narrow set of standards or such great emphasis on the tasks one performs. Secure sexual identity depends far more on how fully one incorporates the notion that one is a male (or female)—how comfortable one feels in one's sex, how acceptant one is of it. This incorporation and this acceptance in turn depend very much on how fully the individual's family of origin accepted him, accepted his sex, and allowed him to develop at his own rate of speed.

Discussing this point at a symposium conducted by the Child Study Association of America, Dr. M. Robert Gomberg noted:

We are moving toward an era when it will be progressively less important to distinguish between male and female on the basis of social activity and responsibility. When the emphasis is put on inner personal fulfillment, it will be less important whether the social roles are diametrically opposed or overlap than that the inner image of oneself be that of a person who is respected, loved, wanted. If a small child in his littleness feels wanted and respected, it is natural for him as he grows to know himself as a loved male child, protected by a family that supports his values, even if society is in transition and is confused in some of its dictates. He will find the strength from within, buttressed by the family, to find his own way and to play out his own role. Conversely, an individual may learn the stereotypes of masculinity. But if he has acquired them in a family that is angry, frightened, and competitive, though he sounds assertive and male, he may be inwardly frightened and need the loud sound of yesterday's maleness to disguise an inner hollowness.

Many people fear the phenomenon of role blurring because they earnestly believe that it will eventually spell the complete eradication of sex differentiation in role and in personality. This seems a needless fear. The biological differences between the sexes will, after all, remain. In fact, sex differentiation may in one sense be more acute when it's not camouflaged by the stereotypes. Robert Sunley, assistant director of the Family Service Association of Nassau County, New York, noted:

> My impression is that the more the roles are blurred, the more the superficial functional differences are eliminated, actually the more essential sexual differentiation occurs. In other words, your more truly masculine and feminine attributes emerge. I think the artificial distinctions don't really fit the people's personalities, and they also don't fit the essential sexuality involved. It confuses it, if anything. I think if you eliminate the arbitrary kinds of role distinctions, then the real sexual attraction—if there is any—emerges.

HOW TO BE MALE, THOUGH EQUAL

There is a new way to masculinity, a new concept of what it means to be a man. It has little to do with how strong the male is physically, how adept he is at ordering people around, how expensive his cars are, how versatile he is with a set of tools or how closely he identifies with all the other stereotyped attitudes and acts. It has everything to do with the way he manages his life—the way he conducts himself as a human being in terms of his wife, his children, his business associates, his friends, his neighbors, and his compatriots in the community—and with his ability to make decisions, with his courage to say no as well as yes, with his perception into the consequences of his actions and decisions. This isn't the easy way. It could hardly be called the path of least resistance. But there's no turning back the clock. With the equality of women an inexorable trend, with the traditional male patterns increasingly losing their significance for a variety of reasons, it is—at bottom—the only alternative to what may well become psychic castration.

What I am saying is that no matter how much American males may yearn for the simpler, more clearly defined times gone by, their yearnings are futile. They have the choice of remaining what collectively they are, a sex at bay, or of redefining themselves in the light of the changing culture. Historically, in the relationship between men and women and between men and men, this is a new approach. And it is the ultimate masculine challenge. It's the ultimate challenge because it does away with stereotypes, guidelines and life plans. It simply requires a man to be more fully human, more fully responsive, and more fully functioning than he has ever before allowed himself to be. This is the freedom that equality of the sexes offers him.

If he's afraid to take this freedom, the American male will wind up enslaving himself all the more. If he grasps it, he may at last come to see that he's not really as fragile as his patriarchal concepts have made him out to be.

Children

Who Cares for America's Children?

by URIE BRONFENBRENNER

Urie Bronfenbrenner is well known as a developmental and social psychologist who seeks to translate the results of social research into public policy. He is professor of psychology and of child development and family studies in the College of Human Ecology at Cornell University. His latest book is *Two Worlds of Childhood: U.S. and U.S.S.R.*

I shall be short, but not very sweet. America's families and their children are in trouble. Trouble so deep and pervasive as to threaten the future of our nation. The source of the trouble is nothing less than a national neglect of children, and of those primarily engaged in their care: America's parents.

We like to think of America as a child-centered society, but our actions belie our words. A hard look at our institutions and ways of life reveals that our national priorities lie elsewhere. The pursuit of affluence, the worship of material things, the hard sell and the soft, the willingness to accept technology as a substitute for human relationships, the imposition of responsibility upon families without support, and the readiness to blame the victims of evil for the evil itself have brought us to the point where a broken television set or a broken computer provokes more indignation and more action than a broken family or a broken child.

America, the richest and most powerful country in the world, stands thirteenth among the nations in combating infant mortality; even East Germany does better. Moreover, our ranking has dropped steadily in recent decades. A similar situation obtains with respect to maternal and child health, day care, children's allowances, and other basic services to children and families.

But the figures for the nation as a whole, dismaying as they are, mask even greater inequities. For example, infant mortality for nonwhites in the United States is almost twice that for whites, and there are a number of Southern states, and Northern metropolitan areas, in which the ratios are considerably higher.

Ironically, of even greater cost to the society than infants who die are the many more who sustain injury but survive with disability. Many of these suffer impaired intellectual function and behavioral disturbance including hyperactivity, distractability, and low attention span, all factors contributing to school retardation and problem behavior. Again, the destructive impact is greatest on the poorest segments of the population, especially nonwhites. It is all the more tragic that this massive damage and its subsequent cost in reduced productivity, lower income, unemployability, welfare payments, and institutionalization are avoidable if adequate nutrition, prenatal care, and other family and child services are provided, as they are in a number of countries less prosperous than ours.

But it is not only children from disadvantaged families who show signs of progressive neglect. For example, an analysis I carried out a few years ago of data on child-rearing practices in the United States over a twenty-five-year period reveals a decrease, especially in recent years, in all spheres of interaction between parents and children. A similar conclusion is indicated by results of cross-cultural studies comparing American parents with those from Western and Eastern Europe. As parents and other adults move out of the lives of children, the vacuum is filled by the age-segregated peer group.

Recently my colleagues and I completed a study showing that, at every age and grade level, children today show a greater dependence on their peers than they did a decade ago. Our evidence indicates that susceptibility to group influence is higher among children from homes in which one or both parents are frequently absent. In addition, "peer-oriented" youngsters describe their parents as less affectionate and less firm in discipline. Attachment to age mates appears to be influenced more by a lack of attention and concern at home than by any positive attraction of the peer group itself. In fact, these children have a rather negative view of their friends, and of themselves as well. They are pessimistic about the future, rate lower in responsibility and leadership, and are more likely to enage in such behavior as lying, teasing other children, "playing hooky" or "doing something illegal."

Our national rhetoric notwithstanding, the actual patterns of life in America are such that children and families come last. Our society expects its citizens first of all to meet the demands of their jobs, and then to fulfill civic and social obligations. Responsibilities to children are to be met, of course, but this is something one is expected to do in his spare time.

But when, where and how? In today's world, parents find themselves at the mercy of a society which imposes pressures and priorities that allow neither time nor place for meaningful activities and relations between children and adults, which downgrade the role of parent and the functions of parenthood, and which prevent the parent from doing the things he wants to do as a guide, friend and companion to his children.

The frustrations are greatest for the family of poverty, where the capacity for human response is crippled by hunger, cold, filth, sickness and despair. No parent who spends his days in search of menial work and his nights in keeping rats away from the crib can be expected to find the time, let alone the heart, to engage in constructive activities with his children or serve as a stable source of love and discipline. The fact that some families in poverty do manage to do this is a tribute to them, but not to the society or community in which they live.

For families who can get along, the rats are gone but the rat race remains. The demands of a job, or often two jobs, which claim mealtimes, evenings and weekends as well as days; the trips and moves one must make to get ahead or simply hold one's own; the ever-increasing time spent in commuting; the parties, the evenings out, the social and community obligations —all of the things one has to do if he is to meet his primary responsibilities—produce a situation in which a child often spends more time with a passive babysitter than with a participating parent or adult.

Even when the parent is at home, a compelling force cuts off communication and response among family members. Although television could, if used creatively, enrich the activities of children and families, it now only undermines them. Like the sorcerer of old, the television set casts its magic spell, freezing speech and action, turning the living into silent statues so long as the enchantment lasts. The primary danger of the television screen lies not so much in the behavior it produces—although there is danger there—as in the behavior it prevents: the talks, the games, the family festivities and arguments through which much of the child's learning takes place and through which his character is formed. Turning on the television set can turn off the process that transforms children into people.

In our modern way of life it is not only parents of whom children are deprived, it is people in general. A host of factors conspire to isolate children from the rest of society: the fragmentation of the extended family, the separation of residential and business areas, the disappearance of neighborhoods, the elimination of small stores in favor of supermarkets, zoning ordinances, occupational mobility, child-labor laws, the abolishment of the apprentice system, consolidated schools, television, telephones, the substitution of the automobile for public transportation or just plain walking, separate patterns of social life for different age groups, the working mother, the delegation of child care to specialists; all these manifestations of progress operate to decrease opportunity and incentive for meaningful contact between children and persons older or younger than themselves.

And here we confront a fundamental and disturbing fact: *Children need people in order to become human.* The fact is fundamental because it is firmly grounded both in scientific research and in human experience. It is disturbing because the isolation of children from adults threatens simultaneously the growth of the individual and the survival of the society. The young cannot pull themselves up by their own bootstraps. It is primarily through observing, playing and working with others older and younger than himself that a child discovers both what he can do and who he can become, that he develops both his ability and his identity. It is primarily through exposure and interaction with adults and children of different ages that a child acquires new interests and skills, and learns the meaning of tolerance, cooperation and compassion.

Hence, to relegate children to a world of their own is to deprive them of their humanity and to deprive ourselves of humanity as well. Yet this is what is happening in America today. We are experiencing a breakdown in the process of making human beings human. By isolating our children from the rest of society, we abandon them to a world devoid of adults and ruled by the destructive impulses and compelling pressure, both of the age-segregated peer group and of the aggressive and exploitive television screen. By setting our priorities elsewhere and by putting children and families last, by claiming one set of values while pursuing another, we leave our children bereft of standards and support, and our own lives impoverished and corrupted.

This reversal of priorities, which amounts to a betrayal of our children, underlies the growing disillusionment and alienation among young people in all segments of American society. Those who grew up in settings where children, families, neighborhoods and communities still counted are able to act out their frustration in positive ways through constructive protest, through participation and through public service. Those who come from circumstances in which the family, the neighborhood and the community could not function—be it in slum or suburb—can only strike out against an environment they have experienced as indifferent, callous, cruel and unresponsive.

The failure to reorder our priorities, the insistence on business as usual, and the continued reliance on rhetoric as a substitute for radical reforms can have only one result: the far more rapid and pervasive growth of alienation, apathy, drugs, delinquency and violence among the young and among the not so young in all segments of our national life. We face the prospect of a society which resents its own children and fears its youth.

What is needed is a change in our patterns of living which will once again bring people back into the lives of children, and children back into the lives of people. But how? The verse in Isaiah says, "a little child shall lead them." I propose we act upon that text. But perhaps to do so one must speak not in the language of Isaiah but in the language of our contemporary times.

What I am proposing is the seduction of America by its children. What do I mean? Let me give you some examples, concrete actions we could take at all levels in our society: business, industry, mass media, communities, local, state and federal governments, right down to the local neighborhood; concrete actions that would have the effect of bringing people back into the lives of children, and children back into the lives of people.

One of these suggested actions comes from the U.S.S.R., which is not the only country that does this; it's also done in Scandinavia. This is the custom for which there's no English word, so I've used the word "adoption," in which a business or an industry adopts a group of children or a children's program with the aim of becoming friends, of acquainting children with the people who work in the world of work.

Dr. David Goslin of the Russell Sage Foundation decided to Americanize this idea, because he felt, as I do, that the values are human rather than parochial. He persuaded the Detroit *Free Press* to try an experiment. Recently that newspaper saw in its composing room, pressroom, dispatch room, city room and other offices young children twelve years of age from two schools in the city of Detroit. It was a fascinating thing to watch.

When we first talked to the people at the *Free Press* they said, "Gee, kids? You know we're a newspaper here. What will we do with them, sit there all day and watch them? Besides, you know, this is a busy place." As one lady in the advertising section said to me, "Professor, you mean you're going to have kids around here—you really mean that?"

On the last day, the same lady said to me, "Professor, it's going to be so lonely here next week—those kids are easier to talk to than people." They were from two schools, one in a slum area, the other in a middle-class area, both black and white. The children were just themselves. They said things like "This is a place to meet, a way to understand people" and "If every kid in Detroit and all around the United States got to do this, I don't think there would be so many problems in the world." It was a two-way street that came alive there. People rediscovered children, and children rediscovered people.

OTHER ACTIONS CAN BE TAKEN

Another idea is the notion of encouraging business and industry to place day-care centers in or near the place of business —not as the only location for day-care and preschool centers, but as one of the options available to parents, so that during the coffee breaks and during the lunch hours people could visit the kids. Perhaps then children would once again become a subject of conversation in places where children don't get talked about as much as they used to.

We are about to propose that every moderately sized place of business or branch of a business in the country establish a Commission on Children to ask how the policies and practices of that business affect the lives of their employees and their children as family members. On such a commission, obviously the employees as well as the management and the union should participate.

We recommend that business explore and maximize half-time and part-time jobs for comparable rates of pay and status so that those parents who choose to work part time may do so, instead of having to make the choice between full-time work and full-time no work, or between part-time work at a reduced rate of pay, reduced status and reduced job security. We're talking about flexible work schedules so that parents can be at home when the kids arrive at home.

We emphasize especially family-oriented industrial planning and development, so that when plants are established, locations are determined and housing is planned, consideration is given to the fact that employees have families and have to be concerned with how and where they can spend time as families. It should be kept in mind in planning the buildings, the apartments and residences that there will be children and parents living in these places. In short, we are asking for a family-oriented business and industrial policy in America. We speak also of actions to be taken in the realm of the mass media and the advertising industry.

We ask that urgent attention be paid to the creation of an entirely new kind of television programming, one which no longer casts the viewer in the role of a passive and isolated bystander, but which instead involves family members and neighbors in activities with each other. That is, involving children, adults, older kids, younger kids and grandparents in games, conversations and joint creative activity. And we assert that there is nothing inherent in television technology which precludes this kind of possibility.

The community, of course, is the family of families. And it is there, perhaps, more than anywhere else that the family needs support. Because the thesis I am presenting to you is that just as children cannot function unless they have healthy and human parents and caretakers to deal with them, so these caretakers, parents and all those who carry the responsibility for children in our society need the support of the community and of the society in order for them to be able to function effectively in their roles. It is not the family that's breaking down, it is not the staff of people engaged in work with children that is breaking down, it is the support in the society for the family and for those who are faced with the responsibility and the delight of raising a new generation of human beings that is being withdrawn.

There can be no doubt that day care is coming to America. The question is: What kind? Shall we follow or reject the pattern of certain other nations in which day-care programs have served further to separate the child from his family and reduce the family's and the community's feeling of responsibility for their children?

The answers to these questions depend on the extent to which day-care programs are so located and so organized as to encourage rather than to discourage the involvement of parents in the development and operation of the day-care program both at the center and in the home. Like Project Head Start, day-care programs can have no lasting constructive impact on the development of the child unless they affect not only the child himself but the people who constitute his enduring day-to-day environment in the family, neighborhood, and community. This means not only that parents must play an active part in the planning and administration of day-care programs, but that they must actively participate in the activities of the program. It means that the program cannot be confined to the center, but must reach out into the home and the community so that the whole neighborhood is caught up in activities in behalf of its children. From this point of view, we need to experiment in the location of day-care centers in places that are within reach of the significant people in the child's life. For some families this means neighborhood centers; for others, centers at the place of work. A great deal of variation and innovation will be required to find the appropriate solutions for different groups in different settings.

In keeping with the foregoing point, I would emphasize that, *in the first instance, children need people, not professionals.* Nowhere is the power of this principle illustrated more effectively than in Harold Skeels's remarkable follow-up study of two groups of mentally retarded, institutionalized children, who constituted the experimental and control groups in an experiment he had initiated thirty years earlier. When the children were three years of age, thirteen of them were placed in the care of female inmates of a state institution for the mentally retarded, with each child being assigned to a different ward. A control group was allowed to remain in the original—also institutional—environment, a children's orphanage. During the formal experimental period, which averaged a year and a half, the experimental group showed a gain in IQ of twenty-eight points, whereas the control group dropped twenty-six points. Upon completion of the experiment, it became possible to place the institutionally mothered children in legal adoption. Thirty years later, all thirteen children in the experimental group were found to be self-supporting; all but two had completed high school, with four having one or more years of college. In the control group, all were either dead or still institutionalized. Skeels concludes his report with some dollar figures on the amount of taxpayers' money expended to sustain the institutionalized group, in contrast to the productive income brought in by those who had been raised initially by mentally deficient women in a state institution.

What accounted for these dramatic gains? The answer is to be found in Skeels's careful observations of what happened on the wards of that institution for female defectives. In each instance, one of the inmates in effect adopted the infant and became its mother, but in addition the entire ward was caught up in activities in behalf of "our baby." New clothes and playthings appeared and the children were lavished with attention. Indeed, the several wards began to compete with each other in terms of whose baby was developing most rapidly.

The Skeels experiment illustrates a fundamental principle: *The extent to which children receive the kind of care and attention which is necessary for their development depends on*

*the extent to which those who have responsibility for their care
are provided with a place, a time, and the encouragement to
engage in activities with young children.* This does not mean
that professionals are not important. Quite the contrary, we
need professionals, but their primary task should be not to
work with the children themselves but to help create the kind of
conditions and situations in which parents and others who
carry the responsibility for the day-to-day care of children can
function effectively as human beings.

There are many other measures we are considering. I will
mention one or two, in relation to the schools. We point out
the sterility of courses in parent education for junior and senior
high school, where there are no children in evidence. We suggest that preschool programs and Head Start centers be located
in or near school programs, that school curricula utilize these as
learning opportunities and opportunities for responsibility. Then
the older children get some notion of what a child is like, what
a child's needs are and how much fun a child is, so we do not
have a generation of young people who don't discover what a
child is until they have one.

These are new kinds of suggestions. They bring difficulties,
but they also bring promise. They bring a very important element into the lives of older school-aged children. If one looks
at the problems of human development cross-culturally, as I've
been privileged to do during this past decade, one is struck by
the fact that American society is characterized by the inutility
of children. We in our country do not give children anything
really important to do. We give them duties, not responsibilities.
And yet there are things they could do if we but looked around.

One of the most important responsibilities that the older child
can have, both as an individual and as a group, is responsibility
for the young. Evidence indicates that older children are very
effective as models, as reinforcers, as praise-givers to the young,
but in our age-segregated society such opportunities are seldom
given.

THE OLD OFFER VITAL ASSISTANCE

Similarly, there is another group for whom children can be a delight and a genuine help, and who in turn can serve a very important purpose in providing a humanizing experience for children. I refer to older people. The pleasure which a child gets from recognizing how much he's appreciated by an older person is a special kind of pleasure on both sides.

There is but one caution to be borne in mind. The crucial factor, of course, is not how much time is spent with a child, but how the time is spent. A child learns, he becomes human, primarily through participation in challenging activity with those whom he loves and admires. It is the example, challenge and reinforcement provided by people who care that enable a child to develop both his ability and his identity. An everyday example of the operation of this principle is the mother who daily talks with her young child and, usually without thinking much about it, responds more warmly when he uses new words or expressions or new motions. And as he does so, she gradually introduces new and more complex activities in her activity with the child.

So it is in this way, in work and in play with children—in games, in projects, in shared responsibilities with parents, adults and older children—that the child develops the skills, motives and qualities of character that enable him to live a life that is gratifying both to himself and to those around him. But this can happen only in a society that lets it happen, and makes it happen, a society in which the needs of families and children become a primary concern, not merely of special organizations and interest groups, but of all the major institutions—government, industry, business, mass media, communities, neighborhoods and individual citizens.

It is the priorities that they set that will determine our children's present and America's future.

Women and Children:
Male Chauvinist Spock Recants—Almost

by BENJAMIN M. SPOCK

While not yet going as far as many women believe necessary, Dr. Spock's current views, as presented in this article, are a far cry from those he once took about such matters as "sex role training" and a child's need for what he used to term "mothering." "Sensitive, enthusiastic . . . care" is now his definition of that last word—something that he has decided can be provided by "loving fathers" or grandparents as well. Because of the impact of Dr. Spock's past views on parents everywhere, his current statement can be read as an historic document in the development of changing concepts about child care and sex roles in America.

When an invitation was wangled for me to speak to the National Women's Political Caucus about The Coalition, an alliance of several political groups to the left of the Democratic Party, I welcomed the opportunity. The Coalition had been put together a couple of weeks earlier by new party groups in a dozen states, the Peace and Freedom Party in California and Indiana, the Wisconsin Alliance, and others. Its draft platform included a vigorous antisexist plank and it planned a national convention late in November to nominate not only a Presidential slate for '72 but a full Cabinet too. But while I was waiting my turn at the back of the hall, along with speakers for other political parties and candidates . . . , it became obvious that many of the women present were more concerned with sexist views in my past writings than with The Coalition.

Several women reporters and delegates came up to ask me suspiciously how I had been invited. Two women told me angrily that my daring to speak would tear the meeting apart. A friend in the peace movement begged me not to talk because the spectacle of the women's movement attacking a spokesman for peace would be bad for the image of both groups. But since my inclusion in the list of speakers had been announced, I saw only more misunderstanding if I ran away.

I started with an apology for some of the prejudiced things I had said about women, and women's roles, in earlier magazine articles and in the first edition of *Decent and Indecent*. I explained that I had written them three to five years ago, when there was no liberation movement, that I had changed my thinking a great deal since, and had rewritten the most objectionable part of the book—Chapter II—for the revised paperback edition published in 1971. Then I spoke of The Coalition.

One member of the audience walked out while I talked, shouting denunciations. Others asked questions about the place of women in the leadership of The Coalition (an equal place already, I could say), about whether I believed fathers have obligations equal to mothers' for the care of children (yes), about whether I would review *Baby and Child Care* and revise it where it is sexist (yes). Gloria Steinem said sternly she hoped I understood that I was considered a symbol of repression, like Freud and other male-supremacists.

Actually, I had already been bruised—and educated—by such attacks at universities all over the U.S. during speaking tours in opposition to the Vietnam war. I had learned that I could be as prejudiced as the next man.

I had begun the ill-fated Chapter II, which was devoted to problems of sex and sex role (the other chapters being about idealism, war, politics and education) by explaining my opinion that men and women have psychological differences not only because of strong cultural pressures but because of inborn temperamental differences between the average boy and the average girl. I admitted I had no proof. I called boys on the average more restless, aggressive and obstinate, citing the greater difficulty in toilet-training them, their endless gunplay in childhood, their obsession with violence, mock violence and power all their lives. I described girls at an ice rink skating amicably in pairs while the boys illegally played tag, skated against the current and darted among the nervous adults. I referred to Erikson's experiment in which he gave dolls representing adults and children, dolls' furniture and blocks to school-age children, as materials for depicting an exciting event: The boys built towering structures and then carried out scenes of violence, most commonly automobile collisions or robberies (the culprit would always be apprehended by the police). Girls used the blocks to outline rooms in a house and then portrayed family scenes. To me, cultural pressure is not an adequate explanation for such differences in the level of aggression.

I've said often in books and articles that, as a result of my own clinical experience as well as training, I subscribe to Freud's formulations about castration anxiety in both boys and girls, and about its persistence in varying degrees into adulthood—most often taking the form in men of doubts about their virility, and in women of rivalry; that small boys' frustration at being forced to admit that they cannot grow babies contributes to the drive to build things, pioneer in the arts, construct theories; that the average young boy's greater unconscious fear of future castration and of his father makes him eventually repress not only his romantic and sexual feelings for his mother but all feelings—more than the average girl has to. This is one of the causes of the greater impersonalness of the average male, the greater inclination to deal in abstractions, even in regard to human affairs, the greater fascination with machines.

Among the psychological problems I discussed in articles and *Decent and Indecent* was the exaggerated aggressiveness, competitiveness or overbearingness of some women. I saw one historic root of this in the rigorous requirements of our frontier society; another in the teaching of the feminists, beginning a century ago, that women not only are entitled to equal justice but are essentially the same as men in drives and needs; and still a third in the fact that as higher education became available for women it held up for emulation the competitive and intellectual triumphs of men, not the achievement, by ordinary men and women, of loving, creative atmospheres in the family and in the community. In other words, I assumed that women are now being drawn by their closer identification with men into a more aggressive rivalry with them. (I was concerned not with the occupational competitiveness of these women, but with their general attitudes.) I explained how the combination of overbearing mother and submissive father causes multiple emotional disturbances in their children, and is passed on from generation to generation.

About fulfillment and jobs for women I came to several conclusions:

Women's frustration with child care is due, among other causes, to the fact that in our materialistic, competitive, profession-oriented society it carries no prestige and requires no academic degree. Since most women will spend several years primarily raising their children, whether or not they have other careers, I said it would be fairer if they were brought up and educated in such a way that they would feel proud of, and fascinated by, the creativity of child rearing. With this attitude they would be more likely, when they went to work outside, to choose fields requiring an understanding of people's feelings and needs, such as medicine, nursing, social work, teaching, architecture, writing. As architects, for instance, they would be more able to make creative contributions to livability, an area in which many male architects have been found wanting. I never said that women's place is in the home. I assumed that mothers would turn increasingly to careers but would make compromises while they had young children. I hoped that parents would bring up their children to be enthusiastic about, rather than minimize, their maleness or femaleness.

Some of these opinions are embarrassing for me to acknowledge now.

It is obvious that I, like most men and women up to a couple of years ago, harbored an underlying sexism (prejudice in favor of the dominant sex) in some matters—for example, my assumption that women will always play the major role in child care, that the mother is more obliged than the father to give up whatever career time is necessary for the care of small children, that fathers' outside jobs will be the main ones. I was right in speaking of the unhealthy effects of domineering mothers and submissive fathers, but I forgot to mention the unhealthiness of the opposite. There was at least a trace of male insecurity and chauvinism in my assumption that men and women should be conscious of distinctly different sexual identities and that parents need to emphasize these during childhood.

In the revised edition of *Decent and Indecent* and in my speeches, I now start the discussion of sex role not with the psychological differences (those are at the end to show that my other points do not depend on them), but with the needs of infants and young children for a sensitive, enthusiastic kind of care if they are to develop into warmhearted, creative people. They can receive this from loving fathers, mothers, grandparents. But each year it is harder to hire a full-time substitute caretaker whose personality and attitude approach those of good parents. (Part-time sitters do not need to be as inspiring.) I am not convinced that group care before the age of three years, in day-care centers, as practiced either in the U.S., the Soviet Union or Israel, can substitute for above-average parental care.

I recognize that, in justice, a wife has as much right to an uninterrupted career as her husband. How they want to reconcile their various aspirations is for them to decide, democratically. I hope that someday the government will pay a salary to a parent who stays at home to care for children, and that his or her seniority in the career position will be maintained. If neither parent is willing to take part time off from a job for a few years, they might do better without children.

Dominatingness and submissiveness are both undesirable, in husband or wife. The effort to dominate a spouse is most often an expression of anxiety about being dominated, usually left over from being dominated in childhood. Spouses should strive to achieve a cooperative balance—in the care of the home and of the children—in which as many jobs as possible are shared companionably, and no one is too important to take his turn at the humbler ones.

As for my belief in inborn temperament and in Freud's basic concepts of psychosexual development, I've searched my mind for evidence of prejudice and do not find reason to recant. (I acknowledge that Freud also had his prejudices like the rest of us.) Perhaps after I have been educated further I will see the light differently.

The overall purpose of *Decent and Indecent* was to make human beings aware of those less visible and less rational impulses of our species which get us into tragic difficulties or deflect us from our conscious aspirations. My principal aim in bringing in temperament was to emphasize to men the dangerousness of the drives which contribute to their bellicosity: their fear of not proving sufficiently virile and courageous, their power-greediness, along with their paranoid readiness to blame others for their own hostile aggressiveness. I also wanted to bring out their inclination to depersonalize relationships, which makes many physicians, lawyers, ministers, bankers, bureaucrats, husbands and other categories of men so difficult to communicate with.

In writing about women's inherent *and* culturally determined personalness, and their understanding of human needs, I admit I was hoping to make them feel good about going into the helping rather than the competitive occupations. I'd like to see more men also choose the helping and creative fields. But I never considered those traits (of personalness and understanding) inferior to the traits the average man has to offer—quite the opposite. I spent thirty-five years of medical-school teaching trying to find ways to inculcate or preserve sensitivity in men students. (At Western Reserve University we effectively countered the student's inclination to dehumanize himself and his future patients during his first two laboratory years by giving him, from the start, a live family to be responsible for.)

I've never thought that inborn differences of temperament were of a type or intensity that could legitimately exclude women or men from any occupation they had a genuine desire to enter. I believe that there are marked temperamental differences between individuals of the same sex, which means that, in any characteristic, a person of one sex may be like the average of the opposite sex. From my point of view, the woman who goes into roller-skate racing or professional wrestling probably had a lot of aggression to start with, and her style was obviously not cramped by the expectations of her family about what a girl should be.

But I agree today that a man has no business trying to tell women what their characteristics are, which ones are inborn, which are more admirable, which will be best utilized by what occupations. So now, in discussions that touch on the question of sex differences, I focus almost exclusively on the male liability to belligerence and to depersonalization.

Growing numbers of young people hope to build, through their individual lives, a more just world in which everyone has a chance to realize his aspirations and potential. They are our main hope of salvation, I feel. In trying to undo discrimination against women—and its ill effects on men—some of these young people will lean over backward to avoid imposing on their children traditional stereotypes of boy and girl behavior, man and woman roles. They will, for instance, be as ready to buy dolls for their sons as for their daughters, if asked, and in no hurry to present dolls to their daughters *unless* asked. The same, in reverse, goes for guns.

Rejecting old stereotypes to this extent may seem ridiculous to some people. It is slightly disturbing to a physician trained in older concepts. But such self-conscious deviations from custom may be necessary if new and perhaps more valid and natural definitions of sex roles are to be tested. Letting children discover their own roles, without coaching, does not mean that they will end up sexually confused. And if roles for women and men in the future are not defined nearly as sharply or as oppositely as they are now, individuals with various personalities may be able to find roles that by today's standards are unconventional mixtures but that they can play out more comfortably.

Meanwhile, other young couples will prefer to stick with the old traditions, at least until the results of experimentation are apparent. Realizing that in all probability the trend for a long period will be to minimize differences, I'll no longer recommend arbitrarily to parents that they treat their sons and daughters differently. I'll define aspects of the issue and leave the decision to the parents.

Child Rearing in Communes

by BENNETT M. BERGER, BRUCE M. HACKETT,
R. MERVYN MILLAR

The authors are now in their second year of a study of child rearing in communal families, under a grant from the National Institute of Mental Health. The article that follows describes some of what they observed in "fourteen communes in northern California, which we studied closely at first hand; two dozen additional communes we studied less closely; and, supplementing these observations, findings from the more reliable literature on communal living which has only recently begun to appear."

The birth of a child in a commune—particularly a rural commune, and especially if the birth is "natural," as many of them are—is often the occasion of a collective celebration of great significance. In the case of the earliest "first-generation" communards, the event can have a virtually *constitutional* meaning, symbolizing the collective property as a home to its occupants and the occupants themselves as members of a single family.

In partial contrast, however, to the solidarity and affirming nature of birth ceremonies, communal children tend to be viewed as rather independent, self-contained persons—although they participate, to be sure, in the higher cosmic unities (for example, in the widespread communal belief and slogan that "we are all One").

In viewing the history of how children are perceived by adults, social scientists have emphasized the differences between preindustrial, agricultural, or sometimes lower-class views on the one side and industrial or middle-class views on the other. In the former view, the status of children is seen as essentially ascribed at birth and rooted in the kinship system. In this view, children are seen as simply small or inadequate versions of their parents, totally subject to traditional or otherwise

159

arbitrary parental authority. The "modern" industrial, middle-class view, by contrast, tends to treat the child as a distinctive social category: children have their own special psychology, their own special needs, patterned processes of growth often elaborated into ideas about developmental stages which may postpone advent to "full" adulthood well into a person's twenties, and sometimes still later. The task of parents and other "socializers" in this view is to "raise" or "produce" the child (the industrial metaphor is often used) according to scientifically elaborated principles of proper child management—a process which in many middle-class families results in the division of family roles in a way that transforms a woman-with-child into a full-time child raiser.

The view that we find prevalent in the hip-communal settings we have studied fits neither of these models with precision. "Young people" are regarded as independent of the family, but not as members of an autonomous category of "children"; instead, their status is likely to be ascribed as that of "person," a development which can be understood as part of an equalitarian ethos, and as complementary to parallel developments in the status of females, from "women" (or even "mothers") to "people," and in the status of men, from being characterized in invidious status terms to being characterized as above all a "human being." Again, "we are all One."

As a practical matter, however, children are not simply independent, autonomous individuals. Age makes an important and understandable difference. Infants and "knee babies" are almost universally in the charge of their mothers, who have primary responsibility for their care. Communards, particularly rural ones, frequently discuss the possibility of "communalizing" even infants—as in the notion of placing infants at an available breast rather than an exclusively parental one, but this proposal seems as yet to be too radical. We have, however, made several observations of what could be called communal child care—for example, collective feedings, bathings and defecations (this last, a rich scene in which three toddlers in the care of one adult squatted in the woods, chatted amiably about the color, smell and texture of each other's productions, then under the ecological guidance of the grownup buried the shit and burned the paper with which they cleaned themselves).

Children aged two to four or slightly older frequently "belong to the commune" in a stronger sense than infants and knee babies do, because they are less dependent upon continuous supervision, although even with children of this age the conventional pattern of sharing their care is largely limited to the group of mothers-with-children. This is not to say that young children do not get a lot of fathering; they do; fathers hold the children often, feed them, cuddle them, and may be attentive in other respects. But this depends upon the personal predispositions of the men involved; there are no strong norms apparent which *require* the attentiveness of fathers.

But for children older than four or five, the responsibilities of either parents or the other adult communards may be much attenuated. All children are viewed as intrinsically worthy of love and respect *but not necessarily of attention.* As they grow out of primitive physical dependence upon the care of adults, they are treated and tend to behave as just another member of the extended family—including being offered (and taking) an occasional hit on a joint of marijuana as it is passed around the family circle. When problems crop up, children are particularly susceptible to being labeled and understood astrologically, in a manner of speaking, as "cosmic wards" with their own karma, or fate, and their own problems that they must work out themselves. They are expected to use first names in referring to their parents and other adults (the children themselves have names like Cloud, Forest, Blue Jay, River, Sweet Pea, etc.), are seen as the equal of adults (they fall quickly and easily into use of the hip vernacular—"far out," "outasight"—as well as all of the routine four-letter obscenities; there are no "bad words" in the language), and are in more than a few instances drawn into doing adult work. In one setting, the children have, with adult approval, established their own separate residences.

In an earlier report last year, we raised the question of whether the variations we observed in the extent to which a child belongs to its parents or to the extended communal family was a variation in types of communes or a sequential development occurring as the child gets older. We are now able to give a fairly conclusive answer: It is a sequential development, but this fact requires a good deal of explanation. Insofar as there exists a role for adults in facilitating the development of children, the role is essentially exemplary (charismatic) rather than paternalistic and authoritarian (traditional), or didactic and hortatory ("rational"). In spite of this limitation which learning-through-imitation-of-adults places on the belief that children must "work out their own fate," attempts are seriously made by adults to allow children to grow "naturally," to be autonomous and free. But the single most important belief governing the relation between children and adults is that *the experiences had by children not be fateful or self-implicating for adults*, that adults cannot be legitimately characterized in terms of what they do with or to their children—in rather clear contrast to both preindustrial and middle-class views in which the behavior of children "reflects upon" their parents, who are in some sense "responsible" for it.

In saying this, some important cautions are in order. First, the great majority of the children we have observed are six or under, and there are numerous communes that are only now beginning to recognize a "schooling" problem; and it may be that in time a distinctive "child psychology" and set of child-management practices will emerge. There may also be important sex differences in the ways adults relate to children; communal ideologies tend to be elaborated by men, and the men are clearly the most mobile sex (from time to time women express wishes that men would spend more time with the children) and therefore most likely to seek freedom from parental responsibilities—*a freedom that is itself legitimated in part by the view of children as autonomous.*

But the women share this view, too, and benefit from its application. One young mother, harried with the care of her two-year-old, said, "What I wanted was a *baby;* but a *kid*, that's something else." That is to say, having "babies" is good because it's natural, organic, earthy, and "beautiful," and besides which babies are wonderful because they represent human potential unspoiled by the corrupting influence of repressive institutions. But "raising" a child involves obligations that they have not "committed" themselves to in the sense that many middle-class mothers, who regard their lives as "settled" and their futures as a working out of what is already implicitly present (home, husband and children), devote themselves to a full-time job called "child rearing." But many hippies, including communal mothers, tend to regard their lives as unsettled, their futures uncertain, and are generally unwilling to sacrifice their own personal questings (for meaning, identity, transcendence, etc.) to full-time devotion to child rearing. And it is in this context that the hippie "theory of children" seems to us most relevant.

Communards generally tell us that "communes are good for the children"—one of the meanings many of their own parents almost certainly gave to their suburban communities; the setting itself may be said to possess medicinal qualities. In this respect there may be an important continuity between the generations, although communards frequently report that their own childhoods were frustrating experiences of little autonomy and little opportunity to develop "real" skills. In relatively isolated and sometimes bucolic rural communes, of course, it *is* possible to grant children much autonomy without much risk of waywardness, and children do in fact enjoy some of what are probably the real benefits of an inadvertent rather than a compulsory education.

FAMILY STRUCTURE AND SEXUAL RELATIONS

Everything we have said about the children of the communes occurs in the context of hippie relationships and family structures, and it is important to understand these because they contain the seeds of the potential future of the commune movement.

The most important single feature of hip relationships is their fragility. We mean by this not that many of the relationships don't last; quite the contrary. In several of our more stable communes couples have been "together" as long as the commune has existed (two to three years) and sometimes longer. We mean, rather, that there tend to be few if any cultural constraints or structural underpinnings to sustain relationships when and if they become tension-ridden or otherwise unsatisfying. The uncertainty of the future hovers over hip relationships like a probation officer reminding the parties of the necessary tentativeness of their commitments to each other.

Very few nuclear (mother-father-child) units, for example, are legally married; neither the men nor the women have the kinds of jobs that bind them to a community. Like many of their parents (who theorists have suggested have been highly mobile), they move around a great deal, getting into and out of "intimate" relations rather quickly through such techniques as spontaneous "encounter" and other forms of "up-frontness." And above and beyond these, there is a very heavy emphasis on now—a refusal to *count on* the future as a continuation of present arrangements—and a diffuse desire to remain unencumbered, a freedom *from* the social ties that constrain one.

Yet despite the fact of (and the adjustment to) the fragility of relationships, there are romantic images also superimposed. Although the fragility of old-man–old-lady relationships is a fact, communards of all sorts are generally reluctant to believe in a future of serial monogamy. Many communards, particularly the women, hope for an ideal lover or a permanent mate but tend not to have much real expectation that it will happen. Instead, compensatory satisfactions are found in the *image* of the communal family and household, always full of people, where a group of brothers and sisters, friends as kin, spend all or most of their time with each other, working, playing, loving, rapping, "hanging out"—where wedding bells, far from breaking up the old gang, are themselves so rare that they are occasions for regional celebrations of solidarity when they do ring out.

Where it exists, it is the fact of communal solidarity which functions as the strongest support for fragile relations among couples. For when the communal scene is a wholesome and attractive one, as it sometimes is, couples whose relationship is very unstable may elect to stay together in order to share those benefits rather than threaten them by breaking up.

In spite of the fragility of relationships in a system which defines the future as uncertain and in an ideology emphasizing spontaneity and freedom, heterosexual couples are the backbone of most communes, urban or rural, creedal or not. They seem more stable and dependable as members than single people do, if only because their search for partners is ended, even if that ending is temporary. The temporary character of the relationships is more pronounced in urban communes, both, we believe, because the very presence of couples in rural communes is itself generally evidence of more stable commitment, and because of the higher probability in urban scenes of meeting another man or woman who is ready and willing to enter into a close relationship at little more than a moment's notice.

When a couple has a child, their mobility is reduced somewhat, of course, even when the child is the product of a previous union of either the female or the male. But only somewhat, because of the importance of what we call the "splitting" phenomenon, particularly as it applies to men. We mentioned previously that children (especially very young ones) "belong" to their mothers, and that norms *requiring* paternal solicitude for children are largely absent. What this means is that fathers are "free"—at the very least free to split whenever they are so moved. Since they are not "legally" fathers (even if they biologically are) they have no claims on the child, and since there is generally a strong communal norm *against* invoking the legal constraints of straight society (i.e., calling the police), fathers have no obligation to the child that anyone is willing to enforce. Moreover, no norm takes priority over the individual's (particularly the male's) search for himself, or meaning, or transcendence, and if this search requires a father's wandering elsewhere "for a while" there is nothing to prevent it.

One consequence of this family pattern is the frequency of woman-with-child-and-without-old-man in many of the communes we have studied—although this occurs as often as a result of the woman-with-child arriving on the commune scene that way as it does as a result of her partner splitting. A situation like this does not typically last a long time in any commune we have studied, although it was present in almost all of them. Even when the women involved say they prefer celibacy, there is some doubt that they actually do. One afternoon in a tepee, three young women (without men) with infants on the breast agreed that they welcomed a respite from men, what with their bodies devoted almost full time to the nursing of infants. Within a week, two of them had new old men and the third had gone back to her old one. Celibacy or near-celibacy occurs only in those creedal communes whose doctrines define sexual activity as impure or as a drain on one's physical and spiritual resources for transcendence.

But although celibacy is rare and although couple relations are fragile, this should not be taken to mean that sex is either promiscuous or disordered. At any given time, monogamous coupling is the norm in all the communes we studied closely; in this respect hippies tend to be more traditional than the "swingers" and wife-swappers one reads about in the middle class. Although there are communes whose creed requires group marriage (in the sense that all the adults are regarded as married to all the others, and expected to have sexual relations with each other), we have not studied any of these at first hand. But even in communes where coupling is the norm, there seems to be evidence of a natural drift toward group—although this may still be ideologically disavowed.

For one thing, when couples break up in rural communes, it is as likely as not that each will remain at the commune; and this occurs frequently in urban communes too. Without a drift toward group marriage, situations like this could and do cause great communal tensions which threaten the survival of the group. On the other hand, a not uncommon feature of communes is a situation in which over a long period of time many of the adults have had sexual relations with each other at one or another point between the lapses of "permanent" coupling. Under these conditions, group marriage can seem like a "natural" emergence rather than unnaturally "forced" by a creed—a natural emergence which, by gradually being made an item of affirmed faith, can conceivably solve some of the problems and ease some of the tensions generated by the fragility of couple relations and the breakups which are a predictable result of them. Broken-up couples may still "love" each other as kin, under these conditions—even if they find themselves incapable of permanently sharing the same tent, cabin or bed, an incapacity more likely to be explained astrologically than any other way. (Astrology is used to explain "problems" with respect to children and intimate relations between couples.)*

But the widespread presence of women-with-children as nuclear units in the communes is not merely the result of the splitting of men nor an expression of the belief of hip parents in the

---

* We think, indeed, that there is a close relationship between the commune movement on the one hand, and the complex of stirrings in the middle class which includes the Encounter movement, swingers, sensitivity training, and the incipient gestures toward group marriage represented by "wife-swapping." Each represents an attempt to cope with similar problems (e.g. alienation, existential discontents with the prospects or the realities of middle-class life) by groups of people differently situated in the life-career cycle: the communards being mainly college dropouts in their twenties, the others being mainly married couples in their thirties or forties with children and already well into their professional careers, with which they may have become disenchanted.

unwisdom of staying together "for the sake of the child." The readiness of hip women to bear the child even of a "one-night stand" is supported by a social structure which indicates its "logic." Unlike middle-class women, for example, a hippie female's social status does not depend upon her old man's occupation; she doesn't need him for that. The state is a much better provider than most men who are available to her. And an infant to care for provides more meaning and security in her life than most men could. In addition, these women are often very acceptable to communes as new members. They are likely to be seen as potentially less disruptive to ongoing commune life than a single man; they are likely to be seen as more dependable and stable than a single man; and these women provide a fairly stable source of communal income through the welfare payments that many of them receive. From the point of view of the hip mothers, commune living can be seen as a logical choice; it solves some of the problems of loneliness—there are always others around. And if she wants to go out, there are usually other members of the family present to look after her child, and other males to act as surrogate fathers.

How is it for the children and what will it be like in the future? It is really impossible to say simply and with any certainty. Do the kids seem happy? Healthy? Will they too rebel against their parents? There just isn't any really reliable information, which means that one can say just about anything one wishes to suit one's prejudices.

There are lots of coughs and runny noses, especially in the wintertime. But there's that in suburbia too. They do smoke dope, but it doesn't take very much to get a little one stoned, so there's a built-in thermostat there.

Are they neglected? By the standards of the child-centeredness model in the middle class, we suppose yes. On the other hand, there is reason to be skeptical about the wholesomeness of the middle-class pattern, among whose major consequences are the prolongation of adolescence and dependency, and whose typical figures are nineteen-year-old boys and girls (instead of men and women) who don't know how to take care of themselves.

There seem to be very few "adolescents" visible in communes, although there are plenty of young persons. And if communal living succeeds in abolishing adolescence, it may have been worthwhile after all.

PART TWO

TRANSFORMING THE FAMILY

Sex Roles, Work and Income

The Breadwinner Trap

by ERICK GRØNSETH

Erick Grønseth is an associate professor of sociology at the Institute of Sociology, Oslo University, Norway. At present he is engaged in research on a dozen "work-sharing" families, where both the husband and wife work only half time, and on a survey of public attitudes on issues of equality for women and men.

With this paper I hope to call attention to the ways in which children and the persons who care for them (most usually their mothers) are economically provided for.

Although other patterns exist, most industrial societies today give their full *sanction* to only one pattern—the Husband Economic Provider Role (which I shall call HEPR). I want to show the many destructive consequences this pattern has for industrialized societies, as well as for the individual members of the family—father, mother and child alike.

Certainly a lot of theorizing (and some research) has already been addressed to the problems not of the HEPR but of modern sex roles generally. However, my proposition is that the HEPR is at present at the *root* of most of the sex-role divisions and of their consequences in modern societies. I don't think that the HEPR is a sufficient condition for all the consequences I will name, or that historically they are not caused by other conditions as well. But I do think that the HEPR is today probably the most *strategic* condition in the sense of being within reach of change. Moreover, *without the abolition of the HEPR (especially as a near-monopoly pattern for economic responsibility of child care) it will be impossible to achieve an end to other destructive sex-role divisions.*

To first illustrate the wide variety of patterns possible, let me briefly note that the distribution of economic responsibility for children and for their "carers" may be arranged roughly as follows:

- As a more or less equal concern of all members of extended families, to which nearly the total population belongs (such as previously in European peasant societies).
- As the concern of the *total society,* implemented primarily through the mother (as in working-class France by means of children's allowances), or implemented through child-care institutions (as in Israel's kibbutzim, where all family members are totally independent of each other economically).
- As the concern mainly of *both* parents of the children (as in many poor, lower-class families and in middle-class double-career families today. Father and mother are here mutually dependent economically).
- As the concern of the father-husband (as in middle-class U.S.A. today), supplemented more or less by public policies, tax reductions, wife's part-time work, etc. Here the emphasis is on the wife's dependence on the husband.
- As the concern mainly of the children's mother, supplemented more or less by contributions from their father and from public welfare (as in the case of single-parent families and of families with unemployed fathers).

In today's industrialized societies the only substantial and socially approved way a child is assured his economic and social place is through the husband-father in his provider role (HEPR). Meeting the requirements of this role is generally possible only by his full-time participation in occupational life. Except in rare and affluent cases, no really adequate source of alternative provision exists for a child whose mother does not have a husband, nor for that husbandless mother herself. Even in their present welfare-state phase, the private capitalist societies have not been willing to provide more than supplements and inadequate alternatives to the HEPR.

WITHIN THE FAMILY

Since a good many of the consequences of the HEPR are seen in the family, let us look at some of these.

There seems to be wide consensus that in spite of important variations, industrialization has thus far led to a kinship structure in which the nuclear family (father, mother and children living alone) is more than ever the pivotal form. With reference especially to the U.S. middle class, Talcott Parsons has shown how this nuclear family is based on the husband's occupational role, the kernel of which is its breadwinning HEPR elements.

The HEPR is what directly establishes the family sex-role divisions—the husband in his "instrumental" income-earning position, the wife-mother in her "expressive" role, the main source of the children's love and comfort and authority. This has led to what in the U.S. has been called Momism, but the husband-father's overall authority has not really been abolished; it has only been delegated.

In spite of reports about a certain amount of equalitarianism in middle-class families, there is evidence that because of the husband's demanding occupational role, sex-role divisions within the family (as well as outside) are as great as or even greater than ever before, with mothers and children often left increasingly isolated in their suburban homes. In stable working-class communities the HEPR contributes to an extremely high degree of role separation between mother and father. And, as I will show, among poor families it leads to a high frequency of mother-headed families.

DOUBLE ROLE OF THE WORKING MOTHER

The HEPR leads, of course, also to the fact that the wife is generally the one who does by far the major part not only of the direct child care, but also of the household chores. And this is largely so even when the wife is herself gainfully employed. A mother's gainful employment thus leads to the *double role* of the working mother, and this is probably because under HEPR conditions it is the husband's job or career which counts the most in the long run, since it is usually the better paid and contains the best promotional possibilities.

As the labor market is now gradually able to absorb an increasing number of subordinate, low-paid women, the number of "double-roled" married women is increasing. We are thus confronted not only with "women's two roles" at different periods in their life, but with a "woman's double role" even during the mothering period—i.e., during the period when the children are more or less dependent upon her care.

With increasing costs of children, with a general heightening of the material standards and aspirations of living, and with the probable increased frequency of housewife isolation, more women are ready to use the opportunities for gainful employment—while the husband for the same reasons does not see fit to reduce his occupational absorption and take his share in child care and household chores.

DISCRIMINATION AGAINST WORKING WOMEN

The HEPR is still—at least under private capitalist conditions —a chief basis for exclusion or discouragement of married women from work life and from higher education, for their general relegation to subordinate and low-paid work, and for the wage discrimination against them.

Such fundamental facts about the sex roles within the occupational structure have important repercussions on the family sex roles. As Astrid Schonberg (*The Concept of the Bread-winner,* 1969) put it:

> If it is always assumed that the husbands have a duty from which their wives are exempted of *providing for their families,*

women only needing to provide for themselves, one might be able to understand the special privileges accorded to men in the form of higher pay for the same work, tax relief, better educational opportunities, better promotion prospects and superior influence in local government, etc.

This discrimination hits especially hard, of course, the women who nevertheless actually are providers, the employed single mothers, the unmarried mothers, but also many divorcees and deserted ones, as well as the widows.

Perhaps a more serious and troublesome consequence of the "breadwinner ethos" is the discrimination that exists regarding *access to the labor market as a whole.* Married women are not treated on the same level as men. Women who have been at home for some time looking after the children and then want to start working again *find it very difficult to get work,* but they are not counted as unemployed. If they are lucky enough to get a job at all, it will generally be on very unfavorable terms.

ECONOMIC DISCRIMINATION AGAINST IN-THE-FAMILY CHILD-CARE WORKERS

The other HEPR-rooted economic and work discrimination against women concerns those women who do the child-care work.* In the U.S., in-the-family child-care work is—except in families of high-income husbands—either unpaid or, when the mother is not doing it herself, grossly underpaid out of the income of the one-man wage of the husband provider (and sometimes also out of the gainfully employed mother's own part- or full-time wage). As long as the economic basis for in-the-family child-care work is mainly limited to the husband's one-man income, this work cannot get an economic remuneration comparable to ordinary occupational work, nor an economic basis independent of a husband and of marriage.

---

* Our concept of child-care work is inclusive and comprises also the nurturance, the emotional care and play, and all the kinds of housework done for or because of the children.

This discrimination against in-the-family child care mainly hits mothers, but of course also hits fathers or other in-the-family child-carers to the extent they engage in such work. Consequently fathers cannot afford to engage much in it, as long as they get better paid in the occupational life than do the mothers. And thus mothers are largely *not* expected to work out of home. Such HEPR expectations also represent obstacles against development of truly satisfactory child-care facilities.

Although this economic discrimination of in-the-family child-care work is as basic and as consequential as the straight occupational work discrimination against women, it has been neglected not only by sociologists but also by many feminists.

ECONOMIC DISCRIMINATION AGAINST FAMILIES WITH DEPENDENT CHILDREN

Economic discrimination against families with dependent children is in its turn a consequence of the two types of economic discrimination discussed above—and basically of the HEPR pattern itself. Since the wage for a provider of one or more children is no greater than that for a childless employee in comparable type of work, it is clear that the members of a family with dependent children have a much lower living standard than comparable persons without dependent children, and that this difference increases with the number of children.

This economic discrimination is only slightly counteracted in a number of industrial societies by children's allowances (which the U.S. does not provide), by tax reductions (which favor the higher incomes and discriminate against the working women) or by other minimal family-policy measures.

The particular economic discrimination against single-mother families consists first of all in the lack of any adequate alternative pattern in cases where there is no man to meet the HEPR expectations. Therefore the single mother is often forced to take full-time employment in order to support her child, even when it is very small. And in her employment she meets not only the same "one man, one wage" principle as do the male providers, but also the wage discrimination against women. In any case such women often have to leave their child for too many hours in what today still may be psychologically inadequate day-care institutions, or under other inadequate circumstances.

Among the one-parent families, those of the unwed mothers are the ones for which alternatives to the HEPR are least well developed. This is probably in part because the unwed mother has so blatantly broken the rule that each woman and child shall have a husband-father provider, so as not to become a burden to the rest of society.

WOMEN'S ECONOMIC DEPENDENCY AND SUBJUGATION

The mothers' and children's economic dependency upon a husband and thus upon marriage follows from the near-monopoly of the HEPR pattern. As a consequence, women generally find themselves in a basically subordinate position in the family.

Contrary to the interpretation of several American-family sociologists, and contrary to a widespread egalitarian ideology, it seems that neither in America nor in any other industrial society is there generally any basic equality between the sexes, neither in childhood nor in adult life, neither inside nor outside the family. The fact of the mother-wife's emotional leadership or even "Momism" does not change this, so long as the husband-father's economic leadership actually sets the basic conditions. The wife is subjugated in the family, because the basic family structure and activities (if not in many day-by-day details) are geared to the demands of the fundamental HEPR and occupational role, as these are interpreted by the husband—and by the occupational structure. The basic frame for the wife's decisions is laid down by the husband on the background of *his* occupational conditions, upon which the mother and the children are economically dependent. The HEPR is the basis for the legitimacy of the husband's institutionalized superior authority—and likewise for his superior status.

And—of course—the persons in the power positions in work life, local, national or international finance and politics, where the conditions for the family's and the women's life are set, are elitist *men*, not women. And the basis for their male monopoly on these power positions is their HEPR-based privileged footing in the occupational and economic life.

THE ECONOMIC TIE ON MARRIAGE

Under the present HEPR conditions the economic dependency of the children and of the mothering wife on the husband remains also after a divorce. And because of the surviving HEPR values, the divorced husband-father is under these economic conditions held legally and morally responsible for their economic provision—on the basis of his one-man income. Now, the costs of financing a family are obviously considerably higher if the family is split into two households than if it remains in one. Even when the moral-legal and emotional obstacles to dissolving a marriage could have been overcome, many loveless marriages therefore remain legally, economically and practically intact. It is too costly to establish a new household; thus very often neither the husband nor the wife is economically free to separate so long as they have dependent children. These circumstances, so repressive of love and sexual fulfillment, are chief economic and social underpinnings of the equally repressive prevailing ideals of lifelong monogamy and "marital duty."

Considering the inverse ratio between frequency of divorce and socioeconomic status—the highest rate of divorce exists among the most poor—it seems, however, that the economic tie on marriage rests on relative, not on absolute economic deprivation. For the economic circumstances referred to become an obstacle to divorce only when the marriage, after all, offers a certain amount of economic advantages through the husband's relatively good income—i.e., when there is something economically to *lose* by divorce.

On the other hand, when we note that the divorce rate is generally higher when the husband's income is lower, this does not necessarily mean that the husband's provision is so little that there is "nothing to lose"—but that the economic difficulties resulting from his minimal income so much increase the emotional conflicts that they become intolerable and outweigh the further increased economic difficulties that follow a divorce.

ECONOMIC COSTS, POVERTY AND FAMILY CONFLICT

Many people have noted the often strongly segregated sex-role structure in lower-class families. Especially in America, the insistence on the full operation of the HEPR is probably another mechanism by which poverty is perpetuated, as a large number of adult males withdraw both from the provider role and from the occupational and the family system as well in face of their failure as adequate breadwinners.

The view that mother-headed families are to a large extent a result of the lack of education and employment possibilities for men has, of course, been advanced by many analysts of U.S. poverty. On such a correct but insufficient basis they have, however, advocated a strengthening of the husband-provider role, bringing the poor man back in it—i.e., to turn the poor man into a middle-class (poor!) man, and to make ordinary middle-class husband-provider-role–based families out of *all* the nation's families, presumably also bringing the poor woman back from work into the family. Such a view skips, however, all the difficulties inherent in the fact that those conditions, from which one wants to salvage the poor, *are the product* of that structure into which one wants to bring the poor! And it skips all the negative factors of the husband-provider role.

If, nevertheless, it really should be possible to secure education and well-paying jobs for all those males who now live in poverty, this would, of course, be extremely desirable. It would, however, be even more desirable if at the same time all *females* got the same chances for well-paid jobs—and if mothers and fathers had equal chances to work out of or in the home, on the basis of an entire abolition of the husband- (as well as of the mother-) provider role.

For in the eagerness to institute the husband-provider role among the poor, one forgets especially how this is itself one of the structural factors which tends to *produce* mother-centered families of both the poverty and the affluent type.

THE NON-AUTONOMY OF THE NUCLEAR FAMILY, AND ITS SUBORDINATION TO POLITICAL SYSTEMS AND CLASS STRUCTURES

Some of the considerations above also bring out another much neglected aspect of the modern family structure: its subordination to the economic and occupational structures and their upper-class political elites.

The large masses of middle- and working-class families have their living conditions established for them with little of their own real say. The central mechanism through which the political domination of family life occurs is, however, through the HEPR aspect of the husband occupational role. Through the absorption of the husband-father, of his time and energies into the elitist-run economies, and through the consequent mother-child isolation, most men as well as women are politically immobilized. For this reason, among others, they have to adjust their family life to the demands of the economic-political system of the society.

The modern family is thus far from that autonomous social unit generally assumed by sociologists. It seems as if sociologists have been so enthused by the discovery of the modern nuclear family's autonomy relative to extended family and kin, that its new HEPR chains to the authoritarian and "patriarchal" occupational and economic structures have been ignored.

POPULATION CONSEQUENCES OF THE HEPR: FABRICATION OF ENFORCED MARRIAGES AND SINGLE-MOTHER FAMILIES, ABORTIONS AND ADOPTIONS

A considerable number of marriages, especially among the very young, take place not for love but in order to save for the mother and child at least a minimum of economic and social status. These marriages are formed for fear of the socioeconomic consequences for mother and child if they do not have a husband-father.

We have already mentioned how the HEPR probably contributes to the divorce rate in the lower classes by way of the severe impact here of the economic discrimination against families with children. For the same reason it contributes also to the especially high divorce rate of early marriages, since many of these generally have an exceptionally weak economic basis. Probably not only the enforced and unhappy but perhaps also many of the emotionally well-founded early marriages break down for such reasons.

A consequence of these HEPR-stimulated divorces is, of course, a corresponding number of single-parent families. Because of the divorcing father's HEPR duties, the mother is most often given custody of the children; consequently the divorced single-parent families are mostly single-mother families.

When—as in the U.S.—the institutionalized prescriptions of the HEPR are coupled with a nineteenth-century individualistic ideology and with a competitive, profit-oriented economic system, the HEPR also contributes to the usual public refusal to provide adequate economic welfare assistance to families wherever an able-bodied male is present in the family household, regardless of the inadequacy of his contribution to the family's income. This in turn stimulates real and fake *desertions* from the families on the part of the male, or to his avoidance of adequately paying jobs. It follows that the HEPR also contributes to the direct formation of single-mother families. This happens when unwed expectant fathers break up the relationship for fear of the provider responsibilities that would follow with a marriage—perhaps often in spite of a love or liking for the woman that might otherwise have been sufficient normal motivation for marriage.

In the U.S. there is a remarriage rate for single mothers with children at least as high as that for the never married childless women, and the period of singleness usually does not last more than a couple of years. Nevertheless, one may ask to what extent these marriages are based on love and to what extent on considerations of economic and practical convenience. One may also ask under what circumstances widowed and divorced mothers do remain unmarried because of a reluctance on the part of otherwise eligible men to take on the economic burden of providing for the children in question.

INSTABILITY OF PREMARITAL LOVE RELATIONS AND CONFLICT IN THEIR SEX-ROLE STRUCTURE

The demand that a man shall be economically able to provide for a wife and children before he marries, along with the HEPR-buttressed ideal of lifelong marriage, seems to be a powerful obstacle to the full sexual love development of many youthful relationships, the frequency of early, often wife-supported marriages notwithstanding. In part, youth may be fearful of full emotional and sexual involvement because of the present economic implications of parenthood and for fear of disturbing their educational or job careers. In addition to such direct obstacles come all the indirect psychological ones, caused by the sanctions against premarital love relations. Thus the HEPR-buttressed family climate and socialization practices typically lead to a basic sexual repression in both sexes, and to a splitting of the originally unitary sexual and love emotion.

An additional and directly corresponding HEPR-rooted difficulty is the difference in the role expectations of the boy and girl in the premarital relationship. These appear in part to emanate from the still widely practiced, if decreasing, double morality. The general expectation is (especially from adult sources) that it is primarily the girl's responsibility to "draw the line"; keeping up the "morality" is squarely put on her shoulders. Correspondingly, it is the general expectation (especially from his peers) that the boy try as much as he can to obtain the forbidden fruit. Thus we end up with the typical young heterosexual constellation, where the boy wants "sex," while the girl avoids it. She wants marriage and HEPR-committed "love," of which the boy is as fearful as he would have been of her natural self-assertiveness. How frequently such constellations occur, rather than the more traditional alternative of the boy having sex with one set of "bad" girls and feeling relatively sexless love and respect for his potential marital partner, would be one of the many interesting things to know.

Undoubtedly, such HEPR-rooted constellations are important elements in the conflicts, frustrations and breakups of premarital love relations, as well as of marital ones. Thus the much celebrated romantic love and the seemingly open field of eligibles in the marketplace for marriage contracts become the first decisive field for the battle between the sexes, where the frustrating affairs of youth are destroyed on a mass scale in the name of sexless romantic love—or of loveless sex—until the third, fourth or twentieth ends with marriage. Even with the spread of new standards of "permissiveness with affection" among the young, the traditional HEPR-based double morality is still living on.

SEXUAL OPPRESSION AND REPRESSION

The strategic relation between sexual freedom (or lack of it) and the HEPR aspects of our family structure has been seldom analyzed.

The HEPR-rooted economic, social and psychological dangers of unwed motherhood contribute, no doubt, to the continuing sanctions against full and regular sexual-love relations among unmarried youth. The fear of motherhood without a legally committed husband-provider also contributes to the oppression of sexual play among younger boys and girls. Where the economic tie on marriage keeps frustrating and repressive marriages of parents going and prevents alternative gratifying relations, they often become even more oppressive of the free emotional and sexual vitality of their children.

These sources of childhood sex repression are decisively supplemented also by the HEPR-based relative isolation of the nuclear family. The parents here become the nearly exclusive objects of the children's unconscious sexual attachments and fixations, while open sexual play elsewhere is prohibited.

FURTHER DISTURBANCES

To the consequences of today's HEPR should in the case of the male be added the general denial and repression of feelings and emotional expressiveness that are still basically expected of him from early childhood. Recent superficial modifications of these expectations hardly do away with the difficulty, but represent what has been termed "a new burden of masculinity."

In the case of the socially well-adjusted males there is the preponderance of steadily more early occurring psychosomatic illness, like stomach ulcers and heart diseases, and the consequently lowered male life expectancy. At the same time a precarious personality structure may easily tip the balance in favor of disorderly behavior. As Holmberg has said: "Men dominate in practically every connection where behavior can be interpreted to be a sign of maladjustment. Men commit suicide one to four times as often as do women. They are qualified alcoholic misusers fifteen to twenty times as often, and are punished for criminality about fifty times as often." Holmberg sees here a direct relation to the general male role in our society.

As for the consequences for women, they are hit especially by sanctions not only against sexuality but against impulses to self-assertion, independence and even normal, constructive aggressiveness. Depression, neurosis, "housewife's disease" are common results.

A further consequence of the HEPR-based family structure is the impoverished, oppressed and infantilized position into which it helps to force masses of retired lower- and middle-class old people. Separated economically and socially from their children's and relatives' families, they are often left to the grossly inadequate public-welfare alternative for support.

ALIENATION, APATHY OR DESTRUCTIVENESS AS FURTHER PERSONALITY CONSEQUENCES OF THE HEPR

The need for mastery of the conditions of one's own life is a primary human need that to a large extent is repressed by way of HEPR-based family and sex-role mechanisms. As mentioned, the HEPR contributes to the general objective alienation and lack of political participation—and consequently also to the subjective alienation, apathy and sometimes desperation of the lower and middle classes in industrialized societies. Furthermore, the economically and socially dependent positions of women may in the general population lead them to encourage the men's family egotism and their absorption in their occupational provider role, as well as to discourage their nonconformist activities in work and politics. Because of male domination in public and political life, the important issues are nevertheless defined and acted upon from the men's point of view.

Equally as important are the types of authoritarian character structures formed by the HEPR-based family structure, so that, as Wilhelm Reich showed, most adults actually desire subjugation and irresponsibility—or to dominate.

THE TOTAL IMPACT OF HEPR IN INDUSTRIAL SOCIETIES

Now, it may be possible that even in the face of the economic and social costs we have mentioned, those, like Talcott Parsons, who believe that the HEPR is perfectly suited to our present occupational and economic system may be right. Parsons, however, seems to dodge the question as to who shall decide which of the conflicting interests of the different social groups shall be said to represent the interests of the total society. And Parsons ignores the possibility that what the achievement-oriented power elites (even with the support of a majority of the subordinated lower classes) define as chief values may in the long run lead to the disintegration and destruction of the society.

And insofar as Parsons is right in his analysis that the HEPR-based family structure is the producer of the type of male achievement-motivated personality which is adequately socialized to function in the present widely exploitative, competitive and alienation-generating occupational and economic life, then not only this type of occupational and economic system but also this family structure and its HEPR basis are in the long run *not functional* but dangerous for the total society, defined in terms of its primary creative life forces.

CHILDREN'S PENSIONS: AN ALTERNATIVE TO THE HEPR

As an alternative for the husband-provider role in modern societies, a "children's pension" can be envisioned, to be given to every child until its economic independence and to be administered by its chief caretakers (usually mother and/or father) until the child's social-emotional maturity. Thus only will parenthood *in all social groups* get an adequate economic basis independent of husband and marriage—thus only can the sex-repressive economic tie on marriage be abolished. The pension should cover the ordinary expenses of housing, clothing and feeding, etc., of the child, as well as a child carer's wage of "average" size but adjusted to the living conditions in question. It should be distributed among the child's carers (father, mother, grandmother, nurses, neighbor, day-care personnel or what). Whether it should be financed through the prevailing tax system from the population at large or be based on funds mainly from the large corporations and enterprises and from their owners (who today are the ones who mostly profit economically from the now gratis child-care work done by the mothers in preparing the children to be "productive" workers) is a question of political feasibility.

A children's pension is simply an extension of present-day welfare-state family allowances now offered through most of Europe. Although this type of change is probably both strategic and *necessary*, it certainly is no panacea for the problems discussed in this paper. It is not a *sufficient* measure for reaching the intended liberating effects. It may, however, stimulate further efforts in the same direction. Along with reforms like equal education, shared work and political opportunities of the sexes (including part-time work opportunities for both sexes, *emotionally adequate* child-care facilities, and free access to contraception) it means a necessary contribution toward equal life chances for men and women. What further political changes in our society would be needed in order to establish a children's pension is the next decisive question.

The Price of Success*

by JAN E. DIZARD

Jan Dizard teaches sociology at Amherst College. In addition to his work on family structure and women's roles, he has written on race relations and social change. He is currently at work on an examination of the limits of reform in contemporary capitalism.

Substantial numbers of married women in contemporary America are living in circumstances that can best be described as "house arrest." The housewife is isolated and alone for large portions of each day. Her social life is largely conducted vicariously through her husband and children. There are, of course, opportunities for neighboring and *Kaffeeklatsch*ing, which means that the isolation is by no means total. But compared to the wider range of contacts her husband and children maintain, the insularity of the housewife's world is apparent.

The oppression of women is, of course, not new, and housework has probably always been something of a punishment meted out to those of low status (women, children, the handicapped). Relatively recent developments, however, have exacerbated the subordination of women to men. In response to the associated changes of urbanization and industrialization, a new family form has emerged, generally referred to as the "isolated nuclear family." It is, I think, no accident that the social strata—predominantly the middle and upper middle classes—in which the isolated nuclear family is most charac-

---

* My wife, Robin, read the early drafts of this essay and, as always, was an invaluable source of ideas and criticism. Her involvement in the women's movement has helped us both understand more deeply the many ways our society has distorted and circumscribed both women and men. It has also shown that this need not happen when men and women struggle together for a better world.

teristic are also the strata from which the current women's-liberation movement has drawn its major support.

The isolated nuclear family's distinctive feature is the relative weakness of its ties to kin and locality. Internally, it is organized around a division of labor in which the husband's primary role is that of breadwinner and the wife's is that of homemaker—caring for the physical and psychological needs of her husband and their children. While this division of labor is obviously not a new one, changes that were initially set in motion by the Industrial Revolution have added a significant new element.

The Industrial Revolution and the rise of the bourgeoisie brought with it emphases on individualism and competitiveness that created a sharp disjuncture between occupational and family roles. Where once both roles stressed cooperation and mutuality, we now find that successful performance of occupational roles generally depends upon the individual's aggressiveness, his willingness to compete and to behave toward others on the basis of presumably impartial estimations of their usefulness vis-à-vis his own ends. By contrast, family members are expected to cooperate, to be willing to downgrade individual ends so that the needs of all family members can be met, and to behave toward others in the family not on the basis of impartiality but, rather, on the basis of love and compassion. In this sense, the division of labor in the isolated nuclear family also entails husbands and wives coming to specialize in quite different kinds of responses. The expectations are familiar: the wife is expected to be nurturant, willing—nay, eager—to allow her husband to eclipse her. The husband is expected, in turn, to be a good provider—i.e., to compete successfully in the marketplace.

As suggested earlier, it is the middle class, and especially the upper middle class, that has been most affected by these developments. It is largely within the arenas of the world of business and affairs, including the academy, that individualism and competitiveness are most highly prized characteristics. It is also within this stratum that geographic mobility is most likely, resulting in the loss of a stable set of peers, drawn from among kin and community, to be close to. The consequences of these combined factors—the segregation of husband–wife roles and the isolation from a stable set of friends and relatives—have rarely been empirically examined. Several years ago, I had the opportunity to conduct an analysis of how the interaction between husbands and wives developed and changed over the course of roughly fifteen years of marriage for four hundred couples.* The findings of this study shed considerable light on the tensions we have been describing, particularly as these tensions affect the wife.

In the late 1930s, a study was begun at the University of Chicago to assess the nature and causes of change in husband–wife interaction as couples progressed through engagement and successive stages of marriage. The couples involved in the study were all drawn from among students and their friends at the university and thus constitute an ideal group for our purposes in that the vast majority were sons and daughters of middle-class families and were themselves to remain within the middle class. All but 6 percent of the husbands had white-collar occupations. Both husband and wife were asked to fill out lengthy questionnaires separately, once when they were engaged to be married, again after they had been married for one to two years, and finally after a period of from thirteen to seventeen years of married life.

The changes that occurred in these four hundred marriages over this period of time were dramatic, especially for the wife. In the early years of their marriages, both husbands and wives reported high levels of satisfaction with their respective spouses. The vast majority expressed happiness with one another, few couples indicated areas of their common life over which there were disagreements, both husbands and wives reported sub-

* Jan E. Dizard, *Social Change in the Family* (Chicago: Community and Family Study Center, University of Chicago, 1968). The following discussion of the study's findings is drawn from this volume.

stantial and satisfying levels of cooperation and sharing, and most indicated that high levels of affection for one another characterized their relationships. By the time of the third and last survey of these couples, the majority of husbands and wives reported deterioration in their relationships to their spouses. Levels of happiness declined for half of the wives and slightly less than half of the husbands. Almost 60 percent of the husbands and wives indicated that they disagreed more frequently with one another and believed these disagreements tended to be of a more serious nature than those they had had earlier. Demonstrations of affection (pet nicknames, terms of endearment, kissing, etc.) had declined markedly for many couples. Finally, roughly 40 percent of the wives and only a slightly lower portion of husbands indicated that since the early years of their marriage, when such thoughts had not occurred to them, they had given serious consideration to divorce or separation.

Had all couples reported declining satisfaction with and commitment to their marriages, we could simply say that time takes its toll. No such bromide applies. In fact what we discovered was that *by and large it was in those couples in which the husband had been most successful in his occupational pursuits that spouses were most likely to report deterioration in the marital relationship.*

Specifically, we found that among the families headed by the least successful husbands (those whose incomes had declined) 23 percent of the husbands and 30 percent of the wives reported declining levels of happiness. Among the families headed by the most successful husbands (whose incomes had increased by a factor of six or more) 50 percent of the husbands and 59 percent of the wives reported declining levels of happiness. Success, in other words, doubled the likelihood that husband and wife's happiness would decline over time.

By examining the data, we were able to discern one of the apparent sources for declining levels of happiness. We reasoned as follows: In order for the husband to succeed occupationally, he must conform to the norms sustained by the firm that employs him, and these norms, as we have pointed out, are contradictory to the norms that family members are generally expected to abide by. We assumed that the more successful the husband, the greater his conformity to the norms of competition. And here the dilemma arises. To the extent that his wife approximates the ideal of wife and mother, she can be expected to hold contrary norms. In short, a gulf develops between husband and wife in which each has increasing difficulty in meeting the needs of the other. This was especially clear in the reports of the wives. In families in which the husband's income decreased, only 30 percent of the wives reported increased conflict with their husbands. But in families in which the husband's income had greatly increased, 64 percent of the wives reported increased conflict!

Pursuing our reasoning, we surmised that when the husband, in addition to succeeding in his occupation, also increased his participation in community organizations, a very familiar pattern in the upper middle class, the gulf between husband and wife should be increased even further and be especially accentuated when the wife remained housebound. Indeed, we found that in no other group of couples was increased conflict and decreased happiness more likely to be reported. Fully 75 percent of the wives in these families reported increased conflict with their husbands, and 70 percent reported lowered levels of happiness. By contrast, in those cases where the husband's income had decreased and his participation in community organizations had also decreased, only 9 percent of the wives reported increased conflict and only 27 percent reported lowered levels of happiness.

Other studies of marriage have reported findings similar to these we have been describing. Blood and Wolfe, on the basis of a study of nine hundred families living in the Detroit area, report the following: "High-income husbands . . . have conspicuously dissatisfied wives. Apparently these husbands are so tied up with their occupations that they are too busy both for housework and for leisure-time companionship." It is under such circumstances that the wife is most likely to feel isolated.

One apparent solution to this dilemma is for the wife to become involved in activities outside the home. Certainly being active in a job or in community life would rectify the isolation from adults that nonworking housewives feel. To assess the effects such involvements have on the wife, we divided our four hundred couples into those in which the wife had worked and those in which the wife had never worked. We found indeed that the couples with working wives were less likely than those in which the wife had never worked to report declining happiness and increasing conflict with the husband.* At the same time, however, the effects of the wife's having worked were not sufficient to remove the deleterious effects of the husband's success.

Working wives of the very successful husbands in our sample were less likely to report declining happiness than the nonworking wives of very successful husbands—but both sets of wives were much more likely to report declining happiness than either working or nonworking wives of those husbands who were not occupationally mobile at all. On the basis of the experience of the four hundred couples studied, it is, it seems, far better— from the point of view of maximizing happiness in marriage— for the husband to scale down his external, especially occupational, commitments than for the wife to emulate her husband's aggressive and competitive actions. In both instances, the wife's isolation is reduced; but it appears that reduced isolation is most appreciated in the context of the increased sharing and companionship that result from the husband's lessening of occupational strivings.

This is not to assert that "the wife's place is in the home." Nothing could be further from our intent. It is, however, to suggest that part of the difficulty—and for the couples we studied,

* The same effect was found in comparing wives who had increased their organizational activity to those who had decreased their organizational commitments.

a large part—that many middle-class couples face is the result of the terms on which men and women are expected to behave outside the family. The very competitiveness and individualism that is expected undermines both men's and women's capacities to relate to one another in equalitarian, noncompetitive ways. Even with this, however, it is better for wives to work, if the choice is only between working and remaining isolated at home. But it bears repeating: the most satisfactory arrangement, judging from the couples studied, was the situation in which (1) the husband was not that successful occupationally and (2) the wife worked. In such circumstances, it seems reasonable to imagine, the possibilities for equality between husband and wife are maximized—both cooperate around the house and share interests and neither spouse is totally dependent upon the other for stimulation and recognition. At the same time, neither is so committed to "success" that concerns about competitiveness and getting ahead dominate their relationship.

The married men and women we have been talking about are all middle-class. Most were well educated, and the vast majority of the husbands held estimable jobs. Even those husbands whose incomes had declined were still earning adequate livelihoods, roughly approximating the median income for the nation as a whole at the time of the interviews. In short, these are not typical American families. What, then, can we learn from them? What bearing does our discussion have on the current reemergence of a women's movement in America?

II

Though the couples we have been discussing are not typical, the problems they confronted derive from basic tensions in American life. On the one hand, these couples, like most, have had to contend with the highly competitive nature of our occupational structure. On the other hand, they have also obviously not been spared tensions that issue from the subordination of women to men. While both these tensions pervade social life in America, the various social classes experience them in different ways and consequently respond to them differently.

Thus, though subordination of women to men is omnipresent throughout society, within the working class this subordination is routinely overshadowed by concerns of economic security, of never having enough to make ends meet. Even more than her middle-class counterparts, the working-class mother is tied to the home, but this appears to her more the consequence of her family's economic insecurity than of her sex. Going out requires hiring babysitters or buying new clothes that are hard to justify, given other, more pressing claims on limited cash. Moreover, her relatively low education, compared to the education of her middle-class counterpart, makes the working-class housewife insecure in the arena of community organizations and thus more resigned to the fate of being homebound.

It should also be apparent that working outside the home is for her generally far from exciting. For a poorly educated woman the jobs available are seldom likely to provide a source of deep comfort and sense of fulfillment. Quite the contrary, they are usually routine, sometimes downright nasty, and pay very poorly. Wives of working-class husbands mainly work of necessity. As a consequence, the home looks something like an oasis, even though there are many frustrations and disappointments in homemaking. Finally, the working-class woman's family is far less geographically mobile than the middle-class woman's, and so she is seldom as isolated from kin and neighbors. Ties to at least the immediate family, often buttressed by still strong ethnic ties, are typically close. Thus, although the working-class woman is easily as subordinate to men as are her middle-class counterparts (and likely even more subordinate), she is not likely to see this subordination as *the* problem in and of itself. Much more salient is her and her husband's relatively insecure economic niche.

By contrast, working-class anxieties over unemployment and having enough to adequately feed and clothe family members are seldom (except in periods of high unemployment) the anxieties of the middle class. For the middle class, economic anxieties are much more likely to be focused on issues about advancement, such as securing a promotion. It is here that the competitive ethos is most pronounced. Few blue-collar jobs demand or, if they did demand it, could expect to elicit the commitments that most white-collar jobs routinely require. In this sense, middle-class wives, over time, are more likely to find themselves in competition with the husband's job for his commitments and energies.

At the same time, what are the wife's alternatives outside the family? For the working-class wife, lack of money and poor education appear as the prime barriers to a rewarding life beyond the home. For middle-class wives, neither barrier is especially pronounced.

An example of one positive alternative for the middle class is represented in those couples we studied in which the husband had, for one or another reason, reduced his commitments to his occupation. In this context, husband and wife seemed able to sustain a satisfactory egalitarian relationship. In other circumstances, the wife's working is a partial solution, though, as we saw, given the nature of work available to women and the competitiveness that many middle-class jobs call for, this response also leaves something to be desired. In sum, it seems quite apparent that individual—or privatized—solutions are not sufficient to deal with the problems that most middle-class *or* working-class women face.

The rebirth of a women's movement is made more understandable in these terms. Individual attempts to resolve the dilemmas posed by competition and hierarchy, in combination with the subordination of women, have failed to sustain meaningful lives for large numbers of women. The frustrations this situation calls forth are especially acute for middle-class women, and they are also, for reasons we have discussed briefly above, the most likely to see these frustrations in terms of their subordination to men.

The women's movement's demand for full and equal participation in the larger society, however, bypasses the fact that
most working-class women (as well as many if not most in the
middle class) still look to the family and their role within it as
their prime source of security and relative protection from *having* to work in menial jobs that pay very little. Subordination is
felt differently in different social strata, and for most working-
class women subordination to men is only a part of a much
larger network of frustrated hopes and bitter, lonely realities.
The women's movement emerged from a stratum in the population in which subordination to men, via the family roles women
were expected to fulfill, appeared to be the root of their problem. If the movement is to broaden its base and increase its
capacities to transform social life in America, it will also have to
address itself to the ways in which the subordination of women
is related to and feeds upon the insecurities endemic in an individualistic, competitive and harshly inequalitarian society.

Training the Woman to Know Her Place

by SANDRA L. BEM and DARYL J. BEM

Determined to practice what they preach—the importance of an equalitarian marriage—the Bems were the first couple to successfully challenge the nepotism rule at Stanford University so that both could be given appointments in the Department of Psychology.

Thirty million women work. That's 42 percent of all American women and over one third of the labor force. Moreover, married women work. Whereas in 1940 only 30 percent of all women workers were married, today that percentage has doubled: today 58 percent of the women in the labor force are married and living with their husbands. That's four out of every ten married women.

Nor is it only the wives of the poor who work. Forty-three percent of the women whose husbands earn $5,000 to $7,000 per year are members of the labor force. And even in families where the husband earns $10,000 per year or more, 29 percent of the wives work outside the home.

Nor does the presence of children necessarily mean that women stop working. Almost half (45 percent) of all mothers with children between the ages of six and seventeen work outside the home. One third (32 percent) of all mothers with children between the ages of three and five are working. And one fourth (23 percent) of all mothers with children under the age of three are working. Furthermore, these percentages refer only to families in which the mother is living with her husband. As might be expected, the percentage of working mothers in father-absent families is even higher.

Finally, it is the woman with more education who is the most likely to work. Of those women who complete elementary school, 31 percent work outside the home. Of those who complete high school, 48 percent participate in the labor force. Of those who complete college, 54 percent are employed. And of those who complete at least one year of graduate study, 71 percent are involved in paid employment.

There is, then, no single type of woman worker. Women of all ages, women of every income and educational level, women both married and single, women with children and without, all participate in the labor force.

Why do women work? For the same reasons that men do. Some lucky women, like some lucky men, work for self-fulfillment. Approximately 20 percent of the married women who work do so for social or psychological reasons. But most women, like most men, work for economic reasons. Single women, widows, divorcees, and female heads of households obviously work in order to support themselves and their dependents. In addition, about half the married women who work cite "economic necessity" as their major reason for taking a job, and still another 20 percent say that they work in order to earn extra money. They supplement their husbands' income; they buy something special which their families would not be able to afford otherwise—a new home or a college education; and they raise their families' general standard of living.

What kinds of jobs do women have? Inferior ones—compared to men. How much are women paid? Compared to men—not much.

Women are concentrated in a very small number of occupations. One third of all working women are concentrated in only seven jobs: secretary, retail-sales clerk, household worker, elementary-school teacher, bookkeeper, waitress, and nurse. An additional one third are found in the following twenty-nine occupations:

Sewer, stitcher	Checker, examiner, inspector
Typist	Practical nurse
Cashier	Kitchen worker
Cook	Chambermaid, maid
Telephone operator	Housekeeper (private home)

Babysitter	Electrical-machinery operative
Hospital attendant	Receptionist
Laundry operative	Charwoman, cleaner
Assembler	Housekeeper, stewardess
Apparel operative	Dressmaker, seamstress
Hairdresser	Counter, fountain worker
Packer, wrapper	File clerk
Stenographer	Musician, music teacher
High-school teacher	Fabric-mill operative
Office-machine worker	

In fact, 78 percent of all working women, as compared to 40 percent of working men, are employed as clerical workers, service workers, factory workers, and sales clerks. Yes, women do work, but they work in dead-end, low-status jobs, not in careers. Indeed, only four of the jobs listed above qualify as professions: elementary-school teacher, secondary-school teacher, music teacher, and nurse.

Only four million women—15 percent of all women workers— are classified as professional or technical workers, and even this figure is misleading. For the single occupation of noncollege teacher absorbs nearly half of these women, and an additional 25 percent are nurses.* Fewer than 5 percent of all professional women—fewer than one percent of all women workers—fill those positions which, to most Americans, connote "professional": physician, lawyer, judge, engineer, scientist, editor, reporter, college president, professor or senator. Only one out of every twenty-five working women (4 percent) is a manager, usually in a small retail store.

Economic statistics tell the same story. In 1968, the median income of full-time women workers was $4,457. The comparable figure for men was over $3,000 higher. According to the Labor

---

* The tendency of both parents and guidance counselors to overemphasize teaching as "the career for women" is now having unfortunate consequences. According to the U.S. Office of Education, 100,000 teachers completing their training in 1970 will have to find something else to do. The teacher glut is overwhelming.

Department, a female college graduate working full time can expect to earn less per year than a male high-school dropout. This is the very best that women have been able to achieve in the world of work.

Why? Why jobs rather than growing careers? Why nurse rather than physician, teacher rather than principal, secretary rather than executive, stewardess rather than pilot? There are three basic answers to this question: (1) discrimination, (2) sex-role conditioning, and (3) the presumed incompatibility of family and career.

DISCRIMINATION

As noted above, women earn less than men, and the gap is widening. In 1955, women earned 64 percent of what men did; by 1968, that percentage had shrunk to 58 percent. Sixty percent of full-time female workers earn less than $5,000 per year; only 20 percent of full-time male workers fall below this level. Only 3 percent of female workers earn above $10,000 per year; 28 percent of male workers do so. And, according to a survey of 206 companies, female college graduates in 1970 were offered jobs which paid approximately $43 per month less than those offered to their male counterparts in the same college major.

There are two reasons for this pay differential. First, in every category of occupation, women are employed in the lesser-skilled, lower-paid positions. Even in the clerical field, where 73 percent of the workers are women, females are relegated to the lower-status positions, and so they earn only 65 percent of what male clerical workers earn. The second reason is discrimination in its purest form: unequal pay for equal work.

New laws should begin to correct both of these situations. The Equal Pay Act of 1963 prohibits employers from discriminating on the basis of sex in the payment of wages for equal work on jobs requiring equal skill, effort and responsibility, and which are performed under similar working conditions. In a landmark ruling on May 18, 1970, the U.S. Supreme Court ordered that $250,000 in back pay be paid to women employed by a single New Jersey glass company. This decision followed a two-year court battle by the Labor Department after it found that the company was paying men selector-packers 21.5 cents more per hour than women doing the same work. In a similar case, the Eighth Circuit Court of Appeals ordered a major can company to pay more than $100,000 in back wages to women doing equal work. According to the Labor Department, an estimated $17 million is owed to women in back pay. In Western Pennsylvania alone, there had been 781 unequal-pay cases as of mid-1970, and thirty-one firms have already been ordered to pay over $450,000 in back wages. At the moment, the 1963 act does not cover executive, administrative or professional employees, but two bills now pending in Congress would include these workers as well.

But to enjoy equal pay, women must also have access to equal jobs. Title VII of the 1964 Civil Rights Act prohibits discrimination in employment on the basis of race, color, religion, national origin—and sex. Although the sex provision was treated as a joke at the time (and was originally introduced by a Southern Congressman in an attempt to defeat the bill), the Equal Employment Opportunities Commission discovered in its first year of operation that 40 percent or more of the complaints warranting investigation charged discrimination on the basis of sex.

SEX-ROLE CONDITIONING:
ITS EFFECTS ON WOMEN'S ASPIRATIONS

But even if all discrimination were to end tomorrow, nothing very drastic would change. For job discrimination is only part of the problem. It does impede women who choose to become lawyers or managers or physicians. But it does not, by itself, help us to understand why so many women "choose" to be secretaries or nurses rather than executives or physicians; why only

3 percent of ninth-grade girls—as compared with 25 percent of the boys—"choose" careers in science or engineering; or why 63 percent of America's married women "choose" not to work at all. It certainly does not explain those young women whose vision of the future includes only marriage, children and living happily ever after; who may at some point "choose" to take a job, but who almost never "choose" to pursue a career. Discrimination frustrates choices already made; something more pernicious perverts the motivation to choose.

AMERICA'S SEX-ROLE IDEOLOGY

That "something" is an unconscious ideology about the nature of the female sex, an ideology which constricts the emerging self-image of the female child and the nature of her aspirations from the very first, an ideology which leads even those Americans who agree that a black skin should not uniquely qualify *its* owner for janitorial or domestic service to assume that the possession of a uterus uniquely qualifies *its* owner for precisely such service.

Consider, for example, the 1968 student rebellion at Columbia University. Students from the radical left took over some administration buildings in the name of equalitarian ideas which they accused the university of flouting. Here were the most militant spokesmen one could hope to find in the cause of equalitarian ideals. But no sooner had they occupied the buildings than the male militants blandly turned to their sisters-in-arms and assigned them the task of preparing the food, while they, the menfolk, would presumably plan further strategy. The reply these males received was the reply they deserved, and the fact that domestic tasks behind the barricades were desegregated across the sex line that day is an everlasting tribute to the class consciousness of the ladies of the left.

But these conscious coeds are not typical, for the unconscious assumptions about a woman's "natural" talents (or lack of them) are at least as prevalent among women as they are among men. When does this ideology begin in the life of a young girl? How does it limit her horizons so that she never aspires to *be* a senator or an astronaut, but only to *marry* one?

From the day a newborn child is dressed in pink, she is given "special" treatment. Perhaps because they are thought to be more fragile, six-month-old infant girls are actually touched, spoken to and hovered over more by their mothers while they are playing than are infant boys. Six months later, these same girls are more reluctant than the boys to leave their mothers; they return more quickly and more frequently to them; and they remain closer to them throughout an entire play period. When a physical barrier is placed between mother and child, the girls tend to cry and motion for help; the boys make more active attempts to get around the barrier. Thus, the mother's overly protective behavior at six months may already have predisposed the female child toward passivity and dependence.

As children grow older, boys are encouraged to be aggressive, competitive and independent, whereas girls continue to be rewarded, especially by their fathers, for being passive and dependent. Little boys climb trees and get dirty; little girls are expected to stay in the yard and keep their dresses clean. Little boys play with water pistols and fire trucks; little girls play with dolls and tea sets. Little "men" fight back; little girls cry and run. Little boys visit Daddy's office while little girls help Mommy bake a cake. And we know of at least one little girl whose goal of becoming a doctor was quickly "corrected" by her first-grade teacher: every little boy in the class got to play the part of doctor in the class play; every little girl got to play the role of nurse.

As children begin to read, the storybook characters become the images and the models that little boys and little girls aspire to become. What kind of role does the female play in the world of children's literature? The fact is that there aren't even very many females in that world. One survey, reported in the book-review section of the New York *Times*, found that five times as many males as females appear in the titles; the fantasy world of Dr. Seuss is almost entirely male; and even animals and machines are represented as male. When females do appear, they are noteworthy for what they do *not* do. They do not drive cars, and they seldom even ride bicycles. (In one story in which a girl does ride a bicycle, it's a two-seater and the girl is seated behind the boy!) Boys climb trees and fish and roll in the leaves and skate; girls watch or fall down or get dizzy. Girls are never doctors. And although they may be nurses or librarians or teachers, they are never principals. There seems to be only one children's book about mothers who work, and it concludes that what mothers love "best of all" is "being your very own Mommy and coming home to you." And although this is no doubt true of many daddies as well, no book about working fathers has ever found it necessary to apologize in quite the same way.

As children grow older, more explicit sex-role training is introduced. Boys are encouraged to take more of an interest in mathematics and science. Boys, not girls, are given chemistry sets and microscopes for Christmas. Moreover, all children quickly learn that Mommy is proud to be a moron when it comes to mathematics and science, whereas Daddy is a little ashamed if he doesn't know all about these things. When a young boy returns from school all excited about biology, he is almost certain to be encouraged to think of becoming a physician. A girl with similar enthusiasm is told that she might want to consider nurse's training later so she can have "an interesting job to fall back upon in case—God forbid—she ever needs to support herself." A very different kind of encouragement. And any girl who doggedly persists in her enthusiasm for science is likely to find her parents as horrified by the prospect of a permanent love affair with physics as they would be either by the prospect of an interracial marriage or, horror of horrors, by no marriage at all.

These socialization practices quickly take their toll. By nursery-school age, for example, boys are already asking more questions about how and why things work. In first and second grade, when asked to suggest ways of improving various toys, boys do better on the fire truck and girls do better on the nurse's kit; but by third grade, boys do better regardless of the toy presented.

In elementary school, with its large number of female teachers and its emphasis on being "good" or docile, girls have a momentary advantage; pleasing the teacher and doing good schoolwork are more appropriate for girls than for boys. Not surprisingly, girls surpass boys in nearly all of their schoolwork in the early grades. And although some of this difference could be due to innate differences in the developmental timetables between boys and girls, research shows that young children do regard school as "feminine."

Soon, however, school becomes more in tune with the earlier socialization of the boys. They are now reminded that doing well will contribute to their later vocational success, and they continue to receive special encouragement in mathematics and science. By the ninth grade, 25 percent of the boys, but only 3 percent of the girls, are considering careers in science or engineering. When they apply for college, boys and girls are about equal on verbal-aptitude tests, but boys score significantly higher on mathematical-aptitude tests—about sixty points higher on the College Board examinations, for example. Moreover, girls improve their mathematical performance if the problems are simply reworded so that they deal with cooking and gardening, even though the abstract reasoning required for solution remains exactly the same. Clearly, the girl's confidence in her ability to tackle a mathematical problem has been seriously undermined.

But these effects in mathematics and science are only part of the story. A girl's long training in passivity and dependence appears to exact an even higher toll from her overall motivation to achieve, to search for new and independent ways of doing things, and to welcome the challenge of new and unsolved problems. In one study, for example, elementary-school girls were more likely to try solving a puzzle by imitating an adult, whereas the boys were more likely to search for a novel solution not provided by the adult. In another puzzle-solving study, young girls asked for help and approval from adults more frequently than the boys; and, when given the opportunity to return to puzzles a second time, the girls were more likely to rework those they had already solved, whereas the boys were more likely to try puzzles they had been unable to solve previously. A girl's sigh of relief is almost audible when she marries and retires from the outside world of novel and unsolved problems.

This, of course, is the most conspicuous outcome of all: The majority of America's women become full-time homemakers. *And of those who work, 78 percent end up in dead-end jobs as clerical workers, service workers, factory workers or sales clerks.* They do not pursue challenging or even well-paying careers. This "homogenization" of America's women is the major consequence of our sex-role ideology.

The important point is not that the role of homemaker or teacher or nurse or secretary is necessarily inferior, but rather that our society is managing to consign a large segment of its population to the role of homemaker—either with or without a dead-end job—solely on the basis of sex just as inexorably as it has in the past consigned the individual with the black skin to the role of janitor or domestic. The important point is that in spite of their unique identities the majority of America's women end up in virtually the *same* role.

Even an IQ in the genius range does not guarantee that a woman's unique potential will find expression. This sobering fact was revealed in a famous study of over 1,300 men and women whose IQs averaged 151. These men and women were followed over a period of thirty-five years, beginning when they were about ten years old. Today, 86 percent of the gifted men in this study have achieved prominence in professional and managerial occupations. But what about the highly gifted women? Of those who are employed, 37 percent are nurses, librarians, social workers or noncollege teachers. An additional

20 percent are secretaries, stenographers, bookkeepers or office workers! Only 11 percent are in the higher professions of law, medicine, college teaching, engineering, science, economics, and the like. Moreover, these statistics refer only to a minority of the highly gifted women in this study. For even at age forty-four, well after their children have gone to school, 61 percent of these highly gifted women are full-time homemakers!

And what does a full-time homemaker do with her time—regardless of IQ? Time studies show that she spends the equivalent of a full working day, 7.1 hours, in preparing meals, cleaning house, laundering, mending, shopping and doing other household tasks. In other words, 43 percent of her waking time is spent in activity that would command an hourly wage on the open market well below the federally set minimum for menial industrial work. The point is not how little she would earn if she did these things in someone else's home; she will be doing them in her own home for free. The point is that this use of time is virtually the same for homemakers with college degrees and for those with less than a grade-school education, for women married to professional men and for women married to blue-collar workers. Talent, education, ability, interests, motivation: all are irrelevant. In our society, being female uniquely qualifies an individual for domestic work—either by itself or in conjunction with typing, teaching, nursing or unskilled labor.

Again, the important point is not that the role of homemaker is necessarily inferior, but that a woman's unique identity has been rendered irrelevant. Consider the following "predictability test." When a baby boy is born, it is difficult to predict what he will be doing twenty-five years later. We cannot say whether he will be an artist, a doctor or a guidance counselor, because he will be permitted to develop and to fulfill his own unique potential, particularly if he is white and middle-class. But if that same newborn child is a girl, we can usually predict with confidence how she is likely to be spending her time twenty-five years later. Her individuality doesn't have to be considered; it is irrelevant.

The socialization of the American male has closed off certain options for him too. Men are discouraged from developing certain desirable traits such as tenderness and sensitivity just as surely as women are discouraged from being assertive and "too bright." Young boys are encouraged to be incompetent at cooking and child care just as surely as young girls are urged to be incompetent at mathematics and science. The elimination of sex-role stereotyping implies that each individual would be encouraged to find and do his or her own thing. Men and women would no longer be stereotyped by society's definitions of masculine and feminine. If sensitivity, emotionality and warmth are desirable *human* characteristics, then they are desirable for men as well as for women. If independence, assertiveness and serious intellectual commitment are desirable *human* characteristics, then they are desirable for women as well as for men. And it is undoubtedly true that many men today would have been more fulfilled if their socialization had permitted them to engage in activity currently stereotyped as female—child care, for example.

Thus, it is true that a man's options are also limited by our society's sex-role ideology, but, as the "predictability test" reveals, it is still the woman in our society whose identity is rendered irrelevant by America's socialization practices.

FURTHER PSYCHOLOGICAL BARRIERS

But what of the woman who arrives at age twenty-one still motivated to be challenged and fulfilled by a growing career? Is she free to choose a career if she cares to do so? Or is there something standing even in her way?

There is. Even the woman who has managed to finesse society's attempt to rob her of her career motivations is likely to find herself blocked by society's trump card: the feeling that one cannot have a career and be a successful woman simultaneously. A competent and motivated woman is thus caught in a double bind which few men have ever faced. She must worry not only about failure but also about success. If she fails in her achievement needs, she must live with the knowledge that she is not living up to her potential. But if she succeeds, she must live with the knowledge that she is not living up to her own—or society's—conception of a feminine woman.

This conflict was strikingly revealed in a study which required college women to complete the following story: "After first-term finals, Anne finds herself at the top of her medical-school class." The stories were then examined for unconscious, internal conflict about success and failure. The women in this study all had high intellectual ability and histories of academic success. They were the very women who could have successful careers. And yet over two thirds of their stories revealed a clear-cut inability to cope with the concept of a feminine yet career-oriented woman.

The most common fear-of-success stories showed strong fears of social rejection as a result of success. The women in this group showed anxiety about becoming unpopular, unmarriageable and lonely:

Anne starts proclaiming her surprise and joy. Her fellow classmates are so disgusted with her behavior that they jump on her in a body and beat her. She is maimed for life.

Anne is an acne-faced bookworm. . . . She studies twelve hours a day, and lives at home to save money. "Well, it certainly paid off. All the Friday and Saturday nights without dates, fun—I'll be the best woman doctor alive." And yet a twinge of sadness comes through—she wonders what she really has . . .

Anne doesn't want to be number one in her class. . . . She feels she shouldn't rank so high because of social reasons. She drops to ninth and then marries the boy who graduates number one.

In the second fear-of-success category were stories in which the women seemed concerned about definitions of womanhood.

These stories expressed guilt and despair over success and doubts about their femininity and normality.

> Unfortunately Anne no longer feels so certain that she really wants to be a doctor. She is worried about herself and wonders if perhaps she is not normal. . . . Anne decides not to continue with her medical work but to take courses that have a deeper personal meaning for her.

> Anne feels guilty. . . . She will finally have a nervous breakdown and quit medical school and marry a successful young doctor.

A third group of stories could not even face up to the conflict between having a career and being a woman. These stories simply denied the possibility that any woman could be so successful.

> Anne is a code name for a nonexistent person created by a group of med students. They take turns writing for Anne . . .

> Anne is really happy she's on top, though Tom is higher than she—though that's as it should be. Anne doesn't mind Tom winning.

By way of contrast, here is a typical story written not about Anne but about John:

> John has worked very hard and his long hours of study have paid off. . . . He is thinking about his girl, Cheri, whom he will marry at the end of med school. He realizes he can give her all the things she desires after he becomes established. He will go on in med school and be successful in the long run.

Nevertheless, there were a few women in the study who welcomed the prospect of success:

> Anne is quite a lady—not only is she top academically, but she is liked and admired by her fellow students—quite a trick in a man-dominated field. She is brilliant—but she is also a woman. She will continue to be at or near the top. And . . . always a lady.

Hopefully the day is approaching when as many "Anne" stories as "John" stories will have happy endings.

THE PRESUMED INCOMPATIBILITY OF FAMILY AND CAREER

If we were to ask the average American woman why she is not pursuing a full-time career, she would probably not say that discrimination had discouraged her; nor would she recognize the pervasive effect of her sex-role conditioning. What she probably would say is that a career, no matter how desirable, is simply incompatible with the role of wife and mother.

As recently as the turn of the century (and in less technological societies today) this incompatibility between career and family was, in fact, decisive. Women died in their forties, and they were pregnant or nursing during most of their adult lives. Moreover, the work that a less technological society requires places a premium on mobility and physical strength. Thus, the historical division of labor between the sexes—the man away at work and the woman at home with the children—was a biological necessity. Today it is not.

Today, the work that our technological society requires is primarily cognitive in nature; women have virtually complete control over their reproductive lives; and, most important of all, the average American woman now lives to age seventy-four and has her last child by age twenty-six. Thus, by the time a woman is thirty-three or so, her children all have more important things to do with their daytime hours than to spend them entertaining an adult woman who has nothing fulfilling to do during the second half of her life span.

But social forms have a way of outliving the necessities which gave rise to them. Thus, today's female adolescent continues to plan for a nineteenth-century life style in a twentieth-century world. A Gallup poll has found that young women give no thought to life after forty. They plan to graduate from high school, perhaps go to college, and then get married. Period.

THE WOMAN AS WIFE

At some level, of course, this kind of planning is "realistic." Because most women do grow up to be wives and mothers, and because, for many women, this has often meant that they would be leaving the labor force during the child-rearing years, a career is not really feasible. After all, a career involves long-term commitment and perhaps even some sacrifice on the part of the family. Furthermore, as every "successful" woman knows, a wife's appropriate role is to encourage her husband in *his* career. The good wife puts her husband through school and endures the family's early financial difficulties without a whimper, and if her husband's career should suddenly dictate a move to another city she sees to it that the transition is accomplished as painlessly as possible. The good wife is selfless. And to be seriously concerned about one's own career is selfish—if one happens to be female, that is. With these kinds of constraints imposed upon the work life of the married woman, perhaps it would be "unrealistic" for her to seriously aspire toward a career rather than a job.

There is some evidence of discontent among these "selfless" women, however. A 1962 Gallup poll revealed that only 10 percent of American women would want their daughters to live their lives the way they did. These mothers wanted their daughters to get more education and to marry later. And a 1970 study of women married to top Chicago-area business and professional men revealed that if these women could live their lives over again they would pursue careers.

Accordingly, the traditional conception of the husband–wife relationship is now being challenged, not so much because of this widespread discontent among older, married women, but because it violates two of the most basic values of today's college generation. These values concern personal growth on the one hand and interpersonal relationships on the other. The first of them emphasizes individuality and self-fulfillment; the second stresses openness, honesty and equality in all human relationships.

Because they see the traditional male–female relationship as incompatible with these basic values, today's young people are experimenting with alternatives to the traditional marriage pattern. Although a few are testing out ideas like communal living, most are searching for satisfactory modifications of the husband–wife relationship within the context of marriage. And an increasing number of young people are entering marriages very much like the following hypothetical example:

> Both my wife and I earned college degrees in our respective disciplines. I turned down a superior job offer in Oregon and accepted a slightly less desirable position in New York, where my wife would have more opportunities for part-time work in her specialty. Although I would have preferred to live in a suburb, we purchased a home near my wife's job so that she could have an office at home where she would be when the children returned from school. Because my wife earns a good salary, she can easily afford to pay a housekeeper to do her major household chores. My wife and I share all other tasks around the house equally. For example, she cooks the meals, but I do the laundry for her and help her with many of her other household tasks.

Without questioning the basic happiness of such a marriage or its appropriateness for many couples, we can legitimately ask if such a marriage is in fact an instance of interpersonal equality. Have all the hidden assumptions about the woman's "natural" role really been eliminated? Has the traditional ideology really been exorcised? There is a very simple test. If the marriage is truly equalitarian, then its description should retain the same flavor and tone even if the roles of the husband and wife were to be reversed.

Both my husband and I earned college degrees in our respective disciplines. I turned down a superior job offer in Oregon and accepted a slightly less desirable position in New York where my husband would have more opportunities for part-time work in his specialty. Although I would have preferred to live in a suburb, we purchased a home near my husband's job so that he could have an office at home where he would be when the children returned from school. Because my husband earns a good salary, he can easily afford to pay a housekeeper to do his major household chores. My husband and I share all other tasks around the house equally. For example, he cooks the meals, but I do the laundry for him and help him with many of his other household tasks.

It seems unlikely that many men or women in our society would mistake the marriage just described as either equalitarian or desirable, and thus it becomes apparent that the ideology about the woman's "natural" role unconsciously permeates the entire fabric of such "quasi-equalitarian" marriages. It is true that the wife gains some measure of equality when she can have a career rather than a job and when her career can influence the final place of residence. But why is it the unquestioned assumption that the husband's career solely determines the initial set of alternatives that are to be considered? Why is it the wife who automatically seeks the part-time position? Why is it *her* housekeeper rather than *their* housekeeper? Why *her* laundry? Why *her* household tasks? And so forth throughout the entire relationship.

In fact, however, even these "benign" inequities are beginning to be challenged. More and more young couples are seeking to enter marriages of full equality, marriages in which both partners pursue careers or outside commitments which carry equal weight when all important decisions are to be made, marriages in which both husband and wife accept some compromise in the growth of their respective careers. Certainly such marriages have more tactical difficulties than more traditional ones: It is more difficult to coordinate two independent lives than just one. The point is that it is not possible to predict ahead of time *on the basis of sex* who will be doing the compromising at any given point of decision.

It is clear that the man or woman who places career above all else ought not to enter an equalitarian marriage. The man would do better to marry a traditional wife, a wife who will make whatever sacrifices his career necessitates. The woman would do better—in our present society—to remain single unless she is able to find the rare man who would put his own work second. For an equalitarian marriage is not designed for extra efficiency, but rather for double fulfillment.

An equalitarian marriage also embraces a division of labor within the home which satisfies what we like to call "the roommate test." That is, the labor is divided just as it is when two men or two women room together in college or set up a bachelor apartment together. Errands and domestic chores are assigned by preference, agreement, flipping a coin, given to hired help, or—as is sometimes the case—simply left undone.

THE WOMAN AS MOTHER

In all marriages, whether traditional, quasi-equalitarian or fully equalitarian, the real question surrounding a mother's career will probably continue to be the well-being of the children. All parents want to be certain that they are doing the best for their children, and that they are not depriving them in any important way, either materially or psychologically. What this has always meant in most families that could afford it was that the mother would devote herself to her children on a full-time basis. Women have even been convinced—by their mothers and by the so-called experts—that there is something wrong with them if they want to do otherwise.

Actually, this is the first time in history that mothers have even been able to think about the possibility of devoting themselves to their children on a full-time basis. Never before has motherhood been a full-time occupation for any adult woman.

In the past, women had to spend a great deal of time and energy running the household: baking bread, churning butter, preserving vegetables and sewing clothing. Children were not neglected, but they were freer to develop the autonomy and initiative and independence so necessary for adulthood. Only in recent times has the homemaker had time to worry about her child's development, to organize his social life, and to discuss his problems.

In fact, there is some evidence that full-time mothering may actually be harmful. Too often, the full-time mother tries to live through her children. The mother whose own identity is defined solely through her children's accomplishments cannot leave her children really free to strive on their own and to learn from their own mistakes. For the child's mistakes are her failures, and so her emotional strength is weakest at that moment when her support is needed the most. Children cannot be hovered over like hothouse plants. Without some identity of her own, the full-time mother is inevitably tempted to bind her children to her in a dependency relationship which only makes it more difficult for them to step into maturity and adulthood. Thus, a high percentage of the psychoneurotic discharges from the Army during World War II was traced to these young soldiers' overdependence on their mothers. Furthermore, the counseling centers of most college campuses are filled with young men and young women who need help in freeing themselves from their dependency on their parents, particularly their mothers.

But when these same female students themselves become mothers, they will be encouraged to perpetuate this cycle of dependency; they will be discouraged from even taking a job, because "the children might suffer."

Research does not support the view that children suffer when Mother works, however. Although it came as a surprise to most researchers in the area, maternal employment in and of itself does not seem to have any negative effects on the children; and part-time work actually seems to benefit the children. Children of working mothers are no more likely than children of nonworking mothers to be delinquent or nervous or withdrawn or antisocial; they are no more likely to show neurotic symptoms; they are no more likely to perform poorly in school; and they are no more likely to feel deprived of maternal affection. Daughters of working mothers are more likely to want to work themselves, and when asked to name the one woman they most admire they are more likely to name their own mothers! If only this last fact could be disseminated to every working mother in America. The other thing that's true of almost every working mother is that she thinks she might be hurting her children and she feels guilty. If only she knew how much her daughter admired her. Finally, research has shown that the worst mothers are those who would like to work but who stay home out of a sense of duty. The major conclusion from all the research on maternal employment seems to be this: What matters is the quality of a mother's relationship with her children, not the time of day it happens to be administered. The conclusion should come as no surprise to anyone; successful fathers have been demonstrating it for years!

Similarly, the quality of the substitute care that children receive while their parents are at work also matters. Young children do need security, and research shows that it is not good to have a constant turnover of parent substitutes, a rapid succession of changing babysitters.

But that is not the same as adding additional, relatively permanent adults to the child's life. In previous years, the extended family accomplished this automatically; any one of several adults might be tending to the child's needs on any specific occasion. Even today, 35 percent of all working women still turn to their own relatives for substitute child care during their working hours. In addition, however, there are many middle-aged women, both in and out of the labor force, whose main fulfillment in life has been the raising of their own children. In preference either to their current idleness or to the dull routine of low-level jobs, such women would probably like nothing more than to have the opportunity to participate in the rearing of still another child.

Even more important is the establishment of government-sponsored child-care centers. All women's-rights organizations, no matter how conservative, are in agreement on this central issue: that free child-care centers should be available, like public schools, parks and libraries, for those who want to use them.

But mothers must feel free to utilize these alternative arrangements for child care. For it is here that America's sex-role ideology intrudes once again. Many people still assume that if a woman wants a full-time career, then children must be unimportant to her. But of course no one makes this assumption about her husband. No one assumes that a father's interest in his career necessarily precludes a deep and abiding affection for his children or a vital interest in their development. Once again, America applies a double standard of judgment. Suppose that a father of small children suddenly lost his wife. No matter how much he loved his children, no one would expect him to sacrifice his career in order to stay home with them on a full-time basis, even if he had an independent source of income. No one would charge him with selfishness or lack of parental feeling if he sought professional care for his children during the day.

It is here that full equality between husband and wife assumes its ultimate importance. The fully equalitarian marriage abolishes this double standard and extends the same freedom to the mother. The equalitarian marriage provides the framework for both husband and wife to pursue careers which are challenging and fulfilling and, at the same time, to participate equally in the pleasures and responsibilities of child rearing. Indeed, it is the equalitarian marriage which has the potential for giving children the love and concern of two parents rather than one. And it is the equalitarian marriage which has the most potential for giving parents the challenge and fulfillment of two worlds—family and career—rather than one.

Do All Women Want to Work?
The Economics of Their Choice

by JUANITA KREPS

Juanita Kreps is Professor of Economics and Dean of the Women's College at Duke University.

We must realize that the working wife and mother is not a modern invention. On the contrary, the nonworking full-time wife and mother is a phenomenon that only modern affluency, that is, modern technology, has made possible.

—BRUNO BETTELHEIM

A willingness to join the labor market clearly exists for great numbers of married women. How many of them elect to take jobs (or, stated differently, what it takes to induce any given number to take jobs) depends upon their evaluation of two sets of advantages:

1. The home set, consisting of more time for leisure, hobbies and community activity; closer attention to the needs of the family; economies reaped through full attention to home management; freedom of schedule, etc.
2. The market set, including earnings and fringe benefits; job status; associations available in the work place; interest in the work itself.

In weighing these two sets of alternatives, the need for income is an overriding consideration for a very large percentage of women. Of the thirty million women now at work, more than twelve million are single, separated or widowed. Many of these women are the sole source of support not only for themselves but for children or parents as well. In addition, almost five million of the working women are married to men who earn less than five thousand dollars annually. Thus *more than half the women in the labor force do not have the luxury of choosing home work over market work;* in fact, there can be little doubt that the relatively low participation rate of women with low educational achievement is due to their lack of job opportunities. If jobs were available to these women, the market set of advantages would surely win over the nonmarket.

For families on very low incomes, the wage necessary to induce the wife to take a job is also low, since the value of each additional dollar of income has high utility. As the husband's income rises, we observe that the wife's willingness to join the labor force declines, other things being equal. We know little, however, about the market behavior of wives in relation to their own possible range of earnings, beyond the fact that the higher their educational achievement (and hence their potential earnings), the more likely they are to work.

The degree of this responsiveness to wage incentive turns on the perceived value of the alternative use of the wife's time. When a man goes to work, no loss in value is imputed to the free time he gives up. On the contrary, any loss in time from work is considered a loss in income, or foregone earnings. But a married woman's nonmarket services are of value; problems of analysis arise from the fact that we do not know, household to household, precisely what value a family places on them.

The maximum value placed on a nonworking wife's services can be deduced from the salary that does in fact induce her to take a job. Similarly, there is some theoretical minimum below which wives at work will withdraw from their jobs and devote their time to home work. The asking price is higher the greater the value attached to home work, and this value obviously varies at different stages of a family's life cycle, each stage making a different set of demands on the wife's time. Between families in the same stage, however, the values also differ; the presence of children in black families has been less of a deterrent to the wife's market work than children have been in white families, where the need for income was less pressing. For any given family size and age composition, the relative value imputed to the wife's home work is obviously lower, the greater the perceived need for additional income.

WIVES' NONMARKET WORK

Since we do not place a price on wives nonmarket work, no value for these services enters the national income accounts. We add in the value of their services only when they take jobs. The gross national product is thus increased by the salaries earned, with no reduction for the loss of home work. Were the wives' employment rate to decline, moreover, GNP would show only the loss in market income, although wives would then perform many services for the family that formerly were not rendered or had to be purchased in the market.*

The National Bureau of Economic Research estimated that the value of housewives' services amounted to one fourth the amount of the gross national product in 1918, and a decade later Simon Kuznets found a value of slightly over one fourth the GNP. Gardner Ackley notes that "not to recognize the value of these productive services is a source of serious bias in the national product." A 1968 estimate of the value of housewives' services again placed the total at about one fourth of the GNP.

Attempts to impute a dollar value to nonmarket work done by wives are hampered by a lack of data on the prices of many services which are typically performed primarily in the home, and by our inability to attach monetary values to certain intangible qualities usually associated with having a wife and mother in the home: companionship, attention, interest in the

---

* In *The Economics of Welfare*, A. C. Pigou cites the classic example: "If a number of bachelors who were employing housekeepers in the customary manner of exchanging services for money decided to marry these housekeepers, then the national dividend would be diminished! Obviously the housekeeper, when assuming the role of wife, regardless of any additional services she assumed by virtue of her marriage, continued to perform those services which she, as a housekeeper, had been performing previously. In other words, the services continued but the value disappeared!"

family's welfare, continuity of relationship with young children. An alternative approach is to estimate the costs of the wife's home work by supposing that its value equals the foregone earnings in the labor market. Although this method would leave many of the vital questions unattended, it would nevertheless allow us to take into account *some* value for nonmarket work, thereby reducing the degree of overstatement in output that occurs when women enter market jobs.

The development and publicizing of such an accounting procedure would not only improve the measure of growth in real output; it might also change attitudes toward market and nonmarket work. On the current scene, one of the most frequently cited complaints of women is the fact that they are expected to do routine, repetitive household chores, for which there is no monetary reward. They are frequently eager to trade this work for a market job which may be equally routine and repetitive; the difference is that the market job pays a salary. An actual payment for home services is not as absurd as might appear at first glance.

Despite our protests that growth in income is not to be equated with improvements in welfare; that society places a high value on the services of wives in the home and in the community; that the absence of a price tag on a particular service does not render it valueless—despite these caveats, the tendency to identify one's worth with the salary he earns is a persistent one. This tendency is not peculiar to men who earn salaries; it pervades as well the thinking of women who work at unpaid jobs.

Within the family, where the market-work–nonmarket-work decision is made, a seemingly low value placed on home work may make the pay offered by an ordinary market job very appealing to the wife.

In her proposal that housewives running their homes be included in the statistics of the active labor force and in the benefits that accrue to members of the labor force, Sylva Gelber of the Canada Department of Labour cites the gains wives would make, even in the absence of money payments for house-work: social-security entitlements (such as pension accumulations) would be conferred for the years of work at home; allowances provided under the Adult Retraining Programme, now available to persons attached to the labor force for at least three years, would be available; a more positive attitude toward the value of domestic work on the part of both society and the housewife would ensue.

It is well to raise the question of whether wives would be entering the labor force in their present numbers if they earned salaries for doing home work (or even if they were made conscious of the opportunity cost of that work).

When some work pays a wage or salary and other work does not, it is difficult for the family or for society to compare by reference to a dollar measure the relative values of the two types of work. The activity which is rewarded with a paycheck is likely to be valued more highly in our society, with the not unusual result that women may strive to maximize their dollar earnings, which may or may not maximize their contribution to family welfare. For women who have no option as to whether they will seek jobs—female heads of households, mothers of children in welfare families, etc.—the social costs of enforced market activity may be higher in the long run than the costs of providing family income in lieu of market work.

These are, of course, two separate issues. In the first instance, women are drawn into the job market because of a systematic undervaluing of their services in the home; in the latter, women are forced into market work regardless of the value they place on the alternative use of their time at home. But payment for nonmarket work would affect both situations: it would improve the base for decision-making in the first case, and provide a market–nonmarket work option in the second.

WOMEN'S ASPIRATIONS: HOW HIGH ARE THEY?

Further documentation of the sex-related differences in earnings is perhaps not necessary; the data indicate that being male pays some wage premium within many of the occupations which utilize both sexes. But a more important source of bias, perhaps, lies in the woman's selection of her occupation. If women persist in going into those jobs which have traditionally paid low wages, improvements in pay scales can occur only if the demand for these services far outstrips the plentiful supply of workers. The reasons why women select these jobs invite further study. Are there nonmonetary rewards in certain careers that more than offset the low pay? Is elementary-school teaching appealing to women because they like the work itself, or because it is viewed as an extension of their feminine roles, or because it can be timed to enable women to perform their regular household duties? How much are women willing to pay (in forgone earnings) for time free of market work at the time of day and year that nonmarket work is heaviest?

Clarence Long emphasized the importance of the short workday to a woman with a reference to her need to be able "to type till five o'clock, and still have time to shop for a cheap roast."

It is not merely that their nonmarket work influences their decision as to whether to enter the labor force; the demands of home and family also influence *which* market jobs women are willing to take. Moreover, the period of heaviest domestic responsibility occurs fairly early in a woman's work life, when she is likely to be forced to make some quite long-range decisions: whether to acquire further job training, or additional formal education; how many children she will have; whether to continue working, at least part time, during the childbearing period. In the face of the demands on her time, the young wife is likely to find that the scheduling of her job is the most important single consideration. Her immediate job choice is dictated in large measure by the time constraint imposed in the short run, and this choice in turn directs her subsequent career development.

THE SLOW PROCESS OF CHANGING THE RULES

If the campaign which many women are now waging on behalf of their right to work throughout life, as men do; to receive equal pay for equal work; to be hired on the basis of credentials rather than sex—if these efforts have the effect of rewriting labor legislation and changing employment practices, there will inevitably be a new look in the sexual division of labor. Both men and women will come to have a wider range of occupations. The change is likely to be a gradual one, however. The number of women willing to forgo marriage and family or to shift child-rearing responsibilities to men or day-care centers cannot be predicted with any accuracy, but changes in attitude toward "women's place" seem to require a basic departure from present thinking.

Writing early in the 1960s, Carl Degler maintained that in this country there is not now and never has been an ideological basis for the movement of women into the labor force. With American women, as with American society, interest in the job is an immediate and practical one; it is jobs, not careers, that women have sought. "To say . . . that men have opposed and resisted the opening of opportunities to women is to utter only a half truth. The whole truth is that American society in general, which includes women, shuns like a disease any feminist ideology." Although he clearly applauds proposals for equality of the sexes, he concludes that most American women still do not want outside work justified as a *normal* pattern for married women; they prefer instead to think of such work as special. And as long as women view their work in this way "the soil is thin and the climate incongenial for the growth of any seed-lings of ideology."

THE QUESTION OF LIBERATION

Degler's appraisal of the limited work interests of most American women in the past must now be cast in the perspective of the new thrust for women's rights. Is something different in the making? And will enough women join to qualify this wave of interest as a woman's movement, even an ideology? Finally, is such a movement an effective tool of change? Answers to these questions lie outside the economists' competence. Yet one can say very little about the future labor force activity of women except by reference to the more pervasive issues affecting women's work preferences.

It is well to remember how far we have come along the path toward sex equality in the labor force, along with how far we have yet to go.

But the questions are now more complex than that of a wife's working or not working. The issues have to do with certain marketplace considerations: the kinds of work available to women, the pay and professional advancement that accompany different jobs, equality of treatment in all aspects of work; and the equally important matters related to the domestic division of labor: whose career takes precedence in job changes, whether the wife assumes complete responsiblity for child care, how much investment the family makes in the education of the female as compared with that of the male.

On the domestic scene, resolution of the current questions has important implications for family living patterns. Along with the restriction in family size, the emphasis on women's right to participate freely in market activities will surely lead the married couple to consider the wife's job more important than heretofore and to plan around her career as well as the husband's.

More women, too, may remain unmarried, or seek divorces; careers will inevitably absorb the interests of many competent women who no longer need the financial support of a husband and who are not particularly interested in having children. Wider social acceptance of the unmarried female is already apparent, and contraceptive methods now make it unnecessary for the single woman to forego sexual relationships.

In the marketplace, whatever progress women make will probably be made piecemeal by arguing each specific issue in the courts and at the bargaining table. Women's emphasis on improved working conditions has thus far paid little attention to the possible advantages of union organization; justice is to be more legislated than bargained, apparently. But some of the new demands can be achieved only through negotiation, and maintained in the way men have maintained their position in the work force, i.e., through day-to-day surveillance.

The strength women have gained from the liberation movement is difficult to assess at this early stage. But the widespread interest in women's rights that surrounded that debate, and the present sensitivity of employers to antidiscriminatory legislation surely attest to the effectiveness of women's activism on their own behalf.

Wives who have no interest in working outside the home—well over half the total number—are less likely than working women to be interested in their sisters' treatment in the marketplace; moreover, we have no data on the proportion of women who think of other women as their "sisters" in the manner suggested by the liberation literature.

The emphasis which female high-school and college students are currently giving to women's rights, job status and freedom of behavior is highly significant, since these women will soon enter the work force. Again, a question arises. Is this generation of young women (and young men, for they too argue for women's equality) typical of those to follow? If so, the relationship of the sexes in both the home and the marketplace will hereafter be different. If, instead, the cohort now in high school and college will be followed by a cohort whose social concerns lie elsewhere, or who actually prefer the more traditional family patterns, the effect of current efforts to improve women's lot will dissipate somewhat.

Even so, it seems unlikely that American women, particularly the college-educated, will again give home work and child care the central role they occupied in, say, the 1940s and 1950s. The greater the societal need to restrict family size, moreover, the greater will be women's participation in market jobs. The one significant deterrent to this movement of women into the labor force would be a substantial decline in the demand for those services typically performed by women. But such a decline would have only a short-run effect, and could easily be offset by opening to women a broader range of job opportunities.

In addition to the question of the extent to which women of all ages and labor-force positions subscribe to the current liberation movement, and the question of whether the cohort of women now, say, aged fifteen to twenty-five will be succeeded by cohorts of similar persuasion, the increased labor-force activity of women raises interesting questions related to the future allocation of time among the three choices: market work, home work and leisure. With the growth in productivity per man-hour afforded by improved technology, and the increased labor-force size afforded by women's entrance to the labor force, a growth in time free of market work should also ensue. Will the change in the sex composition of the labor force have the effect of shortening weekly hours, lengthening annual vacations, or shortening work life?

Productivity gains in this country have conferred increases in nonworking time during the twentieth century, with the forms of the leisure varying from one period to another. Reductions in weekly hours of work occurred mainly in the first third of the century; increases in vacation, sick leave, etc., followed in the decades of the 1940s. In addition to these work-year changes, the age of labor-force entry for males rose significantly and their age of retirement from work dropped, which, with increased life expectancy, added about nine years of nonworking time to the male's life in the first half of the century.

Throughout this period women's labor-force activity grew, albeit unevenly, and one could argue that there has been some tradeoff between the free-time gains of men and the free-time losses of women. To the extent that men take over household and child-care responsibilities so that wives may work, however, the result is merely a redivision of market and nonmarket work between the sexes. But will the fact that both husband and wife have full-time jobs not generate a demand for a reduction in the amount of market work each does? Women have traditionally needed short work weeks in order to meet family responsibilities; increased involvement of men in home work may affect their market-work–nonmarket-work tradeoff in the same way. Given the higher family incomes that result from wives' earnings, moreover, it seems likely that shortened work weeks (or lengthened vacations) will be of somewhat greater value to workers than still greater incomes. The sex allocation of the adult's time between market work and nonmarket activity may thus undergo important changes which, in turn, could affect patterns of working time in industry.

Changing Family Life Styles:
One Role, Two Roles, Shared Roles

by JESSIE BERNARD

Jessie Bernard is professor emerita of sociology, Pennsylvania State University. She is the author of many works, including *Academic Women, Women and the Public Interest* and, most recently, *The Future of Marriage.*

In 1957 the National Manpower Council concluded a survey of the employment status of women by noting that the major concerns of those seeking to advance the interests of women at that time had to do with equal-pay legislation and an equal-rights amendment. The authors commented on the absence of interest in both maternity leave and the expansion of child-care facilities to make employment easier for women. They took it for granted that recent changes would influence future public-policy issues, but as of that moment "the form these future developments may take . . . [was] still obscure." Fifteen years later, the issue of the equal-rights amendment is still hot. And interest in the expansion of child-care facilities has become salient.

I venture here to suggest that future public-policy developments must deal with hours. Not hours in the traditional form of rescinding special protective legislation which can be used as a means of evading antidiscrimination legislation—currently an active issue—but rather concern with implications and ramifications of hours that are far more revolutionary: a concern not so much with the impact of hours of work on productivity or on the economy as with their impact on the relations between the sexes in the family, vis-à-vis one another, vis-à-vis children. Our new concern will ask industry to accommodate to the family rather than requiring the family to accommodate to industry. It calls for extensive increase in the availability of part-time work for both men and women so that fathers and mothers can share roles providing income, child rearing and socialization. It challenges as dysfunctional for men, for women, for children and for marriage itself the exclusive assignments of the child-rearing function to women and the provider role to men, on which all public policy with respect to employment rests.

THE ONE-ROLE IDEOLOGY

Until not too long ago no woman was supposed to work out-side the home unless she had absolutely no other source of sup-port. Only one role was appropriate for any woman, a domestic one which encompassed a variety of related functions, especially childbearing, child rearing and housekeeping, along with pro-ductive activities. Economic necessity was the only acceptable reason for assuming the provider role which belonged to men. Later on it became acceptable for women to hold jobs before they were married but not after, unless, again, they had ab-solutely no other source of support; married women still had only one proper role.

As recently as 1969, one respondent in a Gallup poll was still expressing the one-role ideology: "Women should stay home and take care of their families. Even if the kids are in school, a woman's obligation is still to make a home for her husband." The one-role ideology could prevail so long as all the functional assignments of women—childbearing, child rearing, and indus-trial production—could be combined in one role. When they no longer could—as more and more of the industrial production of the economy was removed from the home—a two-role ideology gained recognition. The function of industrial production—though not of housekeeping services—was split off from the domestic role and a separate worker role for women developed.

When more than half of all the women in the labor force were married, husband present, and when about half of mothers with school-age children were in the labor force, the opinion of the

Gallup poll respondent sounded quaint. It has taken some people quite a while to catch up with the twentieth century. Quaint as they may seem, such attitudes cannot be ignored, for all analyses of labor-force participation by women pay their respects to "social values and attitudes" which "exert a pervasive influence upon women's employment." These attitudes "are deeply rooted and resist change, but they are far from immutable."

THE TWO-ROLE IDEOLOGY

The twentieth century was almost half over when the fallacy of the one-role ideology in this day and age was officially recognized. By that time it was becoming obvious that a modern industrialized society had no choice in the matter; it could not operate without the contribution of women. Thus, in 1949 a Royal Commission on Population in Great Britain reported that it would be harmful to restrict the contribution that women could make to the cultural and economic life of the nation and therefore "a deliberate effort should be made to devise adjustments that would render it easier for women to combine motherhood and the care of a home with outside activities." This was not the reason likely to be given by women themselves if asked, but certainly it was a legitimate rationale for policy. At any rate, the commission's report marked the recognition of the two-role, or double-track, ideology. Now, in addition to self-support, the contribution which women made to the economy was a legitimizing sanction for labor-force participation even by married women.

President John F. Kennedy went along with this ideology. In establishing his own Commission on the Status of Women in 1961, he prefaced his order with a statement including the necessity of making the most efficient and effective use of the skills of all persons to promote the economy, security, and national defense. President Lyndon B. Johnson also played up the we-need-their-services justification for the two-role ideology, pointing out how badly off we would be if women were not encouraged to enter the labor force.

Not until the second half of the century did a third reason for labor-force participation by women, including married women, enter the accepted repertoire of arguments. It was presented in 1956 by Alva Myrdal and Viola Klein in their book *Women's Two Roles*. This book supplied the sober social-science underpinnings for the we-need-them aspect of the two-role policy. It added also that it would be unrealistic to suppose that all the postmaternal years of a woman's life could be left vacant, unfilled. But this book was important because it also added another support for the two-role ideology. Women, no less than men, needed not only "emotional fulfillment in their personal relations" but also "a sense of social purpose." And President Kennedy included self-fulfillment as an acceptable reason for employment also; women "should be assured the opportunity to develop their capacities and fulfill their aspirations." Agreeing with the Royal Commission on Population, he thought women should be helped by provision of services "to enable women to continue their role as wives and mothers" while at the same time "making a maximum contribution to the world around them."

The self-fulfillment basis for the two-role ideology had good research support. There was convincing evidence that if wives wanted to work and did, their marriages were better; in some cases having a job made motherhood itself more satisfying. Many women who gave economic reasons for working said they would want to work even if they did not have to. And in a study of mothers receiving Aid to Families with Dependent Children, four fifths said they would prefer to work even if they had incomes of their own. Some form of the two-role pattern was the preferred one by both young men and women among both black and white students.

Especially persuasive research support for the two-role ideology came from a classic study of marriage inaugurated a generation ago. E. W. Burgess and Paul Wallin had interviewed a thousand couples in the late 1930s and early 1940s; in the late 1950s, four hundred were reinterviewed. Among the most important findings of this unique and unparalleled study was one to the effect that marriages with the greatest role *differentiation between spouses were the least satisfactory*, most likely to have deteriorated into "empty shells."*

Actually, the self-actualization or self-fulfillment argument in favor of the two-role ideology has never been taken seriously by legislators. The nearest recognition of its validity has been the antidiscrimination legislation, and that came almost accidentally; administration has been far from crusading in nature. Self-support, especially in the case of women on assistance rolls, has been aggressively implemented by insistence that women work if at all possible—a policy mean-spirited, almost punitive. The contribution of women to the economy as a basis for the two-role ideology has been given lip service, but, despite the persistent and continuing efforts of women, the facilities in the form of child-care services that would make it feasible have been niggardly. In the case of women pejoratively labeled "career" women, policy has been resistant; one might even say sullen and resentful.†

This, in general, was where our thinking stood in the 1960s. A kind of unwilling acceptance by policy-makers of the basic fact of twentieth-century life: that women's place was not exclusively in the home, that families did not have exclusive claim to the entire lives of women, that, like it or not, labor-force

---

* Jan E. Dizard, *Social Change in the Family* (Chicago: Community and Family Study Center, University of Chicago, 1968), Chapter 5.

† "I have found among the most educated, the most attractive, the most decent husbands . . . a certain more or less rationalized stupidity when it comes to the question of woman's role in science and government—a fanatic refusal to try to understand, which can only be explained as an expression of an underlying panic."—Erik Erikson, "Closing the Gap," in *Women and the Scientific Professions,* Jacquelyn A. Mattfeld and Carol G. Van Aken, eds. (Cambridge, Mass.: MIT Press, 1965), p. 237.

participation was going to play an increasing part in the lives of more and more women.

In the late 1960s and early 1970s a new angle began to appear in the discussions of the employment of women. A new rationale was emerging to add to those which legitimize the employment of women, this time an antinatalist argument.

TWO-ROLE IDEOLOGY BECOMES
ANTINATALIST IDEOLOGY

It had long been known, at first by common-sense observation and later by careful labor-force analysis, that marriage and children were the major determinants of labor-force participation by women, the second more than the first. Arguments against the employment of women had been based on its deleterious effect on the birth rate, the assumption being that labor-force participation was the independent variable. Others saw the decline in the birth rate as the independent variable and labor-force participation as the dependent variable.

For policy purposes, labor-force participation was viewed as the independent variable. Studies of developing countries around the world showed that participation in the labor force by women was related to fertility; thus it came to be argued that women should be encouraged to get jobs as, in effect, a form of birth control. This view not only would discourage anything that interfered with the participation of women in the labor force, but also would positively encourage anything that facilitated it. "As white-collar employment is strongly related to a later age at marriage as well as lower fertility, normative barriers against the employment of women in professional and other white-collar employment should be undermined by government policy whenever possible. Although the employment of women outside the home as well as that of married women should be encouraged, the provision of employment for young, unmarried females upon graduation may lead to an increase in the age at marriage."* Employment, in brief, was to be made an attractive alternative to motherhood as a life career for women. Fewer rather than more children was the goal to strive for. Women were, in effect, to be bribed by attractive jobs to enter and remain in the labor force quite aside from their possible contribution to the gross national product—even, in the case of women who wanted children, quite aside from self-fulfillment by way of motherhood. In the past, contraception had been emphasized in connection primarily with unwanted pregnancies; it was now being emphasized in connection with wanted pregnancies as well.

Strange as it may seem, however, despite the logic of the antinatalist argument for the two-role ideology, it did not seem to work out. For women in the 1960s were learning how to cope with both babies and jobs. Mothers of preschool children were increasingly participating in the labor force, almost a third being in the labor force in the late 1960s. Either jobs were not interfering with having babies or having babies was less and less interfering with labor-force participation. Stuart Garfinkle had noted that "the effect of the birth of a child on work life continuity is rapidly diminishing," and the figures bore him out. In 1969 the fertility of women in the labor force was approaching more nearly the fertility of women not in the labor force than in 1960.

Just as, on whatever grounds, the two-role ideology was becoming accepted and even positively advocated by antinatalists, it was coming under attack by avant-garde women.

---

* Robert H. Weller, "The Employment of Wives, Role Incompatibility and Fertility," *Milbank Memorial Fund Quarterly*, vol. 46 (October 1968), p. 521. See also Judith Blake Davis, statement at Hearings before a Subcommittee of the Committee on Government Operation, House of Representatives, 91st Congress, p. 68.

CRITIQUE OF THE TWO-ROLE IDEOLOGY

One of the most salient issues in the near-future of industrial societies is being gradually formulated not by government, labor or academic economists, but by young radicals, especially avant-garde women, and family sociologists. It is being thought through not in terms of the economy but in terms of the sexual specialization of functions and the roles which implement it. In the formal jargon of economics, implementation will be worked out in terms of hours of work or part-time work; sooner or later the economists will turn the engines of their analyses to show how the goals set up by the critics can be met. For labor-force definition and analysis have always been determined by the needs of social policy. The needs, in this instance, of updating the sexual specialization of functions and the consequent sharing of roles.

The male counterpart in the one-role ideology was the provider role. Talcott Parsons had analyzed the occupational role of men and found it functional for the status quo. But recently Erick Grønseth, a Norwegian sociologist,* has challenged this conclusion; he found the occupational role of men, as structured in modern industrialized societies, dysfunctional. And Jan Dizard had arrived at the same conclusion on the basis of the marriages in the Burgess-Wallin panel, as he reports in his article in this book.

From the point of view of women, as early as 1960 a young woman in Sweden, Eva Moburg, was arguing that as long as the two-role ideology prevailed, women could not really expect equality; discrimination against them was inevitable. There were two fronts in this battle, one in the labor force and the other in the home. No one-front attack could win; both had to be won. In the labor force it involved a more flexible policy, including part-time work; and in the home, a reassignment of

* See his article in this book.

functions: not an exchange of functions—in 1965, about 15 percent of the husbands of working mothers were already taking care of children, and women were performing the provider function in many families—but a sharing of them; not a mere tinkering but a radical restructuring of both labor force and family. Mothers were to be released from exclusive responsibility for child care, and fathers to be given the opportunity to share in child rearing. Everyone, fathers as well as mothers, should share the functions now encompassed in the domestic role.

IMPLEMENTING THE SHARED-ROLE IDEOLOGY

The net effect of this new look at family and work roles of both men and women has been the emergence of a shared-role ideology to be implemented by some form of part-time work for both men and women.

When part-time work was viewed as a solution to women's adjustment to the two-role ideology, it was accepted as a makeshift arrangement by Alice Rossi, but rejected by Myrdal and Klein. But part time in the new context of shared role for both men and women was quite a different matter from part time for women only as a way to make possible the performance of all their functions. The argument now was that child rearing and socialization were far too important to entrust to one sex alone; both parents should participate. If men were to share this function, then they would have to be relieved of part of the responsibility of support. Thus both should have the option of part-time participation in the labor force.

The details for implementing the shared-role ideology have by no means been worked out. Some argue for part time on a daily basis, each working half a day; others argue for an annual basis, each alternating every, let us say, six months. In time implementation will be turned over to the economists. They have been examining hours of work for many years and have accumulated considerable knowledge on the subject under current conditions. A survey of economies around the world leads to the "connection . . . between shorter hours and higher participation rates. Shorter hours—including more part-time jobs—make it easier for more members of a household to take jobs; and reciprocally, a given standard of living can be maintained with shorter hours per worker when the participation rate is higher."* A tenth of the labor force in the country today works on a part-time basis.

Official policy of necessity lags behind avant-garde thinking. But in this case, not very far behind. By 1968 the shared-role point of view had become official policy in Sweden. In a report to the United Nations in that year, the Swedish government stated that it was

> necessary to abolish the conditions which tend to assign certain privileges, obligations or rights to men. No decisive change in the distribution of functions and status as between the sexes can be achieved if the duties of the male in society are assumed *a priori* to be unaltered. The aim of reform work in this area must be to change the traditional division of labour which tends to deprive women of the possibility of exercising their legal rights on equal terms. The division of functions as between the sexes must be changed in such a way that both the man and the woman in a family are afforded the same practical opportunities of participating in both active parenthood and gainful employment.

Hours of work tend to become so highly institutionalized, so much a part of the social structure, so determinative of other aspects of life, so widely ramifying, that change tends to come slowly. And then, say Brown and Browne, only when "workers' preferences for them have had some time to build up and the scope for them has become fairly wide." Avant-garde women, young radicals and academic critics are now, I believe, beginning the buildup of attitudes favorable to the shared-role ideol-

* F. H. Phelps Brown and M. H. Browne, "Labor Force: Hours of Work," *International Encyclopedia of the Social Sciences*, vol. 8, p. 489.

ogy which in the not too distant future will affect the workers'
preferences.

It is, in fact, hard to remain avant-garde very long in a fast-
paced society like ours. In June 1970 a television program, *The
Advocates,* was already debating "women's liberation" in the
form of this question: "So that women may work and men share
the family tasks, should unions demand that everyone be given
the option to work full or half time?" A surprising 46 percent
of the studio audience and a whopping 75.4 percent of the national television audience favored the affirmative. Esther Peterson, the judge in this debate, pointed out the complexity of the
problem and the inadequacy of the way the question was formulated. Then came her conclusion:

> My vote goes to those who are working for a sociey where no one
> is forced into a predetermined role on account of sex; a society
> where men and women have the option to plan and pattern their
> lives as they themselves choose. This society will require many
> things: a new climate of opinion which accepts equality of the
> sexes while still recognizing human and biological differences; a
> society which provides day care and supplementary home services
> which make choice possible; a society where non-merit factors in
> employment such as sex do not count; a society which provides a
> new concept of training for both young men and women with an
> eye to employment and social usefulness along with active parent-
> hood. And most important, a society that provides a shortened
> work day and work week with adequate pay for all workers—thus
> permitting time for families to be together, for fathers to partici-
> pate in family activities (including the care and raising of chil-
> dren) where both parents can develop to their fullest as human
> beings. It's a long way down the road, but it's coming.

Not necessarily such a long way down the road, for, labor
economists tell us, once a momentum has been achieved, hours
have "been reduced substantially in a movement that runs
through many industries in the course of only a few years."

Although the criticisms made by avant-garde women and

their demands that men share in the child-rearing function may sound shrill to some, still even sober economists agree that the shared-roles ideology implemented by way of part-time work could have imponderable benefits for our society. Their studies give them "reason to believe that as time goes on, a labor force that works shorter hours will develop its capabilities as it broadens its interests and education. . . . The hours set free, moreover, although they do not add to the measured national product, are used in practice to add something to the unmeasured amenities of households and to the goodness of life." And, may we add, to the welfare of children?

Lesson from Sweden: The Emancipation of Man

by OLOF PALME

Olof Palme became Prime Minister of Sweden after a long political career in which he played important roles in major national debates and decisions. His party, the Swedish Social Democratic Labor Party, has held government power uninterruptedly since 1932.

In English "man" can mean two things—human being and adult male. What I wish to say is therefore embodied in the title I have given my article—"The Emancipation of Man." We have talked about the emancipation of women, of the problem of woman's role in society. But in order that women shall be emancipated from their antiquated role the men must also be emancipated. Thus, it is *human beings* whom we shall emancipate.

In the long-term program of the party I represent, the Social Democratic Labor Party of Sweden, we say that the aim over the long run must be that men and women should be given the same rights, obligations and work assignments in society. This fundamental idea is now embraced by almost all political parties in Sweden.

For our part we mean that the emancipation of men and women would imply considerable advantages from all points of view. The men should have a larger share in the various aspects of family life—for example, better contact with the children. The women should become economically more independent and have contact with environments outside the home.

The greatest gain of increased equality between the sexes would be, of course, that nobody should be forced into a predetermined role on account of sex, but should be given better possibilities to develop his or her personal talents. The development of the children would also be positively affected by more contacts with both sexes.

Equality also provides prerequisite conditions for better economic security in the family as a result of the double income. If the family is not wholly dependent on only one person's income one can more easily manage temporary reductions in income owing to illness, unemployment, returning to school, etc. Not to say what increased equality means for security in connection with divorce or death. The independence of husband and wife can be protected and the strain on one or the other spouse can cease.

It was not until the 1960s that this way of thinking became more commonly accepted in Sweden after a long and intensive debate. It is still in strident contrast to the factual conditions. I shall first give a short account of the debate and then give a few examples of the practical measures we are taking to make reality move closer to the ideal.

The view of the role of the woman and the man inside the family has gradually changed. Before industrialization, in the agrarian society, the family was to a larger extent than now a working community in which both parents had contact with the children. As a result of industrialization the men began to work far away from home and the most important tasks for a woman began to be regarded as care and upbringing of the children. The discrepancy between different groups was, of course, considerable, and there were many women who were forced into productive activity for economic reasons, although the community had not arranged for any child care and although maybe they had hard household chores to attend to and the conditions in the working life were difficult. But the ideal was that the woman should remain at home and take care of the children. The distance between the world of the men and the women increased. The men were principally looked upon as family supporters. Their relationship to the children was impaired. The women got an increasingly dominating role in the upbringing of the children.

During the twentieth century women in Sweden were given voting rights. They were given the same educational possibilities as men. The standard of living was raised, dwellings became better, household work became easier by means of mechanical aids, more easily handled material, more finished products. School meals were introduced in all schools. Child allowances and other social benefits eased the situation of the families with children. At the same time instruction on family planning resulted in most families planning the size of their family. The average life span was increased. Sweden's modern labor-market policy, which aims at maintaining full employment, was introduced.

These factors contributed to changing the views on the role of women. Childbearing and taking care of children took up an increasingly shorter period of the life of most women. After that they had many years ahead when they often experienced that they were no longer fully employed. Most of the functions which the individual household had to carry out earlier now take place outside the home. One therefore began to talk about the woman's double role, as mother and as gainfully employed. It should be possible for women to have a new life style: first education and work, then child care in the home while the children are small, then a return to gainful occupation. In order to facilitate this life style, demands were raised on, among other things, improved service in the dwelling areas, and adult education for women who wished to return to the labor market after having been at home.

But toward the end of the 1950s a public discussion on a large scale began in Sweden. There was a feeling that the development was going too slowly. Women had obtained practically all formal rights, but they were still considerably underrepresented in politics, and women on the labor market had as a rule low wages and subordinate positions. Women had turned to and had been in demand by a limited sector of the labor market, principally lower positions in retail trade, offices, care and service. Women trying to realize the double-role system often found themselves having double work at home and on the labor market.

A young woman wrote an essay which was entitled "The Conditional Emancipation of Woman," in which she drew attention to the absurdity that woman had been permitted to compete with man on the labor market on condition that she maintained her traditional functions inside the family. Why should a woman have two roles and the man only one? she asked. Is not the role of the father as important as the role of the mother? Should not the household work and the care of the children be shared by the parents while the society simultaneously makes greater efforts for the children? These views were provocative challenges to many people. Their arguments were based on their own situation, which seldom tallied with this idea. They experienced themselves as being attacked instead of seeing the whole as a problem for the society—a problem which demanded reflection, toilsome work and long-term planning. They ridiculed the very idea. Ridicule is probably the weapon which has been most commonly used in the resistance against equality between the sexes. It was a very emotional debate. But during the 1960s a number of books were published which gave an account of inquiries made and contained facts which gradually made the discussion change its character. It became more matter-of-fact and less emotional.

Sociologists, psychologists, social scientists and economists examined the problem critically from different aspects and showed that the role of the woman could not be changed if that of the man was not also changed. They showed how tradition and the expectations of the environment teach the children from the beginning that boys and girls should behave differently and have different characteristics. The so-called "sex-roles," i.e., the culturally conditioned expectations of an individual on account of sex, act as a sort of uniform which represses the individuality of the child.

For example, in Sweden as elsewhere it is usual that parents give mechanical toys to boys and dolls only to girls. This guidance is later on reflected in the sex-determined choice of profession. The female reserve of talents is needed in the technology training, but almost only boys are to be found in this field of instruction. Both children and adults should benefit from being in an environment with both female and male nurses. But few boys are attracted by the nursing profession. Women and men are at an early stage directed toward different spheres of interest, different worlds. The same education and the same role for men and women should not only achieve real equality between the sexes but also increase the communications between men and women and give them more in common.

It is not only the traditional female role which has disadvantages. The sociologists recalled that, according to statistics, the men have a higher criminal record, more stress and illness due to strenuous work, higher suicide rates, and, as a rule, they die at an earlier age than women. In the school it is the boys who have the greatest adaptation problems. Men who are divorced and living alone have greater difficulties to manage than divorced women. The interpretation was that the social pressure on the man to assert himself, fight his way in life, to be aggressive and not to show any feelings creates contact difficulties and adaptation difficulties. Sociologists considered that one should not speak of the "problem of woman's role in society" but of the "sex-role problem" in order to emphasize that the problem also concerns the traditionally male role. This designation has now become generally accepted.

The greatest disadvantage with the male sex role is that the man has too small a share in the upbringing of the children. The ability to show affection and to establish contact with children has not been encouraged in the man. Already from the beginning both boys and girls have a need of having good contacts with adults of both sexes. Studies now reveal a common trait in the picture of children and youths in different kinds of behavioral disturbances. It is that they have poor or no contact with the father or any other grown-up male person.

The sociologists and psychologists drew particular attention to the identification problem of the boys. Already at the age of three the child has need of identifying himself or herself with somebody of the same sex. This process is easier for the girls, because they have constant contact with women. It is more difficult for the boys. In the modern society they grow up practically wholly in a female world. At home they are as a rule taken care of by the mother. During the early school years their teachers consist entirely of female teachers. There is a risk that the boys by means of TV, comic strips and other mass media create a false and exaggerated picture of what it means to be a man. The men are tough and hardboiled Wild West heroes, agents, supermen, soldiers. The boys compensate their lack of contact with kind and everyday men by looking upon mass-media men as their ideal. It should be possible to counteract these problems. The men should already from the beginning have just as much contact with their children as the women. And we should have both men and women as child nurses, kindergarten teachers and infant-school teachers.

Earlier we had a rather intense discussion in Sweden on whether mothers of small children should work outside the home or not. As a result of the new view the problem will be instead whether the *parents* of infants should be employed. One solution is that parents work part time and take turns at looking after the child. Many young families with flexible working hours, for example undergraduates, now practice this arrangement in Sweden. But the psychologists seem to agree that it is not injurious if the child is taken care of by somebody else during part of the day. *Nota bene,* if it is given good care and the parents have regular contact with the child.

The new role of the man implies that he must reduce his contributions in working life—and maybe also in politics—during the period when he has small children. This is what the woman always had to do alone earlier. From a national-economy point of view we could manage this loss in production if we can instead stimulate the woman to make increased contributions there.

We therefore look upon the emancipation of the man as important for the development of our children and for equality between the sexes. Both men and women are working toward this end. The result has been programs, drawn up in the different parties, in which it is demanded that men and women should have the same roles. The big trade-union organizations have prepared their own programs which will make it possible for men to share the child care with the women. The trade-union organizations and the organization of the employers also have a joint-collaboration body which works for equality between the sexes in accordance with this principle. The same views are to be found in the report on the status of women in Sweden which the Swedish government submitted to the United Nations in 1968. These views, which first appeared to be shocking and were ridiculed, have now been officially accepted. Public opinion is nowadays so well informed that if a politician today should declare that the woman ought to have a different role from the man and that it is natural that she devote more time to the children he would be regarded to be of the Stone Age. The supporters of the emancipation of man have, in other words, won the battle, and the ridicule is now directed the other way. In theory, that is. In reality the resistance is still hard. In practical life you find the injustices and one-eyed sex-role thinking.

But when we try to accomplish the ideas of equality between the sexes this is done by means of efforts both in the trade-union and the political field. We do not have any special government body dealing with this problem but regard it as an aspect which is included in the reform work in all fields—in taxation policy, social policy, etc. Let me give one example:

An important reform proposal has been approved recently by the Riksdag (the Swedish Parliament). It is a major taxation reform which implies a redistribution of the tax burden between higher- and lower-income earners. But it also implies a changeover from joint taxation to individual taxation and to a single table giving the rates of national income tax. Hitherto we have had double tables, one which hits unmarried persons rather heavily and one which is less severe for married persons.

The married man had double privileges compared with his un-married colleague. For one thing he was taxed at lower rates and was able to make a tax reduction for his wife. The principle behind the new proposal is that all people shall be regarded as economically independent individuals and that society shall adopt a neutral attitude toward the form of cohabitation which people choose. The support of the society shall be given where there is a need, to children, to the aged, to the sick and to the handicapped, etc.

Now, one cannot carry out such a radical reform without transitional regulations. We have a large group of families where the woman has no possibility to enter into gainful employment even if she wanted to. She may be too old to receive training, or she may be living in a place where there are no job opportunities. For this reason a tax support for women in these families will remain during a transitional period. But it will be given in the form of a reduction of the final tax instead of, as earlier, of the income. In this way we have eliminated a reduction that formerly was of greater value to those with high incomes than to those with low incomes.

The intensity of gainful occupation among married women in Sweden is not particularly high compared with other industrialized countries, but it is now increasing rapidly. If one defines employment as at least part-time work, 26 percent of the married women worked in 1960. In 1965 this share had risen to 33 percent. It is estimated that in 1970 43 percent of the married women will be employed. The differences between various parts of the country are considerable. In some localities more than half the married women are working.

Married women who have been at home and wish to return to the labor market have the right to receive training and a special allowance. The authority which is responsible for the labor-market policy has the duty of activating hidden manpower resources, and this is done, among other things, by providing means of information about job opportunities for women. We regard female unemployment to be an equally serious problem as male unemployment. The labor-market policy shall also contribute to the firms' discarding any irrational recruiting according to sex and giving the same work to men and women.

In 1960 the Swedish Employers' Confederation and the Swedish Confederation of Trade Unions agreed that special female wages would be abolished by 1965 at the latest. But although women in most fields now have the same wages for the same work, they have nevertheless lower wages than men, because women and men do not have the same work and the work carried out by women is more poorly paid. Among the employees in industry women are paid on an average 80 percent of the wages of men. This nevertheless implies an improvement. Ten years ago they were paid only 70 percent.

A study carried out by the Swedish Central Organization of Salaried Employees revealed that full-time working members who in 1966 had a net income below 3,600 dollars consisted of 85 percent women and 15 percent men. In the public sector and in banks and insurance companies the same wages have been introduced for the same type of work. In other fields an equalization of wages paid to men and women has been recommended. Both the workers' and the salaried employees' trade unions regard female wages as part of the low-income problem in general. They pursue a trade-union policy which aims at reducing the wage discrepancies between the different wage earners. The government has appointed a special commission which is surveying the occurrence, causes and effects of low salaries.

In the field of social policy we are working to gradually introduce the principle that the same social benefits should be paid irrespective of sex and civil status. The man who chooses to share the care of children with his wife should not be discriminated against in the social-insurance system.

In urban planning we are endeavoring to design dwelling areas with expanded service in different forms to facilitate the household work. We want to have good mass transportation in order to reduce traveling time and make it easier for both husband and wife to have gainful employment.

The most important form of service is the nursery school, where the children can be while their parents are working. We therefore plan strong expansion of nursery schools. The goal is that all children will be able to go. Some of the children may stay for only three hours, others for a longer period, depending on whether the parents work, study or prefer to be at home. We have become more and more conscious of how important the first few years of the children's life are for their emotional and intellectual development later in life. The nursery school can compensate those children who do not get as much cultural stimulus at home as they should have.

We should also like working hours to be shorter for parents with small children. We are now heading for a general reduction of working hours. The forty-hour week will soon be carried into effect generally, and developments point to a further reduction. If the reduction in working hours is in the form of shorter daily working hours and not a prolonged vacation over the weekends it will be easier for both men and women to combine work with the role of parents.

The old generation in Sweden may consider it correct to *plan* a society with equality between the sexes. But any drastic changes in their *personal* behavior cannot be counted upon. Sex-role attitudes are founded early and are in general too emotional to be changed by means of rational argumentation. As far as the young generation is concerned, one can, however, hope to soften up the tradition that some feelings, characteristics, interests, behaviors and working assignments are suitable only for men and others only for women. Educational policy is an important instrument contributing to a more liberal attitude. Boys and girls in Sweden now receive the same education and are instructed together in all subjects except in physical training. This implies that both boys and girls have compulsory training in textile handicraft and also in wood and metal handicraft. They have also compulsory training in domestic science and child care. One of the aims of the school is to contribute to equality between the sexes in the family, on the labor market and in the rest of the community. This aim is emphasized in the training and advanced training of teachers. Study guidance and occupational orientation will contribute to a more liberal choice of profession irrespective of sex.

But even if the school treats boys and girls alike and has the same expectations of them, they are nevertheless influenced by the environment, parents, mass media, the behavior of men and women outside the school, etc., to regard their roles as being different. It is then up to the school to make the pupils conscious that they are subjected to such an influence and that it is necessary to break an established cultural pattern if one wants to achieve equality between the sexes. The pupils will be stimulated to critically question and discuss the conditions which exist in the society and arrive at a personal opinion which is based on knowledge of the causes and effects of the present sex roles.

My review of some of the practical measures we have taken and plan to take to enable men and women to have the same roles has been sketchy. The problems are connected with other political problems about which I can't go into detail now. The effort to achieve equality between the sexes must be conducted jointly by men and women and not in a struggle against each other. It should be carried out within the framework of strong political and trade-union organizations because it necessitates changing the society. Also in Sweden there are small but loud-voiced groups which maintain that reforms are meaningless and that revolution is the first prerequisite condition for equality between the sexes. This is a romantic attitude. We are working against the pressure of a thousand years of traditions. It necessitates constant stubbornness, toughness and patience in order to change attitudes and to accomplish reforms which gradually change conditions in a peaceful manner. It is in this way that we have changed and are changing Swedish society in many fields. Maybe one can be a pessimist when one observes the big gap between utopia and reality as far as the roles of men and women are now concerned. But already the strong swing which has occurred in public opinion in Sweden arouses hopes that the emancipation of men and women will be possible.

Child Care

Child Care: Destroying the Family or Strengthening It?

by CAROLE JOFFE

Carole Joffe is a doctoral candidate in sociology at the University of California, Berkeley, and a researcher at the Center for Study of Law and Society. She has also been a lecturer in the sociology department at Mills College in Oakland.

> . . . *the vast moral authority of national government* [*must not be committed*] *to the side of communal approaches to child-rearing . . . our response to this challenge* [*child development*] *must be . . . consciously designed to cement the family in its rightful position as the keystone of our civilization* . . .
>
> —President Nixon's veto message on the
> child development bill, December 1971

The issue of a widespread system of federally supported American child care has, predictably, generated a substantial amount of right-wing wrath. When Congress in late 1971 passed a bill authorizing two billion dollars for child-care programs, President Nixon found it politically necessary to denounce it for its "family-weakening" implications, and during approximately the same period Vice-President Agnew in a speech spoke out against the "sovietization" of American children. The core of the right-wing rage about child care focuses on the alleged threat it presents to the integrity of the American family. As the Nixon-Agnew statements imply—and presumably they are not speaking in a vacuum—the logic of the child-care opponents is that if such a national system exists, then parents will see this as a mandate to abandon their children to the state and the moral decay of the American family will commence. In short, the argument is that the existence of child-care institutions will create fundamental changes in family life that do not now exist.

But what is the reality of American families now, particularly with respect to working mothers and their children? The fact is that in a national situation of completely insufficient licensed day-care places, more than eleven million mothers are in the labor force (about one third of them with children under the age of six) and some kinds of arrangements are being made for their children. What these arrangements are, of course, varies greatly and sharply points up what is the real tragedy of the lack of massive child-care programs. Some of these women—the luckier ones—have their children in the approximately 700,000 licensed day-care spaces; others use unlicensed day-care homes, some leave their children in the care of a babysitter or older sibling, and some leave their children alone.

Why are these eleven million mothers working and not at home with their children, as one aspect of Nixon's apparently schizophrenic position on family life would dictate? (The other aspect of this schizophrenia is his endorsement of child-care programs when they are specifically tied to welfare women and job training. In such cases, the White House deems it perfectly legitimate to have working mothers.) Most of these eleven million women have taken jobs because of financial necessity, others have been motivated largely by emotional imperatives. In either case, it is at present clearly *not* the availability of child care that leads to the decision to work. Rather, the important issue should be phrased as the lack of child care and, in many cases, its cost and poor quality, that leads to difficulties for both the working parent and the child—and thus has the net effect of introducing strain to the family as a whole. It is precisely the tension that is generated by the unavailability of adequate out-of-home provisions for young children that should most correctly be seen as having tremendous "family-weakening implications."

In opposition to the premise that child care undermines the family, I believe it is far more realistic to view child care as an institution that in fact might bolster the family in a period of intense social change. As the other articles in this book suggest, we are living in a period in which large numbers of persons are beginning to seriously reexamine their previous notions of sex roles, and as one result the traditional division of labor in many American families is breaking down. What this primarily means to date is that women who formerly did not work are increasingly sharing the role of wage earner with men (and to an infinitely smaller degree, men are beginning to share the woman's role of homemaker). But since this breakdown in division of labor is proceeding largely only in one direction—i.e., both parents in the occupational world—the child of working parents is often in a precarious situation.

There seem to be two general solutions to such a child's problems. One is to exert tremendous social pressure on one of the parents, the woman, to stop working—as happened to women factory workers after World War II and as the anti–child-care forces are seemingly trying to accomplish at present; the other is to create adequate child-care arrangements for this child. The first solution is simply not feasible for poor women, not to mention single mothers, and is grossly unfair to other women who want an occupational identity. The second solution, on the other hand, contains the possibility of meeting a variety of human needs of both children and their parents.

Let us consider what "good" child care would mean for a family in which both parents work (although I would hope to suggest that ideally child care should be seen as the right of *all* children, irrespective of whether their parents are employed).

What child care implies for women in families is by now a fairly well-known argument, as child care has been a central issue of the women's-liberation movement. From a woman's point of view, the existence of child-care facilities means that she can be freed from total responsibility for supervising her children and can then, with ease, pursue other aims—for example, taking a job, or, if she has a job, not giving half her salary to a babysitter.

The question of what child-care institutions might accomplish for fathers has been somewhat less of a topic of public discussion. What a certain form of child-care arrangement, one in which there is regular participation of parents, can do for fathers is return them to the everyday world of children from which our culture has succeeded in cutting them off almost entirely. Child-care centers in which both men and women participate represent a further step in the breakdown of the traditional division of labor along sexual lines that has already started with the entrance of women into the labor force. For both parents the existence of such centers might serve as a vehicle for attaining the new kinds of personal relationships and integrated lives that many persons of both sexes are now seeking. And while ideally men and women are challenging old patterns of behavior at all levels—e.g., within the home—community-based child-care centers, as a relatively new institution, might initially provide the most feasible setting in which to act out these new roles. From an adult's point of view, what child care makes possible are egalitarian relationships in which men and women can both work and be simultaneously involved in the rearing of their children.

For children, the right kind of child care can do several things. It can give them, first of all, a different relationship to and image of their parents and other adults: the little girl whose mother is now able to have a job will grow up thinking the same is legitimate for her, while the little boy whose father makes lunch for everybody in his preschool will not conceive of cooking as women's work. The hopes of many persons who have been affected by the ideas of women's and men's liberation to somehow "raise their children differently" can conceivably be implemented in child-care centers where, in a systematic way, old modes of sex-role socialization can be discarded.

Another function of child care for children is the provision of a society of peers, an experience that in today's nuclear family is normally delayed until the child's entrance, at age five or six, into school. On several counts, it seems unfortunate to deny to children the company of their own peers for so long a time. Educators have recently begun to speak of the critical intellectual functions of the "early childhood" years (that is, ages two to five), and in this respect the stimulation offered by other children and the activities possible in a preschool are seen as invaluable to future intellectual development. And still another stream of thought—this one having roots in the nursery-school–play-school movement, which is now several generations old—calls attention to the social skills children of this age can acquire when placed in a community of peers.

These arguments, which I find essentially valid and in the interests of children, must nevertheless be recognized as adult-developed. Therefore, in speculating what participation in a good child-care center might mean to the child him/herself I would guess that being with other children is purely and simply more fun than being exclusively with adults or with siblings of another age. The children whom I have observed in really excellent nurseries don't "hate school" as most of their older siblings say they do; they in fact are sorry when long vacations come, and in the manner of "old grads" they come back to visit after they have moved on to public school. At the risk of sounding a bit saccharine, I am arguing that good child care means happier adults and happier children.

Throughout my exposition of what child care can mean for each member of a family, I have always added the cautionary adjective "good" or "right." This caution is needed because it is completely clear to one who investigates the issue that while the potential of child care is tremendous, the present reality of much of it is mediocre; perhaps the most significant issue in discussions of child care should not be whether or not it should exist (since it has existed for years) but rather what form it should take. I will not attempt to give here a full rundown of what I think good child care implies in all respects; however, in keeping with our theme of child care's relationship to changing forms of family life, I will mention again what I see as a key element: that of parent participation and local control. (This question of parent participation, it must be noted, highlights a rather ironic aspect of the right-wing hysteria about child care and "weakened families": the bill that the President vetoed in 1971 in fact had reasonably strong provisions for meaningful parental input; in the child-care section of Nixon's own welfare-reform bill, control over the programs is taken away from parents and given to politicians at the state level. It appears that the President was willing to sacrifice his cherished principle of "family authority" if it would also offer the possibility of grass-roots involvement in public institutions.)

These political machinations aside, what are the implications of parent-participating child-care centers? In an immediate sense, parents who with good reason have been made skeptical by previous encounters with poor-quality child care can insure, by their regular presence, that their children are getting the care they want for them. More generally speaking, community involvement in preschools can serve the same function that it does in regular schools, especially for minority children; the presence of parents can reaffirm to the child the integrity of his/her own culture. Parent participation furthermore speaks to a criticism that mass child care has received from the left—namely, the possibility inherent in federally sponsored child care of recreating the most oppressive aspects of most American public schools. Finally, the participation of parents of both sexes in preschools can be especially crucial for the opportunity, already mentioned, of seriously attempting to raise children non-sexistly.

It should, of course, be realized that this type of child care that I am speaking of, one in which parents participate on a regular basis, whether or not there is a teaching staff, implies also a certain flexibility in occupational arrangements that, for most persons, do not now exist. The ability of working people to participate regularly in child-care institutions as well as child-rearing functions in the home is a luxury now available only to a few—e.g., artists, academics. There is thus a third front in the battle for decent child care in this country, in addition to the fronts of individual parents' "consciousness" and political hostility: the corporations of this country which refuse to concede child rearing as a legitimate task of working men and women. (There is some promising evidence, however, of a certain "softening" process among some individual firms in that they have taken the step of providing child care for their employees; the next step, of course, is to allow workers, male as well as female, time off without sanctions to work in these centers.)

To conclude, we can point out that the critics of child care are, in a certain sense, correct: the family, for many persons in this society, no longer holds the same meaning it once did. (Though whether the dreamy image of the family that is invoked by its defenders ever in reality existed is another question altogether.) The phenomenon of child care, I have suggested, did not in itself create these changed notions of the family; rather, the potential of excellent child care is to help implement the new conceptions of family life that people now have—and in this way sustain an institution in transition. The critical question thus becomes—as Pat Bourne spells out elsewhere in this volume—whether child care will be the exclusive province of some members of the upper and middle classes or the acknowledged right of all children and their parents.

The Three Faces of Day Care

by PATRICIA GERALD BOURNE

Patricia Gerald Bourne is now completing her doctoral dissertation at the University of California, Berkeley, on the subject of the delivery of child-care services. She is also a lecturer in urban affairs at San Francisco State College.

We have been told by a mix of strange bedfellows with different priorities why there is such a compelling need for day care: the welfare rolls must be reduced and day care will allow able-bodied mothers to work: millions of mothers with children under six are already working and in need of help; mothers now at home must be enabled to realize their potential through activities other than full-time care of their children; people no longer want to raise their children alone in the isolation of the nuclear family—relief is needed for and *from* the parents; employers of an increasingly female labor force hope that day care may remedy allegedly high rates of lateness and absenteeism due to undependable babysitting arrangements.

All of these arguments for day care have to do with the need for supervision of children while their parents are at work or otherwise occupied in their own pursuits. A final argument is made by psychologists and educators based on increasingly persuasive evidence of the critical importance of the very early preschool years in enriching intellectual and emotional development. This argument is, on one level, the perfect complement to the previous set: day care is needed by and is good for parents, and is also needed by and good for the children. But by the same token this argument is out of key with the rest, for it is the *one* voice whose primary focus is on the perceived needs of children rather than the needs of adults.

There is no reason why the needs of adults and the needs of children cannot be wonderfully complementary—no reason, that is, until the question of our individual and national willingness to pay is faced. Our historical lack of willingness to invest in future generations has been so persistent that it is difficult to be optimistic about the emergence of a day-care system which will be oriented to the needs of children. Let us look briefly at the system of day-care services which has evolved in the United States over the years.

When we talk about day care these days, we are usually talking about three historically distinct phenomena. One is that array of services traditionally called day care—that is, supervision and protection of children whose parents are at work or are incapable of caring for them full time. These programs provide full-day care by definition. The second tradition is that of nursery schools: an enriching experience supplementing family life for the child. These programs have traditionally been half-day or three mornings a week, which means that they are not an option for the children of mothers working full time. The third, so new and so fragile that it is not yet clear that we can call it a tradition, is that of compensatory education. In short, our long-term tradition of day care in America is one of supervision for the children of working mothers and "enrichment" for the children of nonworking parents who can afford it.

THE DAY-CARE TRADITION

The term "day care" still carries stigma. Because it has historically served children whose parents worked, it has been considered as something for people who were either too poor or too crass to stay home with their children. As the combination of work and motherhood roles has spread from the relatively small ranks of the very poor, who had no choice but to work, and the professionals, who chose to work for reasons of self-fulfillment, into the great American middle class, the stigma associated with being a working mother has diminished.

But the stigma associated with allowing, heaven forbid ask-

ing, someone else to *raise* your children for you has not diminished at all. The American commitment to the family as
the sacrosanct child-rearing agent totally responsible for the
emotional and moral development of its children is strong. If
one relinquishes one's children to someone else, it is only to ensure that they are safe and physically taken care of. Day care
serves this ethos well—it is quite plain about being a custodial,
babysitting operation and makes no pretenses at "rearing" children. Even when the well-to-do have gone out to work, they
have hired housekeepers or babysitters or purchased group
babysitting care.

Anyone who may have thought that this particular American
attitude is anachronistic and of no real moving power in the
1970s need only refer to President Nixon's December 1971 message vetoing the comprehensive-child-care bill that would have
provided centers not only for the poor but, at sliding-scale rates,
for the working and middle classes as well. The President, although a passionate advocate of putting *welfare* mothers to
work, objected to committing "the vast moral authority of the
national government to the side of communal approaches to
child-rearing over against the family-centered approach." He
went on to say, "We cannot and will not ignore the challenge to
do more for America's children in their all-important early
years. But our response to this challenge must . . . cement the
family in its rightful position as the keystone of our civilization.
Good public policy requires that we enhance rather than di-
minish both parental authority and parental involvement with
children."

For the same reasons that day care is unacceptable to the
American family ethos, it is also gaining in some quarters a new
kind of stigma. Because day care is clearly hands-off regarding
child rearing, it also lacks the qualities of nurturing, developing
or educating young children. Many feel that such care is not
good enough for "our" children.

Day care has been, and still is, primarily the bailiwick of the
social-welfare profession. Licensing of private day nurseries is

generally done by departments of social welfare (though this varies from state to state); family day-care homes are "caseloads," and the most significant federal support for day care comes from social-security legislation administered by welfare departments. Virtually all federal support for day care has been explicitly for, and limited to, welfare or near-welfare children (e.g., past, present or potential recipients, "target area" residents, etc.).

The backbone of the official day-care-service system is the licensed family day-care home. (The backbone of the "real" day-care system is, by the way, the unlicensed family day-care home and the babysitter—often grandmother or sister-in-law. Studies show that care for 50 percent or more of the children whose parents work is by unofficial [i.e., unlicensed] arrangements.)

The family day-care home has been in low profile during recent discussions of day care; the dazzler has been the notion of a full-day nursery school all abubble with free spirits and the latest in tatami mats and educational toys. Family day-care homes reek of the social-welfare tradition and thus have been ignored in hopes that they may cease to be seen if they are not heard.

A family day-care home is simply a situation where a woman (usually a mother) cares for a few children in her own home. Licensing procedures generally set limits on the number of children she may accommodate and set standards for the physical condition and characteristics of the house in hopes of ensuring the health and safety of the children. Licensing is theoretically contingent upon an acceptable rating by the social worker of the woman's emotional and intellectual suitability for the task of nurturing and caring for young children.

Family day-care homes vary widely in type and quality of care provided. Many writers' favorite day-care horror story is of a day-care home with children tied to beds. Less frequently recounted are the instances of first-rate mini–nursery schools in an atmosphere of affection and freshly baked cookies. Day-care homes often care for children during hours that no group program would contemplate—the split shift is a reality with which it is difficult for group programs to come to terms.

Private day nurseries, run for profit, and licensed (or not) are also a long-standing day-care tradition. As with day-care homes, licensing standards have related primarily to the adequacy of physical facilities and some minimum staff–child ratio of one to ten or twelve. The service provided is basically babysitting, whether you are poor and receiving care courtesy of the welfare department or whether you are paying yourself.

Federal involvement with the support of day care began during the Depression as part of WPA. But the first significant full-day group-care program was created by the Lanham Act in 1941 to provide care for the children of mothers who were desperately needed in the war economy. This federal program was implemented with astonishing speed (and mixed results) and dismantled just as quickly at the end of the war, even though many, many mothers still wanted to work. Continuation of these programs was contingent upon state willingness to assume responsibility; California was the one state to do so, and its children's-centers programs, operated by school districts and paid for by state funds and sliding-scale parent fees, now make it a unique state in extent and quality of day-care services.

Since World War II, federal funds for day care have been almost exclusively tied to the welfare rolls. In the variety of national programs that have been offered thus far for this purpose (such as the AFDC Work Incentive Program and the Economic Opportunity Act's Concentrated Employment Program), three principles of federal policy stand out clearly: (1) The federal government has gone to some pains to stay clearly out of the business of *providing* day-care services; it will pay for services which are provided by a local public agency or a non-profit group. Funds are circuitously routed via state and county agencies (and are contingent upon their commitment to also pay a share) to make sure that there is no such thing as what California Governor Ronald Reagan has called "federal kindergartens." (2) Funding is, with the one exception of an almost invisible program, explicitly for and limited to the welfare or near-welfare population. (3) Funds for day care for the poor are almost always contingent upon participation in the labor force or some training program in preparation for participation in the labor force.

There is one irony in the tale of federal participation in day care, however: in order for any provider of services to receive federal funds, he must meet what are called the Federal Inter-agency Guidelines. These guidelines came about because of the concern with the usual federal lack of coordination and frag-mentation of responsibility. Agencies handing out day-care funds were instructed to get together and thrash out a uniform set of standards. The irony is that the group of bureaucrats as-signed this task came up with a set of standards requiring much more than day-care programs in the traditional sense. The guidelines require a staff–child ratio of one to five (as op-posed to the one to ten or twelve usual in state-licensed cus-todial programs), and as part of the total program they require educational and nutritional features and parent participation as well. Programs which meet the government's own standards, then, cross dangerously over the line into child rearing as de-fined by President Nixon. And, as we shall see, programs which meet the government's own standards are expensive.

THE NURSERY-SCHOOL TRADITION

The nursery-school movement is a complex and shifting phe-nomenon. One might find its roots in the kindergarten move-ment in the 1870s; more usually it is seen as a creature of the '20s and '30s with its intellectual promises drawn from John Dewey and the psychoanalytic movement—both critics of con-temporary educational philosophy. It stressed the importance of the early years, not so much as a time for learning (learning to read before the first grade was, in fact, seen as an evil which inhibited the child's proper experience of childhood), but as a time for critical emotional development. Children needed to learn to play with their peers, to cooperate, to tolerate those restrictions on their freedom arising from their membership in a community. They needed to relate to adults other than their parents and to be provided with a variety and richness of experiences essential to emotional and cognitive development. Nursery schools were not about education; they were about child development.

Public support for nursery schools has been only through state university programs where the nursery school is operated as a laboratory for teacher training. Fees in these schools are usually far below actual cost, and sometimes an effort is made to grant scholarships in order to obtain a socioeconomic mix. But by and large, the values associated with nursery school have been held by and limited to the middle class.

Only recently have the education and learning theorists captured the middle-class imagination. A growing development of "discovery centers" and the like plays on the middle-class absorption with the demands of a meritocratic society to persuade parents that their children will fall behind unless given essential preschool learning experiences. Again, ability to pay limits such experiences to middle- and upper-class children. There is an irony to these expensive preschool learning centers: they developed in emulation (albeit grossly misinterpreted emulation) of a public program for the poor.

COMPENSATORY EDUCATION: A NEW TRADITION?

In 1964, as part of the war on poverty, a bright-eyed, hope-filled new program was begun called Head Start. Putting down Head Start as one of the most misguided of government boondoggles is chic now with both the right and the left. But the influence of Head Start on the public imagination, on the cultural absorption of certain streams of academic research findings and on the current structure, philosophy and politics of child care is undeniable.

A program of compensatory education, Head Start was premised on the notion that success in the educational system was the key to social mobility of the poor and was seen by its creators as one essential piece of a *many-faceted* strategy to break the locked-in class structure of American society.

Interestingly enough, its creators and original administrators were rarely educators, but rather psychologists, psychiatrists and physicians. Like the nursery-school movement, its thrust was child *development*. The key to achievement in school was not seen so much as a matter of giving children a literal head start in learning to read, but rather a catching up on what middle-class children had learned at home.

Originally summer programs, then full-year, half-day and now often full-year, full-day programs, Head Start was endowed with the best the academic research establishment in a hopeful era could muster. But the latest in learning theories, in educational games and toys were just part of the picture. A staff–child ratio of at least one to five was essential to the developmental philosophy. The children were to be given nourishing meals, dental care, eye checks, screenings for early detection of physical or psychological handicaps. A salient part of the program design was the involvement of parents—both in setting policy for their community's center and in the classroom. This effort to pull the community and home environment into a reciprocal link with the "school" was deemed essential to the reform base of the program; but its implementation was also a matter of largely uncharted waters and was thus one of the most vulnerable components of the program.

Head Start, as a program with high visibility, high costs and high pretensions of social reform, inevitably came in for criticism from every direction. Money-savers met with glee the findings of a Westinghouse evaluation study which showed, by their criteria, the "head start" fading out for the children by the second or third grade. Liberals met the same findings with despondency and despair.

The groups for whom Head Start was created also criticized it widely, though, for the most part, they continued to participate and take pride in it. Their complaints that Head Start's "compensatory" ideology, based on a theory of cultural deprivation, was patronizing, middle-class–biased and particularly damaging to black integrity have been largely accepted by those who designed the program. Their plea that Head Start *must* be run by those participating is an increasing imperative. The recipients are right to be vehemently concerned that they maintain effective control of such a program. Their response, as opposed to President Nixon's, is not to avoid the problem with custodial care programs, but rather to struggle for ways of shaping and controlling high-quality educational and developmental programs so that they are in consonance with their own child-rearing values.

COMBINING THE THREE TRADITIONS

We have seen that day care really means three quite different things at this point in history. It means:

(1) Care and protection of children while their parents work. This tradition of day care has steadfastly avoided anything which will *appear* to be a usurpation of the family's child-rearing role.

(2) Nursery school in full-day form. Here child-rearing functions are also carefully not usurped. It is a complement to and extension of the family environment. Nursery schools are often of the cooperative genre, with the mother partici-

pating at least one morning a week and perhaps even taking classes in child development.

(3) Compensatory education. Here we are not really raising the child *for* the parents, but *making up* for an environment which offered limited opportunities for developing certain learning skills. In programs controlled by the local community some effort is also made to educate the parents in the ways of child rearing.

Day care still means day care, but the new voices making themselves heard with increasing clarity rarely mean day care in the sense of a group babysitting venture, but rather as some merging of the two traditions of day care and nursery school with the new tradition of preschool education.

There are a number of programs around the country which do effectively combine care and protection, child development and education. Though often growing out of the compensatory-education tradition, these programs do not think of themselves as appropriate only to the poor. Rather, they are engaged in defining a new principle of early-childhood education for all. This new definition of child care is the bailiwick of the education profession. But to many people the education profession is no more acceptable a purveyor of day-care services than is the welfare profession. Child-development skills are hardly one of the fortes of our school systems, which have been notoriously disconnected from and unresponsive to the child's family environment.

This is not the place to argue the merits of the educational establishment. What is clear, if we admit to ourselves that any program that cares for our children for ten to twelve hours a day is sharing with us our role in raising our children, is that no *single* style, philosophy or type of day care will be either politically or individually acceptable in this country. We simply do not have a counterpart definition to the Russians' collectivist child, nor do I believe we really want one no matter how much more clear and straightforward it would make some of our public decisions.

When one reads over what has been written about day care in the media since it became a flourishing topic, one begins to get some feel that we are coming to a rough consensus about what day care ought to be. It should, of course, care for and protect our children: it should provide an effectively rich environment for the child, one which fosters his development of a sense of self, self-worth and security and his ability to get what he wants and needs from the environment around him, and one which stimulates and develops his cognitive and sensory abilities.

But when we take a closer look, we are not close to an agreement on what day care ought to be at all. Our sources of disagreement are twofold: child-rearing values and the value placed on child rearing. The disagreement is wide on both what *kind* of child care we want and on how much we are willing to spend on it. Nowhere does the nation's diversity and multiplicity of goals and values come to a head more clearly than around day care.

States'-righters on the right and decentralists on the left don't want the federal government to take charge of day care because that would be destroying local autonomy.

John Birchers on the right and some groups on the left don't want the public sector at any level to have anything to do with it because it would be an usurpation of individual freedom.

At the same time, some groups on the right want the state to take over the child-rearing function for the *poor* in order to create a well-behaved lower class; and other groups on the left think it is the state's responsibility to provide free child-rearing institutions for all those who wish to spend their energies on other pursuits.

Some minority groups want a way into the system and say the state must provide institutions to facilitate this. Other minority groups don't want any middle-class establishment inculcating values into their kids.

Some want their young children to play and explore freely in their preschool years; others want their children to sit up straight and learn to read early.

The diversity of views could be spun out almost infinitely. There is only one common denominator: care for the children of working mothers. All groups who want child care want at least care and protection—and beyond that there is no possibility of agreeing on a definition.

The second point on which there is a seeming consensus but in fact a wide disagreement is the amount of money we are willing to invest in care for children. Let us take a very rough look at day-care costs, with school systems as a reference point.

An "extravagant school" district like Berkeley, California, spends about $1,400 per year per child. The national average is more like $800. The *cheapest* custodial day care in California costs $1,200 per year per child. (As with schools, the major costs are for the teachers.) The $1,200 day-nursery figure pays for a program which employs an adult (usually an untrained one) for every ten or twelve children. Federal Interagency Guidelines, mentioned earlier, require one adult for every five children; all instructors must have academic degrees. Israeli programs operate on a one-to-four ratio. An Office of Economic Opportunity–funded study of "exemplary" day-care programs and systems around the country shows that those which maintain a one-to-five adult–child ratio and have first-rate educational developmental, health and parent-involvement components are costing between $2,500 and $3,500 per year per child!

The most striking thing that comes clear from the most cursory look at child-care costs is the importance that staff–child ratios make. It is difficult to imagine how one adult can even just "care for and protect" more than five children at once, especially five children between the ages of, say, two and four. Ask any mother! The danger is that we will start to deal with preschoolers as we now do with older children in schools.

We might well define "quality" in terms of an adequate adult–child ratio as a minimum for all styles of day care—custodial, nursery or educational—but we will then find that the costs of even custodial care are up around $2,500 per year per child.

Now let us look again at the groups which have formed a coalition of sorts around day care and ask whether they would be willing to pay at such a rate.

Will those in favor of forcing welfare women to work be willing to pay $5,000 for care for a woman's two children in order to save $2,400 on her AFDC grant? Will a woman whose earning power is $6–8,000 be willing to spend $5,000 of it for child care in the private market? If she isn't, can the franchisers now entering the business with enthusiasm make a profit? Will industry and labor unions be willing to provide that magnitude of fringe benefit?

The common denominator in the case of costs, then, will very likely be the lowest common denominator. But there are two choices that fall within an acceptable price range. One is the present low-cost, low-quality custodial system mixed with a few low-profile, high-quality programs like full-day Head Start or some of the California children's centers; the other alternative is an extension of kindergarten, in its present format, to include children from six months to five years old.

It would seem that if we are to have quality day-care services in the public *or* private sector—quality even in the most limited sense of a reasonably adequate adult–child ratio—we will have to be willing to assume at least a portion of its costs for all who use it, as yet another public responsibility. I am not optimistic about the possibilities of our doing so, simply because of our long-term national unwillingness to make meaningful investments in future generations.

But if we are even to find a basis of agreement upon which to do so, it seems clear that we must find ways of giving that support in such a way that communities and groups may shape their own services in consonance with their own values and goals for their children. Those groups who argue most fervently that the nuclear family is an anachronistic child-rearing institution would be most appalled and outraged if their children were subjected to child-rearing practices which shaped their children into compulsively achieving, productive, fiercely competitive adults.

Given that we as a nation do disapprove of relinquishing responsibility for child rearing to professionals—or, if not "disapprove" in some ideological sense, then at least are skeptical and mistrustful of the ability of anybody else to do it as we would like—then perhaps the only kind of child-care system that can come into being in this country is one that parents can trust and influence to raise their children as they would like. And if the development of a system which provides real choices and a real diversity of styles of care to the parents of young children is to come about, then we also may have to be willing to think of the rearing of children as *a task with real economic value* and thus be willing to pay a woman or a man to stay home and care for their two preschool children. (And if men agreed to take a full share in the responsibility for rearing children my guess is that this country would come to care in a meaningful sense for its future generations much more quickly and happily.)

In the long run, then, I can *envision* the possibilities of a network of quality child-care services which would be acceptable in the American context. In the short run, however, I am pessimistic about the political acceptability of *quality* child care on either ideological or fiscal grounds. I feel that neither the public sector *nor* the private individual is, at this point, willing to spend sums on the order of $2,500 to $3,500 per year per child for care during the working day—willing, that is, if the issue is drawn solely around the needs of children. I would argue that day care must be placed in the larger context of national priorities in utterly pragmatic American style, given the urgent need of millions of American working mothers and their children.

We must understand that a commitment to quality care will be difficult to achieve. Child care will inevitably be a focus of national concern and debate in the years to come. Even the successful passage of major federal legislation will be only a starting point in this debate.

The debate over just how much we are willing to invest in future generations, either publicly or privately, will continue. The debate over how we can provide adequate child-care services in adequate numbers without threatening the American family ethos will continue. The debate over whether we should continue to allow differentiated systems of child care to develop for the poor and for the well-to-do will continue.

All of these issues will hinge on the real economic value we are willing to place on the "job" of taking care of children. Since we now consider it no loss to the economic well-being of the nation if women stay home to care for their children (unless they are on welfare), that job has no economic value. If we are really to value the role of caring for children, then it seems clear that men must begin to take equal responsibility (at home as well as at child-care centers), since it is only their "man-hours" that society truly prizes. In my opinion, only if we can achieve this basic change in values will we even be able to create a series of styles of caring for children which will meet not only the needs of working parents but the needs of children as well.

Child-Care Communities:
Units for Better Urban Living

by JOHN R. PLATT

John Platt is associate director of the Mental Health Research Institute of the University of Michigan. His books on scientific aspects of social change include *The Excitement of Science* and *The Step to Man*.

The conventional image of the American family is that of a "nuclear family," in which the father earns the money while the mother spends eight to sixteen hours per day taking care of two to four children, handling the shopping and meals, and doing laundry and household maintenance. The mother is supposed to have a car as well as automatic kitchen and laundry equipment, and the children are supposed to have private play space and equipment and neighborhood recreation facilities.

Today this image probably fits more millions of families than ever before, especially in the suburbs and small towns. But there are millions of other families for which this division of roles and this structured pattern of child care and household care are essentially impossible. These include the families of working and professional women—now said to number about one third of all married women—as well as many divorced families and slum families and relief families overburdened by children and poverty. If there is no relative to help take care of the children while the mother works, and no money for a full-time housekeeper, child care may become exhausting, mean or nonexistent. Many of our most difficult personal and social problems are concentrated in such families. It is easy to see how children in such homes may acquire the disconnected and irresponsible images of themselves and their society that lead later to school dropout and unemployability.

The question therefore suggests itself: Can we devise some

new self-maintaining social institution, especially for the central city, that would help out families with working mothers or over-burdened mothers by performing many of the needed child-care and domestic services that are performed by the homemaking mother in the conventional family or by a paid housekeeper in a well-to-do professional family?

The answer is that it might be surprisingly easy to create institutions of this sort, when we consider how close to them we are already. What is most needed for professional families, broken families or slum families is evidently group child care, supplemented by group dining arrangements to reduce the burden of shopping, cooking and cleaning up. If facilities for these could be built into new residential or urban-renewal developments or into large new apartment buildings, it might take only a relatively small organizational effort to make "child-care communities" based on such services. These would meet the needs of a special housing and rental market, they could improve life greatly for both mothers and children, and yet with their group economies they might cost little more than is already being spent by the families and by society on care and preschool arrangements for many of these disadvantaged children.

Today the centralized services provided by a large middle-income apartment building on a private-profit basis are fairly remarkable. Such a building may have (1) a resident manager, (2) centralized janitorial, heating and garbage services, (3) centralized laundry facilities, (4) game rooms, a play lot and perhaps a swimming pool and tennis courts, (5) sometimes a "social director," and (6) sometimes a delicatessen concession or supermarket. To fill out these services to meet the needs of working mothers, such a unit would need to add:

> Larger indoor and outdoor play facilities, recreation rooms and perhaps schoolrooms for older children, with a full-time staff of teachers and a nurse for all-day care of children of various ages.

Lunchroom and dining facilities for children and adults, with centralized kitchens, perhaps run either as a management service, as a cooperative or as a concession.

Various organizational and management systems would be possible. Thus, the families of professional women might form self-help organizations, setting up group child-care and group dining arrangements, say in a university neighborhood or in a large apartment building on a cooperative basis. Or upper-income apartment buildings or condominiums might be designed and managed by realty firms so as to offer such services. At the other end of the scale, especially if such upper-income experiments proved to be attractive models, public housing and urban-renewal housing might be designed and managed with the same kind of facilities and services, but with financial help from projects such as Head Start or city recreation funds to support the child-care program, and perhaps with Aid to Dependent Children funds or food subsidies to help support cooperative dining arrangements.

The nurses, teachers, cooks and waitresses for such services might well come from among the families in a large apartment house, just as the manager and janitor often do today. Grandparents and retired persons might also find useful roles in these programs. Such a child-care community might be organized with as few as ten to twenty families or fifty to a hundred adults and children. Large communities, with fifty to one hundred families, or a total of two hundred to five hundred persons, would probably be able to afford more professional managerial services and a better teaching staff, with separate teachers for different age groups; the quality and efficiency of the dining services would probably be better as well.

Precedents for institutional services of these types can be found in various American institutions. "American-plan" dining rooms are found in many apartment hotels and residential hotels. Low-cost centralized dining rooms are found in university dormitories, and student dining cooperatives have sometimes been organized with as many as three hundred members. Centralized dining is common in low-income public and private nursing homes and old people's homes.

Likewise, half-day to full-day child care is available in public and private nursery schools, in some experimental early-enrichment education programs, in religious vacation schools, and in city and park day-care recreation programs. Working mothers frequently spend a substantial fraction of their salary for such services, as an alternative to expensive or incompetent baby-sitters or maids in the home. The only thing that is different about the present suggestion is the idea of designing these dining and child-care services in advance, so that they would all go under one roof. This offers maximum convenience to busy or overburdened mothers and maintains for the child a sense of home and care; at the same time it permits these care and household services to have the quality and efficiency that can be provided by full-time professional personnel. The mothers would not need to feel guilt, as many of them do now, over "neglecting" their children, and they would not be too busy and harassed to have time for their children after working hours.

With respect to the costs of living in such a "child-care community," it is worth noting that group play areas and dining facilities would reduce the need for play space and for full kitchens and dining areas in individual apartments. The costs of the group facilities could be supported, and perhaps more than supported, from the economies on the individual facilities. If child-care expenses for children of working mothers were made tax deductible, as has often been urged, this would offer an additional financial incentive for improved child-care arrangements of this kind, even at fairly low income levels.

Concerning the acceptability and stability of such a social institution as the community described here, it may be worth noting that group dining and group child care were common in the "extended families" in the poor agricultural households of Eastern Europe in the last century. Some fifteen to thirty people of several generations lived under one roof; the adult men and women all worked in the fields, while the grandparents and older girls took care of the cooking and the young children. Likewise in the hard life of the early Israeli kibbutzim, or collective farms, the women needed to and wished to contribute their labor equally with the men, and this was made possible only by group dining and group child care. In a kibbutz today, because of these services, an Israeli woman of thirty-five works eight hours per day or less and then has many hours free to spend with her children, with no shopping, cooking or cleaning up—a situation that many American women, even in the coziest suburban households, might envy.

Such examples may seem alien to the American tradition and situation. But they show that group dining and group child care may be a useful and stable response to situations where women must work, not only at high income levels but in hard poverty situations, whenever a large group can be brought together by one means or another for the organization of such services. The U.S. today may be becoming more receptive to such ideas than in the past. The addition of such services in new housing projects would provide an integration of the community unit to family and neighborhood problems that would not be out of line with current thinking. Perhaps only a lack of imagination has kept commercial developers and housing planners from seeing what a large potential market there could be for group child care and group dining in urban apartment living. Once introduced, such ideas might catch on rapidly because of their contribution to housing income and management income, to neighborhood stability, and to family satisfaction.

Community

Learning to Cooperate: A Middle-Class Experiment

by WANDA BURGESS

A former social worker, Wanda Burgess is the mother of three children and lives in Mill Valley, California.

In this era of debate over sex roles, I am in full accordance with those trying to break down the old prejudices. We have so many stereotypes about how people "ought" to live and act. Working mothers are still looked on with some disapproval even when they are the sole support of their families or have to work to make ends meet—they get little or no community support. Men who are working at home are still looked on by many people as shirkers or maybe as even being involved with something illegal. (Mostly they are envied—so why aren't housewives envied?)

I know a family in which both spouses are teachers and take turns working and staying home with the kids—one works one year, one the next. And I notice there are increasing couples in similar situations, working part time or reduced hours so they can share in the care of their children, too. The more this kind of pattern develops, perhaps the more we will be able to stop putting everything into special compartments (men's work away from home, women's work at home, education in the schools, religion in the churches, sex in the bedroom) and fragmenting ourselves in the process.

Yet, at the same time as I say this, I have to say I prefer the housewife-mother role for myself at the present. (The crux of any sort of liberation, of course, is being able to answer the question "What do I want?" and then, if the answer differs from society's expectations, having the courage and freedom to stand by one's guns. At a time when a certain portion of society is demeaning the housewife, perhaps it takes some courage to stand by those guns as well.)

I know something about both the work world and the housewife's world. I worked as a social worker and as a teacher of English for several years. And for the past six years I have been a housewife-mother. I found neither situation ideal. Both entail having to do a lot of things I'd rather not do, and both provide certain pleasures and satisfactions. For the time being (I have three small children) I feel the housewife-mother role provides me with the most satisfactions. I have more freedom there, more control over which chores I do, when, how and for how long, and I don't have to follow anyone else's schedule as I did when I was working outside.

But I am also perfectly aware of how trapped most housewives are. Indeed, a great deal of my time and energy the past years has been spent in looking for ways out of that trap.

My first attempt in this regard was to try to organize cooperative efforts in our neighborhood to lessen some of the work and boredom of mothers and to free our time for more interesting matters. I felt we could cooperate on car pools, on shopping trips (why should everyone have to go to the store every day or every week—why not take turns shopping for several families?) and on child care.

However, I found people were generally very wary of such ideas—really afraid to get involved with one another, even to work on such necessities as local fire protection or road improvements. It took me about six months to convince other mothers that cooperative child care had some real advantages. By this I meant that from the age of eighteen months or so until the children were of school age, each mother could take a number of the neighborhood children one morning a week and have the rest of the mornings free.

I found that new mothers particularly, though not always, not exclusively, seemed to feel that they should be the only ones to care for their children. Some seem to feel guilty if they are not with their child most of the time, that they are not good mothers if they sometimes want time to themselves. Others are perhaps afraid that the child will not learn the ideas, values and behavior that the parents desire if they are subject to the influence of others—although they seem to turn them over unquestioningly to the school system at the age of five. Other mothers are frightened of the idea of caring for more than one or two children, particularly if they are not their own; they feel they cannot cope with them, or they feel that the children need constant supervision and they will be unable to keep track of all of them. And some mothers simply dislike the noise and messiness inevitably associated with children and would rather take their own children to a sitter than trade responsibilities.

For myself, I can arrange my time much better if I know that on Tuesday morning I will have several children at my house; I can then organize special activities for them and have other mornings free to do whatever I want. I also feel that contact with other families and their methods of doing things is very educational for my three children. They readily learn that some things are allowed in one place that aren't in another, and as I can't necessarily guarantee that our ways are the best ways, I think it is good for them to see differences, evaluate them and choose for themselves how they later want to operate. Another benefit derived from playing with other children is that children seem to learn much faster, become at ease with others, and become more independent earlier. At any rate, after a lot of effort, we have worked out this arrangement in our neighborhood among a number of families, and it has worked well.

Now our family is embarking on a more structured cooperative venture, of a type that is evidently gaining adherents throughout the country.

Briefly, this arrangement will operate as follows: a group of twelve families will jointly purchase land, each family building the house they desire, with all members helping to build the houses and a community center. The latter will include a workshop, a children's play area, a kitchen and storage pantry and freezer, a swimming pool and tennis courts. There will also be a large organic garden and some livestock.

It is hoped that we will garner ecological as well as economic benefits—we are investigating methods of composting all household and sewage wastes for use as fertilizer and of recycling waste water in the garden. There will no longer be the necessity of each family having two cars. Probably each family will have one, or less; we will try to work up carpools and hookups with public transportation where possible, and then we will have three or four cars for those who remain at home.

Obviously we must set ourselves up on a legal basis to protect our investments and to cover turnover in ownership, and we must set up ground rules for decision-making within the group. At the time of this writing, we are going through the process of evolving common goals. So far we have eleven families committed to this idea, and most of us did not know each other before. After a number of meetings, one family has dropped out, and, admittedly, not without some hard feelings. The process is not easy, but it is fascinating and illuminating. People vary tremendously in their desires and fears, as I found previously in the various mothers' approach to child care.

The common desire which brings people to our group is the desire to get out of the rat race, to simplify our lives, to enjoy living and to reduce the time, energy and money required by our present mode of life to simply maintain ourselves. Sharing possessions and responsibilities seems to be a good solution. But defining exactly how much cooperation we are ready for, and what we mean by it, is difficult. From birth we have been trained to compete with others, to use our individual talents to achieve the highest, the best, the most.

After years of competing, how do you learn to share? How much do you share? On what terms? What does sharing really mean? If a man is very attached to and careful with his tools, will he be willing to put them in a common workshop where others may not care for them as well? Should he have to? How will the group spirit and intent be affected if he doesn't?

Other types of cooperative ventures vary considerably in their expectations of members. Condominiums cooperate only to the extent that the tenants own land and buildings jointly and have to make group decisions regarding them. Any real change in their life style is nonexistent—they simply pay less rent than they might elsewhere. Communes seem to be made up of people who wish to love the whole group and live together, sharing everything. Religious cooperative communities seem to last the longest because the members believe in a set of rules which they regard as final and absolute, so that they can willingly subvert their individualities to them.

We are trying to find some middle road. We are not prepared to submerge our individualities in a group identity. We wish to maintain the cohesiveness of the group without stultifying the individual. Each family will have the privacy of its own home and can partake of the group activities as much or as little as it pleases, outside of various functions which affect everyone and which will have to be agreed upon mutually. But there will be many more of these latter decisions to be made in this group than are required in a condominium, as most areas of our lives will be affected by our living in the group.

For example, most of us have created in our middle-class minds a "dream house," based partly on our experiences living in houses and partly on what has been fed to us by the mass media as what everyone should want; but we find that these cherished ideas may now have to be altered. One may have envisioned a big living room and dining room for entertaining, a large family room for hobbies and children's activities, office or sitting room for the wife, a den for the husband. But now the recreation lodge will be available for many of these functions and probably with better facilities, if one is willing to walk from one's house and possibly have to engage in these activities with other people. Large groups can be entertained in the lodge. The large children's area, which might eventually become a school, could be made a really interesting and educational place if resources were pooled there rather than duplicated in each home.

Our plan also means that the individual houses will be smaller than conventional family homes, because smaller homes also mean that more land will be available for other uses, and, of course, that each home will cost less.

This represents a switch in the plans of most of us, and it is hard to know if this is what we really want, as it is so different from what we have seen before. There is no perfect solution, and one simply has to weigh the advantages and disadvantages as realistically as possible. The economic advantages are obvious, as are the advantages of the recreational and creative facilities. Many of us are hoping that basic needs can be met sufficiently so that those with outside jobs—men and women—can cut down on the amount of time they have to work outside. This would, of course, entail a reevaluation of our real needs and a determination to spend time, energy and money toward fulfilling them, as opposed to the continuing "buy buy" or "achieve achieve" rat-race life styles we have known.

But the big unknown is, how is everyone going to get along? Disagreements are inevitable and may be bitter. Yet no rules can be written to control them, as rules are static and our situation is living.

One of the big concerns expressed is how it will be determined that each individual is contributing his fair share of work to the cooperative effort. This is usually expressed by those who fear they will not have as much time or ability as others and that they will be found lacking. Consideration of this problem becomes, for me, a philosophical journey. Each individual differs as to the possessions, abilities, intangibles and time he has to contribute and is willing to contribute, and it is impossible to measure these relative values. One wonders whether it is reasonable to demand "equal" sharing, whatever that means. Perhaps in the process of this change we are asking of ourselves, each individual must be allowed to evolve according to his readiness and let the group evolve accordingly.

The failure of so many cooperative communities and communes indicates that it is wise and necessary to consider seriously and at length the philosophical and behavioral implications of such a switch in our living patterns. The stories of those with whom I have spoken who have lived in communities which have failed always demonstrate a lack of clearly thought-out understanding as to what was being sought and how. Cooperative living does represent a major change in life style, and therefore in one's philosophy of life, one's values, and ultimately one's behavior. It does not represent simply a way of getting more for less money, as it initially seems to (and which is a value of a competitive society), because when one starts thinking about *how* and *what* one will be getting more of for less, one comes to the conclusion that it will be the result of many major and minor changes in one's life pattern, and obviously each person involved must think long and hard about whether this is indeed what he wants.

I would further like to point out that variations of this type of cooperative plan could actually occur in any neighborhood. I know of neighborhoods which maintain a common vegetable garden. Other neighborhoods have gotten together and purchased an empty lot for a park. A house or storefront could be cooperatively purchased and used as a center. George Dennison, in his book *Lives of Children,* voices the opinion that small neighborhood "block" schools involving parent participation and a lot of normal, everyday activities would be a superior way of learning, as all learning would be directly related to actual living situations and meaningful persons in the child's own environment. Tolstoy said the same thing, as did Rousseau. Such small local schools would be a boon financially as well as being more realistic educationally, as all the taxpayer's money wouldn't be eaten up in cement—buildings and more buildings.

For myself, as I have said, I feel that a cooperative housing group will provide a good environment for individual development. I can envision all manner of problems, as well as all manner of benefits, and I think the latter far outweigh the former. There will be ups and downs, and some problems will be handled better than others, but it will be an interesting journey. It will end, as all things do sooner or later, and that end will be the result of many ends and many beginnings as the process of change evolves. And if the end should be soon, I would not regret the experience, and I doubt that I would cease to pursue the dream.

Communal Living in Old Age

by ARLIE HOCHSCHILD

Arlie Hochschild is an assistant professor of sociology at the University of California, Berkeley. She is the author of *The Unexpected Community: A Study of an Old Age Subculture* (Prentice-Hall, 1972) and has edited a special issue of *Trans-action* magazine on "The American Woman" (Nov.–Dec. 1970).

Along with blacks, women and adolescents, the old have emerged as a "social problem"—a label usually given to people who lack power. There is not one social problem, but rather many. There is the problem of poverty, of poor health and of loneliness. Underlying all three is a condition that is hard to isolate as a "problem," a condition that cannot be changed without radically altering the entire society. Namely this: apart from a privileged elite for whom old age is a harvest of honor and riches, the old in America are not needed by society.

And despite what some of us hope, there is no sign that old people will regain power and many signs that they will continue to lose it. There is no sign that the retirement age will go up and many signs that it will continue to drop. There is no sign that more old people will find work and many signs that young people also will have a hard time finding it. In 1900 two out of three men over sixty-five were working, while today less than a third are.

As work becomes less important as a source of friendships for the old, neighborhoods tend to become more important, especially for the working and lower classes. The old in the United States today either live together with young people (in the same family or neighborhood) or separate from them (alone or with other old people). I will discuss why the first, more common and accepted setting often leads to isolation and why the second, newer and less approved, generally does not. I will also try to show how a new and increasingly common alternative to isolation is communities of old people. Ironically the conservative, fundamentalist widows from Oklahoma and Texas whom I studied are among the least likely to talk about "communal living" and "alternatives to the nuclear family" even while they have improvised something of the sort.

INTEGRATION

When one searches for an example of an old person living with his children, grandchildren and assorted relatives, the mind moves to other times and places—to the grandfather in Thomas Mann's novel *Buddenbrooks*, for example, set in nineteenth-century Germany. The grandfather lived, worked, commanded, protected, bequeathed and finally died in the heart of the Buddenbrook family. He was a powerful man, not a social problem. It was by virtue of him that cousins and aunts and uncles were tied together. For him, biological death and social retirement more or less coincided, so that his old age merely continued the life he knew in what is now called "middle" age. But social conditions were different there and then.

In the United States today only about 8 percent of people over sixty-five live with their children and grandchildren, and probably no more than this ever did in the past. About a fourth to a third of old people now live with an adult child (but not with a grandchild). A widowed grandmother may move in with her daughter and son-in-law, or a divorced man may live on with his mother and father. But it has been rare to see two generations of *intact* marriages living together, and since World War II it has become even more rare.

More often, old people live alone or with friends who are not related. This does not mean that the old are cut off from their children: 84 percent of American old people live less than an hour away from a child. But typically they do not live together. And, more important, most old people do not *want* to live with their children. Many who do live with them do so because it saves money, not because it's a good social arrangement. Less than 10 percent of a recent national sample of old people said they wanted to live with a child or relative. Only 17 percent recommended it to other old people able to care for themselves. Even for ill or disabled old people, more (39 percent) recommended going to a nursing home or getting nursing care than recommended moving in with children (23 percent).

Many young people feel the same way. According to a survey I did of students in two sociology classes at the University of California at Berkeley in 1968, only a small proportion (7 percent) expected their aged parents to live with them, and only 4 percent expected to live with their own adult children. (Even in the counterculture, communes are usually composed of people the same age, generally under thirty.)

Moreover, when the old live near young people outside the family, they usually do not make friends with them. In fact, the old person with young neighbors is often more isolated than his peer who lives near other old people. In a very important and excellent study of Cleveland residents, the sociologist Irving Rosow compared 1,200 old people living in three kinds of housing: one with a mix of ages ("normal"), one with quite a few old people ("age concentrated") and one with almost all old people ("age dense"). Those living with many other old people made the most friends. But even in the normal neighborhoods (with about 12 percent old people), most befriended not young people but others their own age. Finally, a study of five hundred old people in Elmira, New York, showed that the older a widow, the less isolated she was, since she was less likely to be the only widow on the block and more likely to have (other widow) friends.

This means that the more "segregated" the neighborhood itself, the more integrated the old person is *within* it. One survey of older clients of five social agencies in Schenectady, New York, showed that of those needing rehousing, 60 percent did not want to live in a neighborhood with small children. In another case, a retirement public apartment building reserved a third of its units for younger families in order to stimulate friendships across the age barrier. Out of eighty-eight friendships reported, only one old person made friends with a young person. A more recent study sampling the old in the same housing checked this point again and found that of all the old people's neighbor friends, only 4 percent were young.

A mutual disinterest between young and old can, in varying degree, isolate the old. Not all old people are like the widow in the British film *The Whisperers,* living alone in a musty flat with the radio and cat for company. More typical perhaps is the "emancipated" older couple living on their own, separate from their children, in neighborhoods with young working neighbors.

But this situation too can easily dissolve into isolation. Each member of the couple has a fair chance of living alone within a few years. At age sixty-five already 55 percent are widowed or single—30 percent of the men and 70 percent of the women. Poor health and death gradually steal away those special friendships with long histories, and retirement narrows the circle of acquaintances which, on hindsight, rested on having work in common.

It has become a sad commonplace to associate being old with being alone. We call isolation a punishment for the prisoner, but perhaps a majority of American old people are in some degree isolated or soon will be. It has gradually come to seem "natural," and ironically age-integrated settings make it seem more so.

SEPARATION

Old people live together in a number of places: private retirement villages for the well-to-do, public housing projects and rundown hotels for the poor. While most of the 9 percent of the U.S. population over sixty-five live in independent housing in age-integrated neighborhoods, they are only 3 percent of the population in some new suburbs and 30 percent in cities such as St. Petersburg, Florida. Since World War II, there has been a mushroom growth of old-age housing, drop-in centers and retirement settlements such as Ryderwood in Washington, Moosehaven in Florida, Sun City (which has over twelve thousand residents) in Arizona and the Rossmoor Leisure Worlds in California.

Contrasted to the image of Buddenbrook in his family or the widow alone is the new archetype: the sociable, tanned older couple given to organized shuffleboard tournaments, bingo parties and a life of busy leisure. Here the old person is not integrated with the young, but neither is he isolated. He may even find a new mate. One study found that almost a third of the married couples in a retirement community had met and married there.

Many outsiders feel ambivalent toward these new old-age subcultures, partly because they are based on leisure and partly because they separate old people from young people. But according to virtually all the reported research, the old people who live in them like the life and choose it freely.

A CASE IN POINT

I recently worked and observed life in Merrill Court,* a California public housing project for poor people over sixty-two. Initially, I should confess, I felt that there was something sad about a group of old people living together, something artificial, maybe even depressing. But it soon became clear to me that they themselves were not depressed. They saw nothing sad about living together and felt a shade of pity for those who had to live alone. They felt they *had* problems, but they did not feel they *were* one.

The findings of this and other research suggest that the kind of communal life I found at Merrill Court was due more to the

* This is not its real name.

setting than to the particular characteristics of the people who happened to live there. Although the residents are not part of a random sample, their characteristics do not distinguish them so very much from this generation of American old people as a whole. Most of the residents were poor, rural-born Anglo-Saxon Protestant widowed females in their late sixties. And most Americans over sixty-five are poor. (The 1962 average income for couples was about $2,800 and for singles less than $1,400.) Thirteen percent of the population in 1960 was over sixty, and of that strata roughly 60 percent were in their sixties. Most old people today were born in rural areas, although most (70 percent) now live in urban areas. Nationwide, 45 percent of old people are male and 55 percent female; in Merrill Court all but five out of forty-three were women. The residents were probably no more sociable than other old people, since the housing office picked them as their names came up on waiting lists, and they picked the housing not for its social life but because it was cheap.

I should say what the apartment building itself looked like, since the way it was built allowed certain social patterns that might not have emerged otherwise. It had five floors: a ground floor with one apartment and a large recreation room for common use, and four other floors with ten apartments each. On each floor there was an elevator midway between the apartments and a long porch extending the length of all the apartments. It was nearly impossible to walk from any apartment to the elevator without being watched from the series of living-room windows that looked out onto the porch. This was because the chairs inside each living room were arranged so as to face the window and the television at the same time. A woman who was sewing or watching television in her apartment could easily glance up through the window and see or wave to a passerby. Those in the apartments closest to the elevator saw the most passersby and were the "informants" about the whereabouts of people on their floor. I saw more people by simply sitting in one apartment's "television chair" than I ever did knocking on doors.

The residents slept in separate apartments, but they did not live alone. Most waking hours were spent in each other's company, either over the telephone or over a cup of coffee. As a result, they kept an eye on each other and usually noted when someone was deviating from a routine. One day, when I knocked on the door of a resident, her neighbor came out and said, "I don't know where she is, it couldn't be the doctor's. She goes to the doctor's on Tuesday, it couldn't be shopping, she shopped yesterday with her daughter. I don't think she's downstairs, she says she's worked enough today. Maybe she's visiting Abbie. They neighbor a lot. Try the second floor."

Neighboring was also a way to spot sickness or death. As one resident noted, "This morning I looked to see if Judson's curtains were open. That's how we do on this floor, when we get up we open our curtains just a bit, so others walking by outside know that everything's all right. If the curtains aren't drawn by midmorning, we knock to see." (The residents of many midcity hotels make similar arrangements with each other, and in St. Petersburg, Florida, an old person can arrange to be called by a volunteer several times a day.) Some residents also shopped or laundered clothes for other residents, and on several floors they habitually cooked for each other by turn.

In addition to the private apartments, there was a large recreation room downstairs where one came to attend the Monday-morning service-club meetings. If someone stayed up in her apartment during the club meeting on Monday morning it was more often out of spite than indifference. For downstairs was a hub of activity: there people were weaving rugs, knitting clothes, sewing aprons, cooking pies or practicing music—a five-piece band, including washtub bass, played in nursing homes for the "old folks" there. As people worked, they joked and gossiped and, if the mood was right, sang ballads. The activities changed from month to month, but the work, the gossip and the arranging did not. One widow compared the work downstairs to an old-fashioned "workin' in," as she put it: "Neighbors would come in and help out if you were takin' in a harvest or doin'

some cannin'. One time our barn burned down and we had another one up in two days. Doin' it together, we got more done,
see?"

LIBERATION BY SEPARATION

The similarity of the residents liberated them and liberated
their topics of conversation. In a society that raises an eyebrow
at those who do not "act their age," the old-age subculture of
Merrill Court freed the old to dance a jig, to tell an off-color
joke and to flirt without worrying about letting grandmotherly
decorum slip. Among themselves, they developed a backstage
talk about playing the role of old person. Just as one plays the
role of woman to man and black person to white, so one plays
the role of old person to young people. Thus, on occasions
protected from the young, the old are able to drop the role.
Outside such a community old people often try, with powder
and wig, to "pass" as younger, but within such a community
they don't need to.

To bring old people together is not to free them from all
social constraint but to substitute old-age constraints for age-
integrated ones. A typical morning's talk in the recreation room
might move from what Molly had on today when she went
shopping to what Mrs. Barber eats for dinner to whether it is
appropriate to wear hats to church or curlers to the doctor's
office. If a resident broke the rules by wearing a hat to church,
she normally felt it necessary to explain why. On the other hand,
there was much they could do and say together that they could
not—or would not—with young people.

One reason they talked differently among themselves was
simply that some topics were more relevant to them than to
their younger families or friends—for example, whether or not
Medicare pays for chiropractors, visiting hours at various hospitals, the merits of different kinds of dentures, yarn prices, and
the latest episode in daytime TV serials. When daughters

dropped in downstairs, the topic generally shifted to something of more mutual concern, such as whether Jackie had gone downhill since marrying Onassis.

LIFTING THE TABOO ON DEATH

The residents talked with each other about other people's deaths and the prospect of their own quite freely, in straightforward, noneuphemistic language. Death was a fact of life in the community: six residents died in the course of my three years of field work there. There was a collective concern with, as they put it, "being ready," facing up, and each death taught the residents something about it. They felt there was a "good" way and a "bad" way to die. One woman's death especially was the community's example of "the right way to die"—to face death rather than turn one's back on it, all the while living fully to the end. She was praised as much for remaining active as for having her will and burial arranged and being on good terms with her family.

They could not, in the same way, share these concerns with their young family and friends. In fact, it was from the young that they more often heard comments of denial such as "You don't look a day over fifty" or "You get younger every day."

Geoffrey Gorer, in his essay "The Pornography of Death," suggests part of the problem when he notes that death is replacing sex as the new "unmentionable." Compared to those in the nineteenth century, we are more prudish about death, whereas sex, another natural process, is now more open to frank discussion. Death and decay are considered as "disgusting" as birth and copulation were a century ago—a new "not before the children" sort of thing.

However, just as the former taboo on sex tended to be lifted in sex-segregated company, so too perhaps the taboo on death is lifted in age-segregated company. Men alone together and women alone together, even in the Victorian age, may have talked about sex more freely. In the same way, the old among the old feel freer to talk about death.

The age solidarity in Merrill Court tends to liberate the topic of death and the unembarrassed expression of grief. Only a small proportion of old people live in such old-age communities, but it is probably true that in general the old among the old feel less constrained to deny death or to observe the taboo on talk related to it.

STATUS AMONG THE OLD: THE "POOR DEAR" HIERARCHY

Old age has been called a "normal stigma." But while young people may think of the old categorically, the old, especially when they get together, measure small differences between each other, especially differences in luck.

In fact, "luck" is not entirely luck. Health and life expectancy, for example, are often considered luck, but an upper-class person can expect to live ten years longer than a lower-class person. Among the residents of Merrill Court, he who maintained good health, friends in good health, and good relations with children ranked high. Those who fell short on any of these criteria were often referred to as "poor dears."

The "poor dear" system operated like a set of valves through which a sense of superiority ran in only one direction. The hierarchy honored those at the top and pitied (or scorned) those at the bottom, creating status distinctions among those who, in the eyes of the outside society, were social equals. Someone who was unlucky (a "poor dear") did not blame herself for bad luck, nor did she accept the stigmatized status imposed from above by the lucky, and especially the *relatively* lucky. Rather, the "poor dear" would turn to someone she thought still less fortunate to whom she offered solicitude.

This luck hierarchy is only part of a larger old-age status hierarchy which is based on attributes other than luck. For example, at the countywide Senior Citizens Forum, the term "poor dear" often arose with reference to other old people. Senior citizens who are politically active referred to those "poor dears" who are active in recreation. Old people with passive life styles in good health referred to those in poor health as "poor dears," and those in poor health but living in independent housing referred to those in nursing homes as "poor dears." Within the nursing home there was a distinction between those who were ambulatory and those who were not. Among those who were not ambulatory there was a distinction between those who could enjoy food and those who could not. Almost everyone, it seems, had a "poor dear."

The way in which the old look for luck differences among themselves parallels the pattern found at the bottom of other class, racial and sexual hierarchies as well. To find oneself lucky within a generally stigmatized category is to gain the semblance of high status when society withholds it from others in the category. The way in which old people "feel above" and condescend to other old people may be linked to the fact that the young feel above and condescend to them.

CONCLUSION

Deprived of function and power, old people have few clearly defined roles. The former roles that applied to a wife, a worker or a parent have faded with time. But the resulting ambiguity does not obtain in a community of old people such as this. If one is no longer a mother to a brood of small children, or a wife or a provider, one can be the club treasurer, a bowling partner, a volunteer worker in a nursing home or a neighbor's caretaker.

For friends lost through death there are replacements; at Merrill Court whenever an apartment is vacated, it is immediately filled by the first on a long list of applicants at the housing agency. If there is no longer work that "has to be done," something like it is there. With each new role come new customs and new notions of the right and wrong of it. The residents have built themselves an order out of ambiguity, a set of obligations to the outside world and to each other where few had existed before. Lacking responsibilities to the young, they take on responsibilities to each other, and if the outside world watches them less for being old, they watch each other more. They have renewed their social contract with life, on the basis of a new sibling solidarity.

Young people are not alone in their search for "relevant models." Since the parents of today's old people usually died earlier, in the social prime of middle age, an individual does not know what to expect of himself if he lives in pretty good health to a time when he is no longer needed and when he is isolated from others faced with the same dilemma. A community of peers in old life provides models for how to age, when, in this respect, the last generation of old people as well as the young are no help.

Communities of old people need not substitute for warm ties with young family and friends. But the decline of the extended family creates the need for a new social shelter, another pool of friendships, another bond with society apart from family. Old-fashioned values may fade, but the communal experiments of this generation of old people may forecast new social networks for the next.

"Getting It All Together": Communes Past, Present, Future

by ROSABETH MOSS KANTER

Rosabeth Moss Kanter teaches sociology at Brandeis. She has written numerous papers on communes and has recently written a book on the subject entitled *Commitment and Community*.

A few years ago in the springtime of the commune movement, my mother from a Cleveland suburb, like many parents of war babies all over the country, asked me what communes were all about, asked what it was that young people were seeking who left middle-class security for other ways of life.

As I described to her the urgings and yearnings people expressed in their quest for community, she said that a commune reminded her of her family life in the '30s. During the Depression she lived in a large house in Philadelphia with her mother and father, several sisters and brothers-in-law, and a divorced sister and her young son. Since she had a relatively well-paying job as a teacher, she was one of the principal breadwinners for the family, contributing whatever she earned to the support of the others, as did anyone who was working. One of the married sisters kept house, and whoever had a free hand also pitched in. The family was warm and close, sharing intimate experiences as well as a house and livelihood.

Except for the fact that everyone was a blood relation, my mother's house *could* be one of today's communes. In fact, what many communes today are seeking is to recreate their version of extended family of the past, in their search for intense, intimate, participatory, meaningful, group-based ways of life. In the midst of an advanced technological society seen as isolating, meaningless, fragmented and machinelike, today's utopians wish to re-create a shared life together. In fact, they want to be "together" in all the ways that the counterculture now uses this word: inner peace and self-acceptance; whole man relating to whole man; barriers of ego, property, sex, age disappearing; everyone sharing equally.

The result of today's quest for togetherness is the vast number of experiments in communal living springing up across the country. There are small urban groups sharing living quarters and raising their families together while holding outside jobs. There are rural farming communes combining work life and family life under one roof. There are formal organizations with their own business enterprises, like the Bruderhof communities which manufacture Community Playthings; and there are loose aggregates of people without even a name for their group. Some communities, like those forming around personal growth and learning centers, may create a total life style for their members: sleeping, waking, working, playing, loving, eating, even breathing, all guided by the philosophies of the group. Others experiment in more limited ways, several couples, for example, trying group marriage. There are differences in the degree of collectivization—whether the communal group shares only space or also property, money, work and values. There are differences in ideology—from spiritual groups with a religious philosophy to Walden Two groups modeled after Skinner's utopia governed by experts and scientific experimentation, to self-help communities like Synanon or Camp Hill Village, to Open Land communes without any intentional qualities, to friendship groups who want nothing more than to share their lives and their children in a richer way. There are also differences in size—from six people in a house in Boston to two hundred in a Bruderhof village.

The extent of the commune movement is vast, but similarly vast are the problems of building viable communities. Today's communal movement represents a reawakening of the search for utopia that has been carried out in America from as early as 1680, when the first religious sects retreated to the wilderness to live in community. But while experiments in communal living have always been part of the American landscape, only a few dozen of these ventures survived for more than a few years. Building community has proven to be difficult, and today's communes fall heir to the difficulties.

My previous research uncovered some of the things that distinguished successful communes of the past. In order to learn about the kinds of things that make a commune work, I compared thirty nineteenth-century American communes—nine that lasted thirty-three years or more (called "successful") with twenty-one that existed less than sixteen years and on the average about four years ("unsuccessful"). Among the communes in the study were the Shakers, Oneida, Amana, Harmony, New Harmony and Brook Farm. The study asked over 120 questions about the presence or absence of certain social arrangements.

Successful nineteenth-century communities built strong commitment to their group through the kinds of sacrifices and investments members made for and in the community; through discouraging extra-group ties and building strong family feeling within the community; through identity change processes for members; and through ideological systems and authority structures which gave meaning and direction to the community.

Long-lived communities tended to require some sacrifices of their members as a test of faith, and full investment of money and property so that participants had a stake in the fate of the community. They tended to ensure the concentration of loyalty within the community by geographical separation and discouraging contact with the outside. They spread affection throughout the whole community by discouraging exclusive relationships based on two-person attraction or biological family —through either free love (in which sexual contact with all others was required) or celibacy (in which no one had sexual contact) and separation of biological families with communal child rearing. These mechanisms aimed at creating an equal share in man–woman and adult–child relationships for everyone. Family feeling was enhanced by selection of a homogeneous group of members; by full communistic sharing of property; by communistic labor in which no jobs were compensated (everyone shared equally in community benefits, jobs were rotated through the membership, and some work was done by the whole community); by regular group contact through meetings making routine decisions and T-group-like sessions; and by rituals emphasizing the communion of the whole. Identity change processes in long-lived communes tended to consist of T-group-like mutual-criticism sessions in which issues of commitment and deviance and meeting of community standards were examined, and through stratification systems that accorded deference to those best living up to community norms.

Finally, long-lived communes tended to have *elaborate ideologies* providing purpose and meaning for community life and an ultimate guide and justification for decisions. There tended to be strong central figures, charismatic leaders, who symbolized the community's values and who made final decisions for the community and set structural guidelines. That is, while routine decisions might be made by assemblies of the whole or committees with special responsibilities, and while administrative and other work assignments might be rotated and shared, the charismatic leader, as value bearer, still was the ultimate source of authority. Long-lived communities also tended to have fixed daily routines for carrying out tasks and personal-conduct rules —all deriving from ideology and informing an individual of his responsibilities. Finally, they tended to require ideological conversion for admission and did not automatically admit all applicants.

What I found, then, in the successful nineteenth-century utopias, was a number of ways of dealing with group relations, property, work, values and leadership which created an enduring commitment—the motivation to work, the will to continue, fellowship and cohesion as a group. The successful much more than the unsuccessful groups organized their community life in these ways. At the same time that this enabled the successful communities to survive in terms of longevity, such practices also created strong communities in the utopian sense and fulfilled those desires impelling people toward community today. The successful groups provided for their members strong feelings of participation, involvement and belonging to a family group. They built a world centered around sharing—of property, of work, of living space, of feelings, of values. They offered identity and meaning, a value-oriented life of direction and purpose.

TODAY'S COMMUNES

I have applied the lessons of the past in my research on modern communes, looking for those things that make community work. (I have also lived in a communal situation as well as visited many communes, and lived with the issues first hand.) What makes today's communes different from those of the past, however, is that the vast majority of them tend to be small in size, anarchic in philosophy. There *are* a number that resemble the successful communes of the past—Synanon, the Bruderhof communities on the East Coast, some religiously oriented groups, a few older, more established communes. But most of the new communes range in size from six to forty people and reject the rigid structuring of group life true of past communes. "Do your own thing" is a pervasive ethic.

It is impossible in this paper to do more than skim the surface. And I can't do justice to the range and variation in today's communes. But I will try to shed some light on one important issue in communes: becoming a group. Regardless of the eventual outcome or the special characteristics that result, all of today's communes have to make a group out of a diverse collection of individuals.

The kind of group today's communes wish to build is one that provides the warmth and intimacy that is found in a family; they want to become, in fact, extended families. For some communes becoming a family means collective child rearing: shared responsibility for raising children. Children as well as adults, for example, in a Vermont commune have their own separate rooms, and they consider all the adults in the community their "parents." Other communes are interested in sexual experimentation, in changing the man–woman relationship from monogamy, an exclusive two-person bond, to group marriage, in which many attachments throughout the community are possible and encouraged. The sharing of sexual life and children as well as living space are all attempts to bring people closer together, to liberate women from exclusive domestic responsibility, to free couples from all the weight that a two-person bond must bear, and to free parents and children from excessive dependence on one another.

Behind these practices lies the desire to create intense involvement with the communal group as a whole—feelings of connectedness and belonging and the warmth of many attachments.

GROUP ISSUES

While communes seek to become families, they are, at the same time, something different from families; they are groups with their own unique form, something between communities, organizations, families and friendship groups, and they may contain families in their midst.

Certain issues that are faced by all human groups affect communes even more, because they do not yet have the legal status or wide legitimacy that the family has in American society. One important concrete consequence of this lies in the childhood socialization of today's commune members. Not only were they probably socialized from birth to be members of conventional families and thus not given the skills and experiences to deal with the issues they face as commune members, but they also may have to unlearn some of the lessons gleaned from living in conventional families.

Each commune must create anew its own social form from scratch; it must cope afresh with those group issues that are at least partially presolved for families or for other institutions in our society. Part of the definition of a commune, in fact, is that it is a group which comes together to create its own form. No matter how much a commune participates in the emerging counterculture, I still think that to some extent each group seeks to create and control its own existence and to meet its own particular needs in its own way.

Communes, like other groups, start with certain goals or ideas, sometimes well-defined, sometimes vague. Their structure comes about through the process of coping with several important group issues, in the context of their ideals.

The first important issue is admission to the group: how does a person become a member? There are socially delimited ways of entering a family—through marriage, birth or legal adoption —but no similar guidelines for joining a commune. In American society, strangers do not knock at the doors of residences inquiring about whether they can become a member of your family, but they *do* approach communes with this request. And many modern communes began with the wish to be open to all comers, to be places where everyone is welcome and no one is excluded, where anyone can automatically "belong." Some still operate on the "open land" concept: anyone can come and stake out a bit of territory on the property.

In strong contrast to the successful communities of the past, which required an ideological commitment for membership or had some screening procedure, some of these communes do not even make a member–nonmember distinction; whoever is there at the time "belongs." But as the group begins to define itself, it also begins to define criteria and procedures for membership, an issue that many communes are reluctant to face. But some limit membership by the size of their property, others ask that people come in for probationary periods first, and gradually, I think, even some of the more anarchic communes are beginning to control entry. The consequences of failing to control it are sometimes demoralizing for the group, as Kenneth Lamott said in 1967 about Morningstar Ranch's open-admission policy: "It's not like it used to be. Too many outsiders have been coming up here during the summer—Hell's Angels, tourists, people who come up for the wrong reasons. I don't know if Lou's right, letting everybody in." By contrast, the enduring communes of the past all had selective entry procedures.

"Getting it all together" is a central group issue—to find sources of cohesion, to create and solidify the bonds holding the group together as a group. I've heard members of urban groups, in particular, ask themselves what it is that makes them a commune. In this there is a searching for the basis of solidarity and a reaching for the specialness of the *group* as an entity beyond the collection of individuals present. I'm struck by the tendency of even new groups of limited duration to reach for the blanket that wraps the separate individuals together.

In communes, several things may happen to provide sources of cohesion. One is the development of belief in the groups' superiority. Nineteenth-century communities had elaborate beliefs of this kind, including the fact that they were heralding a new age, bringing about the millennium, and that, by contrast, the surrounding society was evil, wicked and sinful. The Oneida Community felt that contact with this outside was sufficiently contaminating that the whole community joined together after visitors left, to clean the buildings in a ritualistic purification. What a sense of membership in their own special group the Oneidans must have had, to scrub away traces of contact with non-Oneidans. And the Shakers developed their condemnation of non-Shakers and the previous non-Shaker life of Shaker converts to a high art. One example is a hymn in which Shakers indicated their great love for other Shakers after first expressing their deep hatred for their biological families:

Of all the relations that I ever see
My old fleshly kindred are furthest from me.

O how ugly they look, how hateful they feel!
To see them and hate them increases my zeal.

We can see parallels today in the bitterness with which some communards condemn their parents or, more often, the life that their parents have led. The firm rejection of other ways of life, particularly those representing options the commune members once had, helps reinforce the belief that the commune is indeed a special, valuable, worthwhile place.

What parents also represent is a set of ties that not all members of the commune share—yet the cohesiveness of the group is dependent in part on elevating that which is shared to a higher moral and emotional plane than that which cannot be included in the group or shared by all members. "What we have together is more beautiful than what we have apart" is echoed by many communes. Also recurrent is: "What we have and are *now* is more important and worthwhile than what we may have been separately." On some communes this results in a noticeable lack of interest in members' pasts and even resentment at talking much about life before the group—in group language, the "there-and-then" rather than the "here-and-now." A researcher at a communal farm in Oregon reports that the ten adults there knew relatively little about each other's backgrounds, that they said instead that what matters is what you are and do *after* you come to the commune, not what you were before. "We accept a person for what he is, not what he was."

Such reasoning is part of the elevation of the group's present existence to a higher moral plane than past or outside lives. Even when these sentiments are not voiced explicitly, even when the group is content with a loose federation of individuals rather than a close-knit entity, I still believe this is an underlying theme in communes. A woman I know, living with her husband in an urban commune that they intend to leave at the end of the year when they've finished school, still reported to me the awkwardness and uneasiness she experienced when her parents came to visit her in the commune. They were a reminder of her noncommunal past, of course, as well as people with whom she shared something that other commune members couldn't share.

The issue of outside relations and friends visiting can be dealt with in many ways, of course, that enhance rather than detract from the commune's cohesiveness. Some groups take over visitors as the property of the group, no matter whom they have come to visit, and visitors may find themselves overwhelmed by greetings, by curious children, by the desire to find them a place in the life of the whole commune rather than just those they come to visit. With a friend of mine who is a frequent visitor I recently visited a West Coast commune where members had small separate dwellings—log cabins, tepees, one-room plastic houses—and did not spend all their time in the communal house which held the kitchen and dining room. It was interesting to notice that my friend tried to get around to *all* the houses and say hello to everyone. In other communes the process of visiting and the role of visitor may become a matter of group policy and decision. Drop City in New Mexico built a special visitors' dome, particularly for parents who wished to visit—in a sense putting them in their place.

Belief in the group's specialness is one step away from belief in its superiority—and a big theme in the commune culture is superiority of their way of life over others'. One rural commune prides itself on the purity and naturalness of its existence as opposed to the corruption of the city. A member said, "In the city you don't even know your own *motives.*"

Many of these sources of solidarity I have been describing are dependent on the existence of a wider society—the group becomes special by delimiting who and what it is not, who and what it rejects. But at the same time communes struggle with defining what they *are*. At this point the issue of common purpose becomes essential: What are we trying to make happen together? What goal or idea or symbol "gets it all together"? This is a major problem for many modern communes, particularly anarchistically oriented ones. They tend to come together in the shared rejection of the established society, particularly of its structure, and wish to make no demands on members that would detract from doing their thing. This lack of a common purpose has been cited by the member of one now defunct commune as a reason for its failure: "We weren't ready to define who we were; we certainly weren't prepared to define who we weren't—it was still just a matter of intuition. We had come together for various reasons—not overtly for a common idea or ideal, but primarily communitarians, or primarily farmers, or primarily political revolutionaries—or just plain hermits who wanted to live in the woods. All these different people managed to work together side by side for a while, but the fact was that there really was no shared vision."

Defining "who we are," by the way, is particularly difficult for urban communes where members hold outside jobs. It is much easier when members work together in commune jobs, as was true of all the nineteenth-century utopian communities. Some urban groups deal with this by trying to find employment as a group.

In the absence of elaborate integrating philosophies, of a sense of destiny or mission such as the religious groups have, or of an essential, overriding goal, many groups develop a sense of purpose by finding shared tasks that represent a common endeavor. Construction—building—seems to me to be the most important of these, for it leaves the group with a permanent monument to the shared enterprise. The emphasis on constructing and shaping one's own environment that is so central to the commune movement may have roots here. The end, the actual building, may not be as important for the group's identity as the means by which the building came about. I have felt on many communes an infectious sense of group pride in the self-made buildings, like the gala celebration in the Connecticut Bruderhof community after the construction of new beams in the dining hall.

Rituals and shared symbols also tell a group what it is, particularly those that are unique to it. Ritual was an important part of the life of many communes of the past, especially for the Shakers. Every evening each Shaker group gathered to dance, pray and express the togetherness of the group. Many aspects of the Shaker ceremony resemble encounter-group exercises in their use of energetic body movement and emotional outburst; after the ritual one Shaker reported that the group felt "love enough to eat each other up." The Shakers also had a number of special ceremonies in which spiritual or imaginary events occurred. Some of these centered around spiritual fountains on magic hills near the villages, reputedly populated by angels and spirits—but spirits that only Shakers could see, of course. Among them were such luminaries as Napoleon, George Washington and Queen Elizabeth. Present-day communes often create their own rituals, some with the same special or hidden elements that only group members share. Particularly those groups oriented around religion or mysticism find ritual an abundant source of group feeling. But even creedless communes develop ritual. One group begins its "family meetings" by sitting in a circle and chanting "Om." A number of communes use sensory awakening or encounter exercises as a kind of ritual. In the community to which I belonged one summer, we arose around six-thirty and met on a grassy lawn at seven for T'ai Chi Chuan exercises—a beautiful flowing Chinese moving meditation. For an hour we stood in rows and moved together, all following the pattern, and then went in to breakfast.

The desire for the group to become a group sometimes means that members feel a pressure to take pride only in things which are held in common, shared by the group, rather than those which belong to them separately. This, of course, was an explicit norm of the communistic groups of the last century who held all property in common—including clothes in Oneida—and found that joint ownership was an important source of community feeling. But even in "doing-your-own-thing" communes today that maintain a great deal of individual ownership and resist making demands on each other, I have still found that some people feel it important to take pride only in that which is shared. In a rural hip commune I spoke to a woman, a particularly respected member of the commune, who had just finished building a very striking-looking one-room, two-level redwood house, with the help of some others in the group. It was very cleverly and artistically created, with windows that were really sculptures, framed with pieces of twisted wood found in the forest. She expressed both great pride and guilt— guilt that she should have such a nice house for her own.

A group can become a special entity if members value it above other things. It is very difficult to maintain outside allegiances in a commune, for there is often pressure from the group to be fully present and fully involved. Most of what a commune is, after all, is the devotion and energy of those who belong—it *is* the group composed of specific people and needs *those* people to be what it is. Some of the nineteenth-century communities solved this problem by eliminating the possibility of conflicting loyalties; they tended to break ties with the surrounding society and moved to isolated locations which the average member rarely left. But even for rural communities this is rarely feasible today, and for urban groups it is impossible. So an important source of interpersonal friction in communes is how involved and present a member is. Meetings in which tensions and hostilities are confronted often revolve around this kind of theme. There is a dilemma here for many present-day groups, for while there may be a group pressure for involvement, there is sometimes an accompanying reluctance to make demands or to create norms that will regulate the individual's involvement—even in such simple matters as doing his share of domestic work. Yet the failure to make such norms explicit undermines the groupness of many communes and helps lead to their dissolution. So the member still feels the weight of group pressure, but there are no clear norms that pull the commune together as a group.

The reluctance to make formal rules is pervasive through the commune movement, and communities such as Synanon that *do* have a highly developed structure are viewed by many other communes as authoritarian. There is a real split among communes around the degree of organization they are willing to create; those that fail, however, to organize their work and their decision-making procedures tend to find that work stays undone, some decisions never get made, and group feeling develops only with difficulty. The unwillingness to make decisions or impose order is to me a function not only of a "do-your-own-thing" ideology but also of a lack of trust in the group. One hip commune reported the difficulties in the group's working together on construction. "Everything was a hassle, an object for discussion. Even how many hammer blows to use on a nail. Should it be five or seven?" Those communes, on the other hand, in which there is enough mutual trust and commitment to the group—often through the sense of shared purpose mentioned earlier—find that they can build organization and that this enhances rather than detracts from their functioning as a group. In fact, I have found among residents in the very anarchic hip communes a longing for more order and groupness than they have. Kenneth Lamott, a resident of Morningstar, made this remark about Tolstoy Farm: "It's a groovy place. They don't let *everybody* in—just people who really believe in it. They've got some organization there. Everybody knows what he's supposed to be doing." Tolstoy Farm, of course, is now almost ten years old and in this time has developed its structure, and there are other more mature communes that have evolved toward building cohesiveness through becoming a well-defined group.

THE FUTURE

I am usually asked to make predictions about the viability of today's commune movement. First, many of today's groups are not looking for the same kind of permanent, stable community that utopians of the past sought, so while it is true that many of today's groups are temporary and subject to much change and turnover of members, it is this kind of temporary system that some communes themselves seek—feeling that nothing should be forever, that change is part of life.

On the other hand, a number of groups do *wish* to create long-range viable alternative communities, and to these the lessons of the past well apply. Those communes that develop common purposes, an integrating philosophy, a structure for leadership and decision-making, criteria for membership and entrance procedures, that organize work and property communally, that affirm their bonds through ritual, and that work out interpersonal difficulties through regular open confrontation have a better chance of succeeding than those that do not. They will be building commitment and also satisfying their members by creating a strong family-like group. The failure rate of communes is high, but so is the failure rate of small businesses. And no one suggests that small business is not a viable organizational form. As the commune movement grows, so do the number of groups that build for themselves what it takes to succeed as a commune.

The movement is part of a reawakening of belief in the possibilities for utopia that existed in the nineteenth century and exist again today, a belief that by creating the right social institution, human satisfaction and growth can be achieved. John Leonard wrote in the New York *Times* at the turn of the year 1971: "The romantic notion of the perfectibility of man is all we have left to sustain us. The rest is rhetoric, and the romantics have the best rhetoric."

Lesson from the Kibbutz: A Cautionary Tale

by MENACHEM GERSON

In addition to being a kibbutz member, Menachem Gerson is associated with Israel's Institute for Kibbutz Education.

From the beginning, women have had an equal share in shaping kibbutz life. The kibbutz founders, deeply rooted in socialist philosophy, were convinced that changed social conditions would quickly bring about a decisive change in the traditional feminine character exemplified by Nora in Ibsen's *A Doll's House*. While Freud deeply influenced the kibbutz movement's approach to child rearing, his theories regarding the character of women were rejected as a typical example of middle-class prejudice, as were all theories proclaiming an essential inferiority of women.

ACHIEVEMENTS

There can be no doubt that the kibbutz has achieved fundamental change in the social status of women; most of the goals of the women's-liberation movement in the United States have been realized in the kibbutz:

1. Women in the kibbutz are no longer economically dependent on men; since every woman works at a job, there is full economic equality.

2. The conflict created in women by dual roles has been resolved. The kibbutz enables a woman to do justice to both roles, without fear of losing her job during pregnancy or of her children being neglected while she works outside the home.

3. Official kibbutz philosophy demands that women take full part in all spheres of social activity.

4. The sexual double standard has been eliminated in the kibbutz. Needless to say, birth control is the established practice.

5. The kibbutz has developed a dual-centered system of education that provides the best of both family and institutional settings. The child-centered kibbutz community offers a full-fledged education that in no way resembles the custodial care that so often characterizes day-care projects.

6. Household tasks in the kibbutz are fewer than elsewhere; cooking, laundry and mending are provided for by the kibbutz. The jobs that remain, such as cleaning the flat and taking care of the garden, are generally divided by the spouses, though the fine touches of homemaking remain specifically feminine tasks.

TENSIONS

The above are achievements of which any society could be proud. But age-old problems of women persist in the kibbutz. Many women of the founder generation are dissatisfied and disillusioned. Now middle-aged and older, they find that many of their once meaningful jobs have become too strenuous. Kitchen and dining-room, laundry, and tailoring chores are often too hard—or too boring. Middle-aged women who used to find satisfaction working in early-childhood education often have difficulty cooperating with younger, second-generation women, whose style of work with small children is more easygoing.

Older women frequently feel that their kibbutz career has not provided them with a skill, that women are more restricted in their choice of work than are men. Whatever the reasons, kibbutz women are less active than men in fulfilling prestigious tasks, such as the central-managerial ones, and they are less vocal in the weekly general meeting, where many kibbutz problems are decided. Quite a few women in the kibbutz still struggle with traditional feelings of female inferiority or dependence on male esteem. For most women in the kibbutz, then, it is not their work and social activity but their marriage and family that form the center of their lives.

FAMILISTIC TENDENCIES

Women have often become proponents of "familistic tendencies" in the kibbutz. This term, introduced in kibbutz research by the late Yonina Talmon of Hebrew University, denotes the demand of the family for greater authority in decision-making, a demand frowned upon in kibbutz practice. It also conveys the family's desire to increase contact between parents and children by having the children sleep in the parents' apartment rather than in the children's houses.

These familistic tendencies exist in a small minority of kibbutzim; currently, only twenty out of 230 kibbutzim have private sleeping arrangements for children. Supporters see the tendencies as a way to win back women who feel estranged from kibbutz life, but I find them regressive from two points of view. First, studies carried out by Yonina Talmon and, later, by Joseph Sheffer (both unpublished in English) have shown that supporters of familistic tendencies conceive of the woman's role in a traditional, rigidly sex-typed fashion inimicable to the desired change in sex roles. Second, it is fundamental to kibbutz life that the economic production of an individual not be motivated by personal or family gain; thus, it follows that the family must not exist as a self-interested economic unit.

As does every healthy social body, the kibbutz is steadily changing. But, as I have noted, familistic tendencies, far from being consistent with this process of healthy change, strike at the very root of kibbutz existence. Thus, the attitude of the second generation, the kibbutz-born generation now taking center stage, is of great importance. Evidence to date has indicated that familistic tendencies are no stronger in the second generation than they are today in the founder generation. In February 1971, for example, the largest of the three kibbutz federations held a national convention at which problems of early child care were discussed by delegates, and they were taken up in all seventy-three member kibbutzim. It is noteworthy that of the hundreds of convention delegates, mostly second-generation parents of young children, only nine delegates voted in favor of private sleeping arrangements for children.

But the emergence of women's problems in the kibbutz raises nagging questions. Doesn't it support Freud's view of women? If changed social conditions do not bring far-reaching change in feminine characteristics, does that not prove the existence of an essential feminine character, rooted in biological structure? The scientific approach does not permit us to shy away from facts, even if they challenge our beliefs. But acceptance of this traditional image of women would mean renunciation of the egalitarian character of kibbutz society, and would entail a serious setback for women's emancipation movements everywhere. Before drawing conclusions, then, it would be well to examine the historical conditions that have affected kibbutz women. In doing so, we will consider three stages of development that every kibbutz went through.

FIRST STAGE

Initially, there was a period of great hardship and great enthusiasm. On a spot of arid land, far from the urban centers from which most of them had come, the settlers—all young and often threatened by hostile neighbors—had to build a flourishing farm and a new way of life. The elation of starting from scratch, the once-in-a-lifetime opportunity to found a new society, pervaded every sphere of a life reduced to bare essentials—physical work by day and standing watch by night. In this highly emotional atmosphere, women struggled from the outset to be equal partners with men, demanding their full share both in work and in communal life. The members, intoxicated with longing for new styles of life, often regarded the family with suspicion, seeing it as a remnant of their bourgeois past. Family life was restricted both by circumstances and by outlook. Life in tents, wooden huts or, later, small rooms in concrete buildings, life within one age group, many of whose members had spent years together in a youth movement abroad, life with children few and far between—all restricted traditional family functioning. The goal of a new brotherhood of all community members further discouraged public demonstration of family ties; spouses took their meals separately in the dining room and sometimes even sat apart at the weekly general meeting.

Work was the overriding element of the new life, and women regarded it as both duty and privilege to participate fully in hard physical labor. Agricultural work was not only basic to the kibbutz economy, it was also the major proof of belonging to the budding new community. In this atmosphere, how could a woman pay attention to her looks? How could she dare to cultivate her natural beauty? This would have taken her back, both in her own opinion and in that of her male companions, to the much hated doll's house of Nora. While it was necessary that some women take on traditional female tasks in the kitchen and the nursery, this work did not share the glory of labor on the land. And, for both economic and ideological reasons, it was not regarded as productive labor. Many women doing this traditional duty contributed far more than a mere "productive" day of work. They laid the foundations for a communal education, and they created a common kitchen that provided tasty food in an atmosphere of concern for the comrades they fed. But they rarely met with the appreciation or encouragement reserved for women who worked in agriculture. And among those whose activities embraced various areas of public life (politics, education and cultural and organizational work in the kibbutz movement), it was usually the politically active women who were singled out for public praise and esteem.

During this initial period of enthusiasm, the women of the kibbutz voiced no complaints; the spiritual rewards of this unique and creative period were high indeed. But looking back, one fact becomes strikingly clear: the concept of women's equality was greatly distorted. Women's striving was toward identification with men, toward an equality that disregarded sex differences and that set forth male qualities and activities as the model for both sexes. This distortion of the concept of sex equality has occurred in the early stages of other women's-emancipation movements. There is little doubt that this period in kibbutz development was tinged with an unconscious postulate of male supremacy. It is likely that it left kibbutz women with a hidden distrust of women's liberation slogans, and that it planted the seeds of their later disillusionment.

SECOND STAGE

The second period of the kibbutz came into being with the easing of the economic situation. As living conditions improved, couples began to have more children. Dwellings were enlarged, and often a garden plot was attached to them. The recognized functions of the family became less restricted, and the new, more spacious homes became natural centers for weekend family gatherings. Along with this general improvement, women had more time and resources to provide homemaking for their families.

The initial, ecstatic expectation of revolutionizing social relations by tearing down all barriers between members of the community began to give way to a more sober and realistic understanding of human relations in the kibbutz. As a result, the early suspicion of the role of the family eased, and slowly the family came to be regarded as a cornerstone of stable kibbutz life. While, earlier, the parents' role in education had purposely been restricted, parents were now regarded as significant partners in the socialization of the child. The children's houses were now open to parents at all times, and the care givers (*metatloth*) were told to seek cooperation with parents on an equal, nonauthoritarian basis. With the increase in children, the work of the care givers was held in greater esteem, and a network of training courses for them was established at Oranim, the pedagogic center of the three kibbutz federations. As the extreme hardships of early kibbutz life gradually eased, members conceded that a higher standard of living was not a betrayal but a realization of socialist principles.

It was in this atmosphere that some important changes in the status of women occurred. As the increase in children required that more women work in child care, the former one-sided emphasis on agricultural work came to be seen as a contradiction.* At the same time, with the standard of living on the rise, the kibbutz members placed increasing value on the contributions of those workers whose efforts went into making life more comfortable and pleasant. As a result, training facilities for service workers began to be developed.

Another development indicative of greater understanding of women's special interests and problems was the shortening of work hours for both middle-aged women and mothers of young children. Theoretical understanding followed: the former male-oriented and mechanical interpretation of women's equality gave way to a recognition of differences in the interests and capacities of men and women—differences that in no way render women inferior to men. It seemed now that positive solutions to the problems of kibbutz women were finally at hand, that the conflict between women's sense of their social achievement and their remaining feelings of inferiority and dependence would soon be resolved.

There were hints, though, that women in the kibbutz did not yet fully understand the historic perspective of their problems. This came to light in the reaction to two proposals put forth by some members—both men and women—who felt that the solution should not be left solely to the efforts of individual women, but should be advanced through organizational means as well. The first proposal was that women establish their own organiza-

---

* For all its progress toward equality, the kibbutz apparently still persists in thinking of child care as women's work.

tional framework, a women's movement within the general framework of the kibbutz movement. Its advocates hoped for greater participation of women in public affairs, and believed that organization would help women compete with men in public speaking and politics, where long experience had given men an advantage. Organization, they felt, might also make it easier for women to verbalize and discuss their problems. The second proposal was to assure a certain percentage of participation by women in every elected committee, both in the individual kibbutz and in the framework of kibbutz federations.

Both proposals were fiercely rejected by the majority of women. They felt offended by the suggestion of a special women's problem in the kibbutz. They condemned the proposals as violations of the principle of equality, declaring that they wanted to be elected as individuals, as were men, not as members of a weak sex that needed organizational propping up. Only in one of the three kibbutz federations was the second proposal accepted, apparently with some positive results. The view of the great majority of kibbutz women indicated that they were not yet prepared to admit the existence of the age-old problem of women's liberation. This lack of historic understanding was in fact a symptom of an erroneous emancipationist approach that would have women be like men; it was a bad foreboding for future developments.

THIRD STAGE

In the third (present) period, the kibbutz-born generation has come of age. Many developments that began in the second stage have reached completion. The majority of kibbutz families now consist of three generations, and the family is fully recognized as a cornerstone of kibbutz life. (Indicative of this elevation of the family are the changes in attitude toward marriage and children. In the early stages of kibbutz life, the marriage ceremony was a private occasion, with few guests present. Now a special marriage ceremony has been created, a festive affair with all members of the kibbutz and hundreds of other guests attending. At the same time, the average number of children per family has risen from one and a half in the initial stage to three.) Large-scale mechanization has further decreased the number of women working in agriculture. Training facilities for child care, and, to a lesser degree, for maintenance services, have increased. The beautician's is now one of the recognized women's professions. The image projected by the young woman in the kibbutz today is a less strained one than that of the woman of the founder generation. And while here and there one may detect a longing for what women in other societies call "the drudgery of housework," the great majority of young kibbutz women are opposed to such regressive tendencies.

There remain, however, problems and tensions specific to the young woman in the kibbutz, some of which may be attributable to the dissatisfactions expressed by their mothers. One such tension has become explicit in the strong trend to early marriage. Marrying at about twenty years of age, at the conclusion of military service, has become common. While the tendency may be observable in other societies as well, young kibbutz couples who wish to live together do not face the moral qualms of their elders and the economic problems that often confront couples outside the kibbutz who decide to live together before marriage. Thus, one might expect that they would not rush into official marriage—especially when it means that the woman has to give up plans for vocational training outside the kibbutz.

These early marriages are particularly puzzling given the great desire for vocational training among the youth. For the founder generation, the transition to the physical work that went into creating the kibbutz was in itself a great and satisfying achievement. The kibbutz-born generation shows an astonishing degree of work capacity, and for its members to find self-realization in work, greater expertise is necessary. This is particularly true for women in the kibbutz, to whom there are comparatively few occupations open. And while some women, especially those seeking to enter one of the glamour professions such as physiotherapy, delay childbearing until the completion of their vocational training, these seem to be the exception.

These observations may be summarized as follows: (1) Young women, rejoining the kibbutz after army service, wish to begin as early as possible to build their family nests. We can only speculate about their reasons. The framework of the kibbutz is much smaller than that of the army, and many young women seem to feel that it might be more difficult to find a man in the kibbutz if they delay. (2) Job involvement seems to be weaker among young women in the kibbutz than are family considerations; when job and family conflict, preference is given to the latter, as indicated by the trend to early marriage.

Thus, with all of the achievements of the kibbutz, two basic problems of women remain: dissatisfaction in the sphere of work, and comparatively little participation in civic activities and the management of the society.

CONCLUSIONS

It would be easy enough to play down the problems I have raised. One could say that such dissatisfactions and tensions are typical of middle-aged women everywhere. But they appear to affect young kibbutz women as well, and that is harder to dismiss. Or one could say, "Accept the fact that women are not interested in civic activity and careers, stop forcing them into a role that fits only your own utopian ideals of kibbutz society—and all the so-called problems will disappear!" Perhaps. But other things will disappear as well, including the hope of active women fighting in the kibbutz and elsewhere for a change in the traditional image of women. And without this hope the kibbutz is doomed. Its very existence, as a socialist cell within a capitalist society, is a miracle. But if its women continue to find life frustrating, it is hard to expect the kibbutz to survive.

Both intellectual honesty and socialist values demand that we refrain from quick conclusions, such as "Freud was right." One theoretical conclusion, though, appears to be proved: radical change in social conditions does not immediately bring forth a corresponding change in psychological makeup; new social conditions do not automatically create a new woman, one who finds satisfaction both in family life and in civic activity. The principle holds for men as well as women. From a historic viewpoint, it is clear that a change in fundamental attitudes can be accomplished only over a prolonged period of time; the changes in attitudes and belief systems accompanying the transition from feudalism to capitalism have been part of a long and complex process, as Max Weber has shown.

In this light, we may begin to understand some of the tensions faced by kibbutz women in the transition to a socialist form of living. The radical and exaggerated egalitarianism that characterized the early period of kibbutz life must have left its mark on the first generation of kibbutz women. The misleading assumption that feminine psychological makeup would quickly change with the change in social conditions may have led to a kind of psychological short-circuit. Certainly it is easy to understand the deep disillusionment of kibbutz women who discarded their traditional role only to find that the fulfillment they expected did not materialize in their lifetimes.

LEVERS FOR CHANGE

The significant question to be asked, now that we have examined both the achievements and the limitations of women's progress in the kibbutz, is what practical measures might further that progress. In discussing the women's problem in the United States, I have often been asked: Why doesn't the kibbutz draft women into managerial jobs, even if they are not inclined to accept them? Why doesn't the kibbutz draft men into early-child-care work, in order to loosen up rigid sex typing? In general, the experience of Soviet Communism can hardly encourage any socialist to rely on such dictatorial measures. Specifically, this sort of coercive action would be diametrically opposed to the voluntary structure of kibbutz life.

The main avenue of action open to the kibbutz is in the direction of a determined attempt to deepen the involvement and satisfaction of women in their work. There are three aspects to this undertaking:

1. The final uprooting of prejudices stemming primarily from early periods in kibbutz life, as described above. The "cult" of agricultural work, which created great stress for many women, no longer exists, but remnants of the male tendency to demean women's work as unprofitable may linger. These are gradually disappearing as the importance of child care and work in the services to the individual kibbutz member's sense of "feeling at home" is perceived.

2. Providing better training for child-care personnel and service workers. Good training is not only an important vehicle for deeper work satisfaction, it is also an indication of the social prestige of an occupation.

3. Providing greater choice of occupation for women. Certain prejudices of sex typing still must be overcome: There is no reason, biological or social, why a woman cannot be an electrician or a technical draftsman; why a woman cannot be a chief accountant rather than one of his assistants; or why women teachers cannot make up 50 percent of the high-school staffs, rather than being limited to primary schools, where they hold 90 percent of the positions. Some women have already entered these occupations, as well as those of registered nursing, physiotherapy, and special education, and their number must grow. But it is not sufficient to increase the number of women working in prestigious professions. The number of professions accorded such status will itself have to increase; such

diverse job categories as social worker, artist, pediatrician and efficiency expert will have to be accorded recognition in the kibbutz equal to that of the admired agricultural and service trades. The kibbutz has already broadened its framework to take in a variety of professions that were not originally planned; in doing so, it has set up the professional training and higher education they require. What is needed now is a concerted effort to enlarge the proportion of women benefiting from these new training and study facilities.

Educators in the kibbutz have to do a great deal of new thinking in order to overcome remnants of traditional rigid sex typing. The pubescent girl who joins the boys on the football field is too readily called a tomboy; the young male introvert who lives in his own world of art and literature is too easily called a sissy. One of the great advantages of the kibbutz is its capacity deliberately to pursue a modified line of education, embodying new thinking based on collective experience. This teaching should not be conveyed by an authoritative imposition of "new" sex characteristics and roles, but in a manner that will help individuals of both sexes to choose their areas of interest freely, without fear of transgressing time-honored sex roles.

Redefining Marriage
and Parenthood

The Case against Marriage

by CAROLINE BIRD

Caroline Bird's best known work is her book *Born Female: The High Cost of Keeping Women Down.* She is a contributing editor to *New Woman* magazine, from which this article is taken.

At graduation, Barbara Ballinger, Barnard '71, was introduced by her friends as the only member of her class who was getting married. The distinction may have been exaggerated, but breakdowns from the 1970 census available about that time were a surprise even to those who knew that getting married the year of graduation was no longer important to women college students.

Since World War II, most American women have married and had their babies in their early twenties. In 1960, for instance, only 28 percent of the women twenty to twenty-four were single. But in 1970, 36 percent of the women in the marrying ages were single.

The increase was dramatic. Young unattached women are highly visible. They are a lush market for everything from hair curlers to airline tickets. And since the population grew during the 1960s, the increase in absolute numbers means that there are now more than twice as many of them running around the country.

Why didn't they marry?

There are now so many exciting alternatives to marriage—alternatives that include sexual relationships—that the brightest women no longer have as much incentive to play dumb. They've raised their aspirations, particularly their aspirations for self-expression.

Talk to the graduates of 1971 and you find them full of unfinished personal business. The best of them are surprisingly unworried about the decline in entry jobs. "There is so much I want to do," they'll say. "I want to travel. I need to grow up. I want to find myself before I settle down." Young people of former times have postponed serious thought of marriage because they "wanted to have a good time." Now they postpone it because they don't think they are ready for it. Marriage sounds too hard. Because they don't have to get married to have sex, young people of the 1970s can be much cooler-headed about the kind of marriage they demand. As the urgency declines, the standards rise to clearly impossible levels.

The new Puritanism demands that sentimentality be examined not as decoration or lubrication for a relationship difficult at best, but with the literal eye of a child. In the past, the hypocrisy of the wedding ceremony has been endured with help from corny jokes, and a ritual nervousness on the day itself. But the brides of the 1970s won't say what they don't mean. To be honest, they are rewriting the ceremony. Many marry themselves, Quaker style. They read favorite poems, or make up the vows they pledge, or insist on being married in bare feet, or even naked. Parents are sometimes excluded, or the mother as well as the father of the bride stands at the altar. It's a way of saying, "Our marriage is not for society. It's for us."

Another expression for the new Puritanism is the refusal to marry a mate on the grounds that you can't be sure how you are going to feel about anything next year. Far from promiscuous, these openly declared "arrangements" are actually conscientious objections to marriage. In practice, as well as in theory, the young people of the 1970s are developing two-step marriage: "living together" and then, if children are desired, legal marriage. Many of the couples who have formalized their marriage after living together for years buy the whole traditional package, including a church wedding and solid silver.

Young people are delaying having children, and the demographers studying the abrupt drop in the fertility rate of women twenty to twenty-four no longer think that the babies will come later. It's not like the Depression of the '30s, or World War II, when deeply desired babies were postponed for practical reasons. Many young women now frankly say they don't like taking care of children; or, more often, that they simply aren't up to rearing them, even if adding to the population were desirable. Increasingly, too, they have "other things" they want to do.

Are young women staying single because they have been influenced by women's liberation? Maybe. But I'm inclined to think that the causal relationship is the other way around. It wasn't until a critical mass of young women remained single in their twenties that it was politic to admit out loud that marriage isn't essential to happiness. Feminism has never been deader than it was during the 1950s, when the marriage rate hit a new high, the age of first marriage a new low, and the ideal of universal, compulsory marriage boomed marriage counseling, psychiatric therapy and romantic portrayals of married life.

A half century ago, when a fifth of our women never married, marriage itself was psychically undemanding for those who entered it. But in midcentury, marriage became the impossible thing that all but 8 percent of women tried at some time in their lives to do. Everyone was led to expect a marriage that was a great personal achievement, like the celebrated love affairs of history. Everyone was required to improve his sexual performance to virtuoso standards, on pain of neurosis. Married couples expected their marriage to grow, and a marriage that served as a means to any other end was snubbed as mean-spirited if not actually immoral. Rising divorce rates and disillusion with domesticity were the inevitable result, and thoughtful sociologists were beginning to lay the blame not on the frailties of human beings, but on impossible standards for marriage.

"I sometimes wonder where we would be now if the Standard American Marriage had been enforced in the past," Dr. Leslie Koempel, professor of sociology at Vassar College, wrote in a popular article, "Why Get Married?" Medieval monks, explorers, immigrants, schoolteachers, and women like Florence Nightingale and Clara Barton were necessarily unmarried, she pointed out, as were many of the greatest of our great men.

> The faculty of Princeton once named the ten biggest contributors to the advancement of human knowledge [Dr. Koempel wrote]. Of the ten, Plato, Newton and Leonardo da Vinci never married; Socrates couldn't make a go of it; Aristotle and Darwin married long after embarking on their work; and domesticity does not seem to have made many demands on Galileo, Shakespeare, Pasteur or Einstein. Similarly, Michelangelo and Keats never married. Milton, Lincoln, Edgar Allan Poe and Shelley were "failures" at marriage. How many self-respecting modern American women would excuse Nobel scientist Irving Langmuir, who fell into shop talk on his way to pick up his wife and walked by her, tipping his hat to her vaguely familiar face?

The Saturday Evening Post printed Dr. Koempel's views in its St. Valentine's Day issue of 1965 as a "Speaking Out" column devoted to opinions not necessarily shared by the editors, and blurbed the title "Why Get Married?" on the cover just above a luscious pink heart framing a woman contemplating roses who was obviously happy to be a sex object. Her answer was obviously that of the management: "For love, of course!"

The media were not, however, hitting young women where they lived, as the rising average age of the readership of major women's magazines attested. All through the 1960s, each college generation of women differed in its outlook so radically from those in college just before them that seniors complained that they were as out of touch with the freshmen as with their own parents.

The economic base of traditional marriage was eroding much faster than its ideological base. Men no longer had to marry to get sex. Women no longer had to marry to get financial or even social support. Meanwhile, more young people went to college, remaining single or contracting companionate-style marriages in which the wife was more likely than the husband to bring home the money.

The case against marriage is getting its day in court. Some of the evidence:

1. *Health.* The health of the married is generally better than that of the single, but the difference is nowhere near as great for women as for men, and careful breakdowns by age, sex and marital status suggest that there are many ways in which single women are better off than married women. This is the surprising finding of a U.S. Public Health Service inquiry into symptoms of psychological distress which was published in August 1970. The researchers asked a cross section of the population whether they were troubled with nervousness, inertia, insomnia, trembling hands, nightmares, perspiring hands, fainting, headaches, dizziness and heart palpitations. Contrary to expectations, single women simply aren't the Nervous Nellies they're made out to be. Never-married people reported fewer symptoms than the married, with never-married white women strikingly free of nervous symptoms, in spite of the fact that women as a sex were twice as apt to complain as men. It certainly looks as if the institution of matrimony was harder on the nerves of women than of men, and the suspicion is confirmed by the further finding that housewives report more psychological symptoms than wives who have jobs. The investigators discerned a new disease, "housewife syndrome."

As for physical health, there is much less difference between the longevity of married and single women than there is between the life expectancy of married and single men. Whatever the reason, marriage is more life-prolonging for men than for women.

2. *Happiness.* Studies of mental health made in midtown Manhattan and in New Haven, Connecticut, as well as elsewhere, report the same relationship between mental health and marriage. Married people are better off than single people. They have fewer neurotic symptoms, are less likely to be admitted to

mental hospitals, are more likely to score high on the Bradburn "happiness scale." But marriage makes a much bigger difference for men than for women, and in some ways single women are stabler, less anxious and "happier" than married women. Studies of happiness in marriage find that men are more satisfied with their marriages than are women.

3. *Credit*. Marriage subjects wives to disabilities as credit risks and candidates for job promotion. A woman lawyer I know who has worked herself up to a senior position with a federal agency recently married a man who earns less. As a single woman, she had been paying much less rent than she could swing, but as a married woman she is not the "head of the house" and so landlords refuse to count her income. When she was single, department stores were delighted to give her credit, but now when she went to open an account with a new store she found that the store insisted on going by the credit available to her as the wife of a man who was temporarily unemployed.

4. *Job Opportunities*. The most serious disability, of course, is the custom as well as the law which decrees that the "domicile" of a married couple shall be the place in which the husband resides. This means that wives cannot move to new job opportunities as easily as husbands.

5. *Social Life*. Marriage was regarded as insurance against loneliness, and in the regimented life of the 1950s this was frequently true. Except in bohemian quarters of the big cities, parties were given by and for couples, and single women and men found themselves handicapped by their lack of a spouse. But the advantage is beginning to fade. Even in the 1950s the ritual round of suburban parties was boring to many of those who participated in them, and was frequently blamed for a rise in alcoholism. Parties in which men talked shop in one corner of the room while women talked shop in the other corner were the inevitable result of social life based on couples rather than individuals.

The fact of the matter, of course, is that the old deal of sex for support has long been a dead letter. Marriage is no longer the only way to fulfill any basic human need. It is still the most satisfactory as well as the easiest way to do a great many things, such as rearing children, but it is no longer the *only* way to make a success of even that. The Israel kibbutz and communal child-rearing experiments in the United States turn out acceptable human products.

Wives can no longer do as good a job of catering, cooking, baking, butchering, nursing, teaching, sewing, child training or decorating as the specialists their husbands' money can buy —nor can a wife expect to be as good a dancer, hostess, sounding board, business adviser, sexual partner or showpiece as some woman he can find to specialize in one of these feminine roles. So women who are modestly affluent through their own nonbedroom efforts are finding that one man is not necessarily the best partner for chess, sex, camping, party giving, investing, talking plumbing, vacationing, gallery going and all the other activities which the city offers.

Traditionalists who subscribe to the sex-for-support theory assume that marriage will break down if women can support themselves. One sociologist thinks the sex-support deal can be salvaged as long as "working in the bedroom" is easier for women than jobholding. But what happens when sex is divorced from pregnancy and women want it as much as men? What happens when sexual intercourse occupies the same role in the life of a woman as it does in the life of a man?

There remains, of course, "love." Love may be grand, but it was never the original purpose for which marriage was intended, and it now has to compensate for a growing list of inequities and inconveniences. At the risk of spoiling St. Valentine's Day, it is relevant to ask exactly what love does for people and whether Standard American Marriage is any more essential to love than it is to sex.

The answer is long, but to put the question is to suggest that love and marriage may not be as inseparable as the horse and carriage of the popular tune. If love is a commitment between persons which provides emotional support, then it is obvious that traditional marriage is not the only institutional framework that can nurture it. If love, mutual support, face-to-face daily relationships are essential or desirable—and I am sure that they are—wouldn't we do better to start from scratch and design an institution specifically for their benefit? Work groups, play groups, the "gang," the "outfit" in the armed forces, "friends" colonies, collectives, communes are all doing this work now. Some of them have advantages over traditional marriage, and not the least of these is the frankly experimental and informal character of the group which encourages exploration of the psyche of the other and dispenses with sanctions that shrivel mutuality.

Which is not to say that marriage won't survive. The most probable future is going to be the most difficult social situation of all: many life styles coexisting among which young people must choose and, as they grow, choose again and again. Traditional marriage will satisfy many men and women, but it will never again command the prestige of the "one right way" to live, so it will never again confer on those who choose it the security available only to those who may not choose.

Redefining Motherhood

by ALICE ABARBANEL

Alice Abarbanel lives in Berkeley where she is currently at work on a book about motherhood containing a fuller version of the segments of her journal printed here.

I

I want to write a kind of journal/commentary about myself as woman and as mother. In writing it down I feel I will explore my feelings and thoughts in a deeper, more coherent way than I have done before. I also want to share with my sisters my own struggle, because if I had been able to read something like this, I would never have felt so alone, so full of doubts about my terror, my hate or my joy.

At age twenty-three, two weeks after my second wedding anniversary (and after three years of being with David), I found out I was pregnant. A diaphragm baby—a diaphragm used carelessly because, well, I believe I wanted to be pregnant and have a baby. We had talked about it and more or less planned to get pregnant in a year or two's time. This planning was very much on a fantasy level, because we couldn't imagine actually having a baby around—our friends were all childless and I couldn't imagine *my* being pregnant.

What do I mean "more or less planned"? I always thought I would get pregnant after I got my career together. We had fantasies of each of us getting half-time jobs while we had babies so we could share in their care, and taking turns working once the children (notice the plural form) were older. But as a first-year graduate student in sociology at Berkeley I was beginning to realize that I was not going to get one of those "careers" together. I knew I wasn't going to be able to be a traditional academic woman. Yet I saw no alternate life style that appealed to me—regular movement politics or hippie hang loose. I knew I wanted to do "meaningful" work, but I felt confused about what kind of work to get into.

So there I was, dissatisfied with school and work and vaguely figuring I could get some kind of fulfillment out of parenthood. Also it was a very natural thing, given my particular family, for me to have a child. My father is an obstetrician, my mother a nurse who identified herself as part of the medical world even though she was always a full-time mother. She had worked six or seven years before marriage and until a few weeks before my older brother was born. Pregnancy and birth had been dinner-table conversation in my house. The whole process didn't scare me at all. In fact, I had always looked forward to it as a beautiful time.

It really was a matter of timing. On the one hand, when David and I talked we figured there never was a perfectly right time. There was always something else to do—travel, work, education. On the other hand, "If not now, when?"

Then one day I woke up and vomited. Suspicions aroused, I got a pregnancy test and in an impersonal and alienating situation I was told that I was pregnant.

As soon as I left the clinic, waiting for David to pick me up and to tell him, I cried. My sadness came from three places. I felt cheated because I had always looked forward to deciding very consciously to get pregnant, to stop using that awful diaphragm and then to joyously, even mystically, make a baby. I felt like a failure because I saw myself as someone who had control over such matter-of-fact processes as birth control—I mean I was an obstetrician's daughter. And finally I realized that David and I would no longer be alone, totally independent and without responsibilities. One of my reasons for putting off getting pregnant had been that I wanted more time alone with David.

Should I get an abortion? was one of the first thoughts that came into my head. It seemed silly to abort this baby when I would be making another one so soon. But perhaps if abortions had been both physically and psychically more easy to obtain, that would have been my course. Now that I look back on it, however, I see that my strongest emotion was shame that I, a modern woman, did not plan to have a child.

Perhaps at this point more details of my personal biography are needed. This was February 1969. The summer before, I had heard about women's liberation and welcomed it wholeheartedly as very relevant to my life. When I was married in 1967 I thought I legally had to change my name. I did for over a year and always hated being Mrs. Him. When I arrived in Berkeley in the fall of 1968 I changed my name back to my "maiden" name. I realize it is my father's name, but it was me for twenty-two years and I never felt I was Mrs. David Rice. I went through all kinds of bureaucratic and emotional hassles making that change, but I knew I had to do it for my own state of mind.

That fall upon coming to Berkeley I sought out a small women's-liberation group. I went to two different ones. One had been going on for a while and I felt I needed to be in one from the beginning. The next was very in-groupy. I felt left out, so I didn't go back. But I read literature that was available and saw my marriage as being "liberated." Today I would never begin to claim that, but then I believed it was for a few reasons: I no longer was Mrs. D. R.; also I felt I shared the household tasks equally with my husband—cooking, dishwashing, shopping and cleaning. I was unaware that I still felt and acted on the total responsibility for that work, but more on this later. At that time I believed I had an equalitarian marriage, that when we had a child we would continue being equal in child care.

So when I found out I was pregnant and decided not to have an abortion, I used to say, "*We're* pregnant." We planned to share the experience in as total a way as we knew how. After all the hassles I had gone through to become publicly Ms. Abarbanel, when I went to an obstetrician I told him my name was Mrs. Rice! I didn't want the doctor to label me as an unmarried mother or a weird feminist. I didn't have the self-confidence or support from others to be straightforward with the straight doctor.

I got into being pregnant. I had always looked forward to that time as one of joy and beauty. I didn't feel *I* was creating a being. I used to tell people, "It is creating itself." I read all kinds of books about the natural process of pregnancy. I found one other woman who was also pregnant and we shared experiences, pains and aches, doctor stories, and information on natural childbirth. I loved to watch the changes in my body and to fantasize about the growth of a human being going on right inside me! Always worried about being too heavy before, I felt for the first time in years that my body looked really beautiful and I got positive feedback about that from my friends. It was a happy exciting time for David and me.

Now when I look back on those months I can see some things going on that I was then blind to. What I thought was sharing being pregnant wasn't really sharing at all. Yes, on one level, we didn't see the baby as *mine*, it was going to be ours in a real way. But I was the one who desperately needed another woman to talk to. I was the one avidly reading pregnancy books. David read sections I suggested in various books, but he didn't feel the absence of an expectant father to talk to. When you get down to it, I, not we, was biologically pregnant. David got into taking care of plants, I got into my own core and body. When the Third World and People's Park crises came, I stayed home to protect the unformed child inside me and David did battle on the streets. No tear gas for my baby. As I remember it now, I felt annoyed that David didn't feel a need to share his prefatherhood feelings and that he wasn't reading those books. I also felt glad that I had an excuse to stay out of the streets and avoid police attacks and busts.

About two weeks before the due date I and we were ready, and we waited in a time frame that very definitely belongs to pregnancy—a feeling of days being epochs, a time frame Doris Lessing captures and relates so well in *A Proper Marriage*.

At last labor began. It was slow and long. I spent a day at home and we kept saying, Is it really, really happening now? What does it all mean? I was very well trained in the process of natural or prepared childbirth, and David and·I made a very good team of breather and coach/timer.

The whole birth experience was one of joy and pain. It was a physical and emotional high unlike any I had ever experienced. "Pain and pushing and feeling relieved," I wrote in my journal. David got tears in his eyes when I was finally dilated and started to push; I was totally involved in the physical process, with no energy to reflect. How rare for me not to always be watching and analyzing with my inner eye. I felt very together with David, that we were sharing a unique and loving moment. I couldn't have endured it alone or unprepared. I mean I would have coped, but I feel like we did more than that.

For many reasons the hospital stay was bad. Mainly I was immediately separated from David. He had been with me in labor and the delivery room. Once I knew Amanda was a girl who was perfectly physically formed, my main desires were to be with David and share our news with our family and friends. But I was left alone in a hospital that was very crowded. "It's the full moon at the end of September," the nurses said, "the Christmas and New Year's babies are being delivered." The nurses were hassled and bothered. I saw David three hours in total between Friday noon—the birth—and Sunday after lunch.

After great protest and maneuvering I was put into rooming-in with three other women for my last night. Rooming-in means the babies and fathers are with you all day. The women were saying things I couldn't identify with: "I was my husband's bride, now I'm his son's mother." Great discussing about endless shopping for the perfect crib and clothes went on, and I felt left out. They told how being pregnant was *their* secret and how each decided the right moment to let their husbands in on it. They were three very prepared white middle-class women all into Lamaze natural childbirth and nursing—all with very fancy layettes to put on their infants despite the Indian-summer heat. I just had a little baby blanket and undershirt to bring Amanda home in. I had enough consciousness then not to put down those women, but I felt sad that this experience was their only thing in life. What it was for *me* I didn't know; I was clearer about what it was not.

II

Amanda, David and I came home from the hospital Monday noon. My mother was there. Thank goodness. She is so casual, experienced and a very open-minded teacher. She showed us how to change and bathe the baby. She accepted my ideas on nursing. We immediately got into a pattern. Since I was nursing I was always around, but David, Mom and I took turns taking Amanda—burping her, holding her, and putting her down to bed again. She stayed up an hour or so and slept for two or three. God, was I tired. My body ached.

I remember the talks with my mom in the small hours of the night—asking her about me and my siblings as infants. I remember her quiet kindness and warmth that set one of the tones of that week. I remember feeling glad that she must have treated us as groovily as she was treating Amanda.

But even then I flashed on the fact that one reason my mother was so helpful was her almost total adjustment to my trip; that was her life story with four children—she put herself last. She adjusts to those around her with very few if any of her own opinions entering in, and it was those that entered that I reacted to. When her own demands emerged around food and cleanliness I balked in my gut, resolved to be different, yet could I really be?

When I look back on it and reread the occasional journal I kept those first few months, I see my mom's presence in another way. I wrote, "Wanting to stop the clock. Always be a child. Cause I don't know what it is to be a woman. Abarbanel or Rice? Career. My own thing." In my first week of motherhood it was I who desperately needed to be mothered. I needed to be taken care of, and my mom came through. Not only did she care for me and my body, she was calm, secure, and very very competent, and, most importantly, she trusted in my ability to be the same.

Once Mom left, I felt enveloped (imprisoned?) by Amanda and my bodily needs. I couldn't relate to there being an outside world of other people, graduate school, work or politics. I was caught up in a new time dimension very different from the internal waiting of the last weeks of pregnancy. I was on Amanda time, my body belonged to her still, but in a different way. I felt like a cow. I remember sitting there dripping and spouting milk.

I guess you could say I had a postpartum depression. After all I cried a lot, wanted to forget the whole thing, wanted to kill the baby. We live on a hillside, and one of my ideas was to take her by her tiny leg and fling her off the cliff. In all the literature I read it said, at first it's hard, just take it easy and the new rhythm of your life of motherhood will naturally evolve. Just get a good cry out and all will be well, you'll adjust to your natural role. Forget it. What does this say about my role conflict and isolation?

Some things helped me through:

1. Repression. I'm pretty good at it, as it turns out, and the daily demands of coping with an infant are strenuous and didn't give me much time to analyze my situation and reflect on it.

2. I had a sense of personal security with respect to knowledge and even experience. This came from my mother as a model and her trust in my competence and common sense and therefore my own belief in it.

3. My relationship to David. I could talk and cry to him. He was accepting of my negative feelings. In fact, he wrote a song that kept my spirits up. I'd like to quote part of it here. The first three verses are like a conversation—first Amanda, then me, and then David. The last part is David suggesting a way to deal with our feelings about our past plans and our new future. This song was very important to me.

Amanda:

If you want to get along with me, we'd better get things
    straight
I love smiling for no reason, but I don't like to wait.
& I love yawning without a warning, but I don't like to
    suddenly awake.

Alice:

If we want to treat each other right, we'd better understand
I don't mind working through the night, but I hate to rise
    without a helping hand,
& I have fun making faces for everyone, but don't start
    asking me to lead the band.

David:

I have noticed times of troubled cries, that sometimes
    tears overwhelm your eyes,
Well I'm sure we can arrange a way to ease your fears
    smoothly away
I'm sure we can except where we're inside.

If I want to watch the different hopes, that come and
    go before we speak,
I'd try to remember about the past, without forgetting
    the future so unique,
I'd try to forget about outdated plans, without upsetting
    what I seek.

4. My vague identification with the women's movement. I
knew somewhere out there my feelings of conflict were not dis-
approved of.

III

Slowly, I began to feel confident that I could manage an
infant. Caring for a newborn is really a matter of interpreting

her cries—does it mean gas, hunger, cuddles, or is she simply trying out her baby lung power?

David and I felt together, and five minutes of hug time became a precious gift. He was in school and although I was a registered student I basically was not a student in practice. But knowing that I had that other identity was very important to me.

A new pattern began to emerge. We felt we were very explicit about sharing the tasks of child care equally, and I felt content that it was what we were doing. I spent hours nursing Amanda and reading at the same time. To show you where my head was at, I was avidly reading two kinds of things: infant-care books and women's-liberation literature. I remember feeling like a schizophrenic—*The Golden Notebook* in one hand and Dr. Spock in the other.

Then one day I read "The Politics of Housework." Zonk! That was perhaps the most important article I have ever read. I suddenly had the following realization. David and I certainly shared the Amanda tasks, but *I* was the one responsible for her. I was the one who thought of what to do and then delegated the responsibility. I was aware she was about to run out of clothes and said, "It's laundry time, it's time to change her crib sheet, what about the relief apple juice bottle?" And then I reevaluated our preparenthood existence. I felt we both had unconsciously acted upon my ultimate responsibility for the housework and later for the child.

And there began enormous fights, misunderstandings and anger. And was I alone! Here I was with what most people considered to be a model husband—Oh, you're so lucky Alice—and I had always felt lucky (read: better). The shit hit the fan, so to speak. I had had talks the previous spring with a woman who had two children, ages seven and nine. She and her husband explicitly delegated jobs. At the time I felt David and I had a "greater" mutual understanding and we didn't need such artificial job outlines. Our commitment to equality was enough. Forget it.

We started to assign specific jobs. That wasn't so bad; it was figuring out a joint agreement as to what needed to be done. I resented that *I* was the one who always thought of what to do. We tried to change that, but I had been socialized well and so unfortunately had David. In many ways our struggles were those many sisters have gone through about housework; but ours were complicated by Amanda's total presence and dependency. Our life in every way was no longer our own—alone or together.

The struggles were hard. For one reason, they were our first ones specifically around conscious women's issues, and a few words of awareness do not break up old patterns. The change is painful and very scary when you feel like a fanatic unappreciative bitch. Compared with anybody else's situation I was lucky —a helpful hubby, a student, both of us on fellowships. So my feelings of frustration and anger were turned inward, repressed, sometimes expressed to David. But to nobody else. I didn't want to admit being a failure. "If it's so bad, why did you have a baby in the first place?" I said to myself and imagined others would say to me.

I felt guilty for resenting David. I turned a lot of anger on myself and felt I should appreciate his helpfulness. I'm frankly not sure what he was feeling. Frustration, I imagine. Every time he turned around I had a new task I thought of. Oh, those arguments about whether and how much her room should be dusted. After all, we never dusted *our* room. But she's an infant, and the germs are out to get her. All should be sterile and as clean as the picture in the books. So we had to mutually agree on tasks. I probably felt more should be done than was necessary; David, less than necessary.

During Amanda's first four months I was involved with the Woman's Caucus of my graduate program. I had a dim realization that that contact was very important for my sanity—but exactly why I didn't know. It was my only contact outside of my world of Amanda, David and the house. And it was a contact that represented a new kind of yet undefined "liberation" even

though as a mother I felt unwelcome in the world of professionally oriented graduate students. Winter quarter began and I
took some classes. Despite the fact that school was unsatisfying,
I clung to that identity and in fact ego-tripped on the fact I
never dropped out of school—after all, I had a husband who
took the baby half time.

I remember tripping on how atypical (read: better) I was.
I didn't see nursing as an orgasmic mecca—although I dug it.
Now I see that a lot of my words to other people, especially
women's-liberation women, were partially to impress. I feel I
bragged about my negative fantasies of killing Amanda and
didn't talk about or let myself feel many positive or "typical"
ones. This is really difficult for me to admit. I dug acting cool
and indifferent. I dug being a liberated mother. I dug not being
dragged down by Amanda in the typical way. I dug nursing
her so casually and successfully and bringing her to my women's
meetings. At the time I wasn't conscious of doing this bragging.
After all, I really did have fantasies of escape from this drama,
of feeling it was all a temporary game, of feeling, Well, I've
experienced the pregnancy-birth-nursing trip, I might as well
kill the kid. After all, we hadn't established any mutual-love
relationship. I knew it really didn't matter to Amanda who was
holding her, but then again I did know she preferred the breast
over the bottle. And I was the one with those lactating breasts.

As my body recovered and we got into a routine, David and
I could talk and reflect, as opposed to react, more. He realized
that he also related to a lot of taking care of Amanda as a
burden and a constant responsibility. I felt the same way, because David and I are in a world of childless graduate students
and I was jealous of their freedom and embarrassed to say so. I
feel guilty and ashamed even in writing this today, because I
am thinking what does this say about my feeling the joys of
parenthood—grooving on the amazing growth and world of an
infant. I guess I have to admit these moments of joy were there,
but they were never long-lasting.

I can barely admit this even today because it means I was

not a free agent. If I had been I would have planned my child and been in a situation to totally dig her. I know this isn't really true, but somewhere in me I feel Amanda is cheated to have a mother who is so totally ambivalent—who finds her boring in long stretches of hours, who resents her constant demanding dependence. My impulse is to say, "But I also dig her." I do and my love grows as she does, but here I want to stress the more difficult aspect.

The above describes my situation until Amanda was about eight months old. By then I could ask my friends to babysit or to take Amanda for a couple of hours here and there. Still it was me and not David who did the organizing of others to do that baby care. I was aware of this, but I still felt that responsibility.

We had pretty well settled into a pattern. I felt great resentment at doing more than my exact time allotted share of baby care and therefore kept very keen watch on the division of labor. When I wrote some papers for school and David seemed willing to do more than his share, I felt amazed and guilty because I knew I wasn't willing to do the same for him. God, I thought, I was selfish, but I kept my principles because I felt a vague unspoken support from some women in my life.

I would like to explore these feelings about David some more. I was angry and I was jealous. I was jealous because he not only had the rewards of parenthood, he was into work he could relate to. I think one reason I nursed as long as I did was to keep myself as Amanda's most special person. It was also difficult to share the one area of competence I felt I had.

Once, I remember, Amanda fell off the bed. David was in the room with her. One of my gut reactions was it wouldn't have happened if *I* had been there. I rushed in to comfort her when David called for me, and silently felt, *I* can comfort her better than anyone. After all, if she prefers David, what else do I have? I am woman therefore mother. I held on to my ambivalent identity as student in order to have something of my own.

I didn't trust my own feelings and so felt very uptight and

rigid about exact equalization of Amanda responsibilities. Because I didn't feel I had anything else important or satisfying of my own, and because of a guilt inside somewhere of what kind of mother I really am, I'd slip into doing more out of a kind of inertia.

I couldn't believe David didn't feel as isolated as me and have the desperate desire for another person to identify with or to talk with about everyday issues of infant and baby care. I don't know why, but perhaps one reason he didn't was that fatherhood wasn't his whole identity. Being a father was another something he did, not "was." Being a mother was who I was.

Finally somewhere in me I felt gypped and unrecognized. I was an unusual mother because I didn't groove all the time on my daughter and my new status. David was unusual because he even noticed her at all. He was the focus of attention as being so nice, caring, tender and oh so responsible for his child. "Oh, Alice, he is amazing and you're so lucky because most men don't have that special feeling and intuition for babies," said my mother and her friends. He got the public accolades from my mother and my friends as well, for what was expected from me and therefore only noticed by its absence. I felt competitive then for Amanda's attentions and for those of others. I got approval from some by expressing my cool negative feelings. From others I was considered lucky or selfish.

IV

Of all the mothers I knew who had a baby near Amanda's age, the one I felt the closest ties with was Marianne. She was the first mother I had met whose feelings to a great extent coincided with mine—she was into motherhood *and* women's liberation. Earlier that summer another mother and I had talked about how sick she was of the women's movement "ripping off" mothers, especially mothers with male children. I remember feeling she had some good points, but it took a couple of months for my reaction to penetrate to my guts.

In August, Marianne and I started talking about how to reach out to other mothers. From our talking emerged the idea for motherhood rap sessions. Marianne and I decided to lead sessions concentrating on mothers of babies. We decided to offer it as a "course" in the Free University, beginning in October. The course description went like this:

> We want to talk about ways society puts its trip on women as mothers—ways this oppresses us as well as the benefits we may get from this role. Myths to be explored (and probably exploded): Mother-earth concept, maternal instinct, good mothers are nursing mothers, motherhood ties you down, etc.

We planned questions for the sessions, and although we were apprehensive about our abilities of leadership, planning the sessions met some need in both of us.

I can't speak for Marianne, but here's what I wanted. I wanted to meet more mothers like me. Simple as that. That didn't happen and I was disappointed. The women who came felt alienated from the women's movement, and I could identify with part of that. I realized that it was true, people into women's liberation were hostile to and about motherhood—many of them were very busy being "not-mothers."

Finally I articulated my feelings and wrote down some of my ideas about mothers and the movement and presented them to my women's-liberation consciousness-raising group. Below is part of what I wrote.

> We talk about white skin privilege. In the women's movement there's that with respect to all women. But within our movement, there also is an unspoken Brownie-point elitism—unmarried and childless.
>
> Women's liberation has been emphasizing the negative aspects of having a child. But I have one and so do most American women. Are we interested in including them? me? What does that mean

for the women's movement in general, and for this group? I see this group as some kind of paradigm for the women's movement as a whole.

In general it means the movement has to help mothers get some free time so they can begin to experience a self—feel they are important enough to be taken seriously. It means other women *besides* mothers should do something about child care, because otherwise the mothers' free time is spent in procuring that child care! It means we who identify with the movement have to come to terms with our own feelings about motherhood and children. How do we reconcile those who don't want or like kids, and those who do?

My own feelings are ambivalent. I dig Amanda, but I often hate being a "mother." I hate being tied down, but what being tied means to me is probably different for you. I have most of the negative feelings you all have. I *also* have positive ones, but being so into women's liberation it is hard for me to separate out the myths from the good parts, the benefits from the guilts.

On one level it is the most meaningful "work" to be with children and babies. It is interesting to watch them grow and be part of that growth. It is rewarding to be needed. It is important for us as full human beings to be with *other* than one generation. But what our society defines and makes people do who have kids is crazed. Our whole basic conception is wrong, yet to get out of it now means individual solutions.

That night our group talked about feelings about motherhood. Each of us was freaked about our own mothers and what kind of mothers we would end up as. I say "end up" on purpose. "End up" means not breaking out of the cycle of generations. After that session I could accept a woman's choice to not be a mother more easily, without jealousy on my part and/or anger at feeling like I'm being considered a kind of copout. This acceptance comes from my own working out of what motherhood means for me, my understanding of how frightened many women are of becoming like their own mothers. I don't feel tension in my small group, but the place of mothers in the women's movement as a whole is still dubious.

V

I still see myself as both lucky and isolated. I can't imagine being where I'm at today if I had had a different marriage or if I had been a woman alone with a child. Yet I feel an urgent goal is to make it possible for women who are not connected with a man, as well as those in couples, to have, if they want it, the freedom I sometimes am able to feel—to feel in control of their lives. It's probably an even more difficult and lonely struggle for women without men unless they can find a community—of sisters or of sisters and brothers to work with and relate to.

Women also must have the choice not to have a child. This is happening a lot and is really necessary. I hope, however, that women don't stop at the *not*-being-a-biological-mother state. If women are merely "not-mothers," then we stay in our old cycles by doing the opposite. We do not explore new forms of sisterhood and community. What we need is a new definition of motherhood.

My experience is very specialized with respect to my individual life situation and the historical time in which I became a mother. A big reason David and I both had free daytime hours for Amanda is that as students we both had fellowships her first year, so we didn't have to earn money. This year I'm a teaching assistant and David has a fellowship. In most families at least the man works all day, so obviously the job structure in our society will have to change if we are going to take the burden of responsibility off the mother. At the very least, however, we need quality child-care arrangements.

David and I are extremely privileged in our living and financial arrangements to have had the space to experiment with new definitions of parenthood. Even so, it wasn't until after Amanda's first birthday that I could say "I am a mother," because finally motherhood could have a new meaning for me; it didn't define my whole identity as a woman and a person.

And what about Amanda? I want her to read this one day. I sometimes still feel bad for her that she got stuck with such an ambivalent mother. But I feel stronger now and more affirmative of myself—and therefore of her.

A goal I have for my relationship with Amanda echoes Jane Fonda's feelings about her daughter Vanessa:

> I feel like a person with another person, an extraordinarily beautiful person who teaches me things. I mean, I realize that she is not a belonging of mine, that I won't have and will never have any right to her. So I do not ask her, and I'll never ask her, to love me as I love her. I do not want her, and I'll never want her, to respect me and to obey me. I want her to be free.

I also want that for Amanda. How we as mothers try to create or allow the space for that freedom will differ for all of us. Some women think marriage will prevent it. For myself, I see a continuation and development of my life as it is now—living with David and Amanda, and perhaps other adults and children someday.

I want Amanda to be free, and the only way that's possible is for me to taste my own freedom, so I will not demand respect and love. So I do not, out of desperation and lack of any other meaningful work to do, try to possess and live through her soul.

This journal describes my personal solution. Another "solution" would be to have lots of money and pay various babysitters to care for Amanda. This, however, would not indicate change in the larger society. The implementation of my ideals needs to be done in a revolutionary social context—and as soon as I think of one change another presents itself. For example, if both men and women take care of children, we need a different job structure; if couples don't live in isolated units, it's the end of the old type of nuclear family and marriage; if children belong to society, there should be quality communal child care.

VI

Amanda just had her second birthday. I am amazed by the difference in my feelings from the time of her birthday a year ago. When she turned one, I felt like celebrating *my* getting through one year of motherhood. A couple of months later I started my journal. The experience of writing about and rethinking my feelings about motherhood has somehow freed me from constant but unverbalized feelings of anxiety and ambivalence. I have had a chance to reflect instead of merely react.

Also, Manda has emerged in my mind as a very separate child, as opposed to a baby. At two she is on the verge of really talking in full sentences. I love this special moment, the beginning of language. I love her separateness and ability to express it, I love her spontaneity, games and fun. It is probably a mixture of my own feelings of connection to meaningful work (I am at last doing something that feels like it has potential for me) plus her age and her beautiful energy—I really appreciate Manda in a new way.

One final point. Because neither David nor I refer to each other or ourselves as Mommy or Daddy, Amanda calls us David and Alice just as she calls other people she knows by their own first names. However, all the other children in her play group call their mothers "Mommy," so Amanda knows about that word. At about nineteen months she started saying "Mommy" as a general refrain when she wanted something. About a month ago she expanded her use of the word. Now she occasionally addresses both David and me as Mommy Alice or Mommy David or just plain Mommy.

To Manda, Mommy is a word like "Give me" or "I want." She is beginning to also associate it as a person's name, but frankly I think her initial perception of its use is accurate. She is a fine sociologist; to a child Mommy is the person who takes care of me, who tends to my daily needs, who nurtures me in an unconditional and present way. Manda has two mothers; one is a male, Mommy David, and the other a female, Mommy Alice. I suppose she also has two fathers—if father love is supposed to be more instructive and limit-setting, and breadwinning. But I am not sure of these words anymore. We are still trying to redefine what motherhood and fatherhood—and therefore parenthood—can be.

Redefining Fatherhood: Notes After Six Months

by DAVID STEINBERG

David Steinberg is now at work on a book about free schools. He was part of the collective at San Francisco's New Vocations Center which put together *Working Loose,* an excellent "book about people looking for good work."

Dylan is napping. A chance for me to unwind and settle into writing. Dylan is six months old. I still find it hard to write in tune with his schedule. Like now I've just started and he's woken up crying. I have to stop and take care of him.

* * *

When Susan was pregnant, I imagined that writing and taking care of a baby would fit together well. I figured that as long as I was home taking care of him I would do some writing as well. It seems incredible now that I could have so completely misunderstood what it would be like to have a baby.

* * *

I have resisted the shift from working on my schedule to working on Dylan's. I've tried to hold on to my old pattern, and built up a lot of resentment in the process. Now as I begin to accept the new pattern and find that I can work with it, I feel better all around.

* * *

After six months I'm finally letting go of my old life for the new one that includes Dylan. I see now that my old life is really gone and that the job is to build a new one that I like as well or better. Letting go means that my energy can go into building instead of mourning what has died. One day, I cried at the

368

ocean, saying goodbye to a life that I loved and had worked hard to create.

*　*　*

Having a baby has brought an astounding amount of day-to-day work. It's not that doing the work has been so hard. It's what gets lost in the shuffle: time to sit and relax, to talk about things that are hard to say, to sort out feelings and become whole again, Sunday-morning pancakes in bed.

*　*　*

Recently, though, I've gotten better at making time to work out tensions, unraveling all the muck that's built up over these months. I'm fitting into a new rhythm, making use of free space as it becomes available.

*　*　*

The consumerism of the baby industry is overwhelming. So many special fancy things to buy so that you can feel like a good parent and provider. Dylan does fine with his used crib, toys made from little things around the house. There are a dozen ways to use a plastic infant seat, and a hundred things to do with a single piece of cloth.

*　*　*

Once a salesman came to sell us a piece of baby furniture that converted into fourteen different things, all of which, he insisted, we would buy sooner or later. It cost four hundred dollars. When we didn't buy one he accused us of not caring about our baby. He said he made eighteen sales pitches a week, fourteen "successful." I believe him.

*　*　*

We don't have very much money, and don't have any immediate prospects of earning more. I could make more money, but I would have to give up a lot, including my relationship with Dylan. So far it hasn't been worth it.

* * *

So far, Dylan hasn't dramatically changed how much money we need. We've moved into a two-bedroom place, so the rent is a little higher. We spend more freely on conveniences to make up for the time Dylan consumes. And I guess we'll need a car now in place of the scooter that's served us so well. Before Dylan we were spending about three hundred a month. Now we spend about four hundred.

* * *

Susan and I agree that neither of us should work full time. We'll both work and share taking care of Dylan. That way we'll both have outside lives in addition to a baby. Susan is driving a school bus and teaching piano. I'm free-lancing and writing a book.

* * *

I get an empty feeling when people ask me what I'm doing. Most of my energy in the last six months has focused on Dylan, on taking care of him and getting used to his being here. But I still have enough man-work expectations in me that I feel uncomfortable just saying that.

* * *

I'm not willing to be the second, somewhat foreign, parent. I tried that for a couple of days in a pique of frustration with Dylan. I felt very distant and alienated from him almost immediately. It was horrible. I decided it was better to share responsibility for him, which we've done ever since.

* * *

Right after Dylan was born, we both spent almost all of our time with him. We both cleared out a month when there was nothing else we had to do. As other demands pressed, we began setting aside time to be alone. I took three hours a day for writing and Susan took three hours in return.

*　*　*

Now, with both of us working, it's a bit more complicated. We've drawn up a schedule, evenly dividing housework, cooking, miscellaneous chores, and Dylan. It feels a little formal and cumbersome, but it's helping me get into honest work-sharing habits, and it's relieved a lot of other-person-not-doing-his-share tension. If the schedule becomes too burdensome, we'll do something else instead. I think that once sharing work comes naturally the strict sense of schedule will loosen up by itself.

*　*　*

I wish now that I had prepared myself better for having a baby. I let myself get caught by surprise, and then felt resentful, as if I had been cheated out of something I couldn't quite define.

*　*　*

Having Dylan has made me feel confused, overwhelmed, uncertain, then bitter and resentful. The feeling of being up against a situation that I couldn't handle, that was too much for me. So many things needing to be done, so many emotional pieces to be put together, and my energy outside of Dylan very, very low. Everything has seemed very complicated. I have felt the jaws of middle-aged American mediocrity open wide.

*　*　*

Often my anger and frustration come out at Susan. It seems ridiculous to rage at Dylan, and I'm too defensive to blame myself. Whatever goes wrong somehow becomes Susan's fault.

*　*　*

The more I am ready to have things come out badly from time to time, the more I allow myself to be imperfect, the less angry I get at Susan.

*　*　*

I knew nothing about babies when Dylan was born. I'm an only child and have never spent any time at all with babies. My confidence in myself as a father was very shaky. I felt deeply afraid of Dylan, always fighting an urge to close my eyes and shove responsibility for him over to Susan. I could hold myself together as long as everything went smoothly, but when something unusual happened I quickly panicked. I got very depressed at my lack of intuitive baby sense.

*　*　*

One evening, feeling very tense, I let all the fears and insecurities come tumbling out in a heap. Seeing it all together, I got even more scared. I cried for a long time. I felt completely weak, that I had failed at something very important.

*　*　*

Once I admitted all that to myself, and to Susan, I stopped putting up such a brave front and allowed myself to have times when I just couldn't handle being with Dylan. Starting from where I was, instead of where I wanted to be, I could face my weaknesses and work against them. I began to see that there were times when I was really good with Dylan, when I really did have good baby sense.

*　*　*

I had wanted to jump right in, confident and competent, and be a father who enjoyed taking care of his baby half the time. I wanted to cut all the American-father bullshit out of me in one slice. I learned again that coming out from under basic cultural habits isn't that easy or dramatic. But after six months' work I can see that it's happening after all. And that makes me feel that it's been worth all the trauma and tension after all.

❊ ❊ ❊

Writing about all this is making me jumpy. I'd better stop and do something else for a while.

❊ ❊ ❊

My fear of Dylan comes from feeling so much responsibility for him. When he cries I'm supposed to make something right. If I don't know how to do that, I panic. I do best when I'm ready to make mistakes, even serious ones.

❊ ❊ ❊

I know that I will make major mistakes with Dylan, and that I'll cause him a good amount of grief. I try to keep that in front of me, to expect it, and to accept it when it happens.

❊ ❊ ❊

As soon as I get oriented to one of Dylan's patterns, he changes and a whole new pattern begins to evolve. It's like standing up in a roller coaster, a little unnerving. I'm finding that the more I accept this constant change, the more I can enjoy the dynamics of it, the constant growing. Dylan is deepening my sense of change as a way of life.

❊ ❊ ❊

When I trust my intuitive sense with Dylan, I generally do pretty well. It's when I lose touch with that intuition that things fall apart.

❊ ❊ ❊

Susan wanted to have a baby at least a year before I did. Being a father was a rather frightening idea to me. I kept waiting to be more together, to have my life be somehow more resolved. Susan said that I could wait forever before things would be exactly right, that the only way to feel good about being a father was to have a baby and work through the hassles. That made sense to me. We decided to have a baby. Susan became pregnant immediately.

* * *

Sometimes I've thought that we should have waited a little longer, maybe another year. That then the adjustment wouldn't have been so traumatic. Now I think that adjusting to a baby is a traumatic process by its nature, and that it would have been the same thing a year later.

* * *

Deciding to have a baby was a little like when we decided to start our own school. A chance to do it right without artificial external limits. A chance to see what happens when we can't blame anything on what other people made impossible.

* * *

While Susan was pregnant, my relationship with her, and my relationship with myself, went through a beautiful time of growing and deepening. It was a very exciting time. I think now that I was getting ready for Dylan, unconsciously preparing for the upheaval that my conscious mind refused to acknowledge.

* * *

I feel myself moving out of stereotyped father roles into a relationship with Dylan that comes from me, that expresses who I am and how I feel. It leads me into some pretty strange situations, but as long as I'm clear on what I want I won't become nervous about the strangeness.

* * *

I've gone through a similar process in building my relationship with Susan around our particular personalities. The sense of creatively building the relationship that best suits us has been one of the most exciting things I've ever done. There's been lots of doubt and uncertainty, but we've built something that I find very nourishing and beautiful, that gives me strength and energy.

* * *

Remembering how uncertain I felt after we got married and seeing how far we've come from there gives me courage to work out all the stuff with Dylan. After all, six months is really a short time. It took about two years of being married for Susan and me to become ourselves instead of playing out traditional young-couple roles.

* * *

It really helps me hold on when I keep my eyes on the prize. It's so easy to take values and roles for granted, particularly basic ideas about being a husband or a father. By looking carefully at what's going on I can shape what I really want and throw out the garbage. Then I'm actively deciding who I want to be and what kind of life I'm going to lead.

* * *

Another help is being close to other people who are building new life patterns that suit their needs. I learn from what they do, and with their support I don't feel so self-conscious about rejecting TV-America.

* * *

It would be easy to fall into sitting around the house all the time. Doing things with Dylan often seems like a lot of trouble. But he's really pretty flexible. The more we've dared try with him, the more seems possible. He goes to sleep in strange places and survives being carried home on a bus. He jounces around the city in his back pack, goes on long car trips peacefully and has been camping in the country, diapers and all, for a week at a time.

* * *

Having a baby doesn't need to mean settling into a regular, repetitive life pattern. I can't go on as before, but whether the basic quality of my life changes now is up to me. I like the flexible, spontaneous, growing, changing life I've been living, so I'll work hard to find a way to integrate that with Dylan's demands.

* * *

It's always a shock when I remember that Dylan is related to me in a more basic way than that I take care of him, to realize that he is of my body, grown from my seed. My son. Occasionally it hits me from behind. I still don't know what to make of it. I suffer from not having been pregnant.

* * *

Dylan has been sleeping for three hours while I've been writing. Susan has gone to her bus-driving job. When he wakes up he's going to be hungry. I'd better go make a bottle.

* * *

Most of our friends don't have babies and don't relate to Dylan very closely. I remember that before we had Dylan I often felt put upon by the noise and demands of friends' babies. I feel that same tension now from the other side of the fence. I can see how couples with babies tend to socialize with each other almost exclusively. Still, I don't want to give up my relationships with friends who don't have babies. We'll have to work something out.

* * *

We exchange child care one afternoon a week with another couple. The free time has been important to me as a period of regeneration. A break from Dylan's unending presence, a chance to walk undisturbed along the ocean, to have some daylight time alone with Susan.

* * *

I would like to be living in a larger family group. It would help to have other people share responsibility for Dylan and help with the basic work he requires. It would also be good for Dylan to have intimate relationships with other adults than Susan and me. We have pursued various possible living arrangements with friends, but right now none feels good enough to actually do.

* * *

Dylan makes it much harder for me to control my environment, to plan ahead, to predict what's going to happen. He makes me realize how important control and planning have been to me. Now I'll have to loosen up, learn to flow more easily with things as they happen. Again I'm thrown into growing.

* * *

I can't impose my rules on Dylan. All my persuasive skills, the ones I use to get other people to do things my way, are totally useless with him. It forces me to accept the validity of his rules and then learn to integrate that with my real needs. The trick is to become less of a control freak without sacrificing myself to Dylan entirely.

* * *

Being with Dylan gives me a chance to express my intuitive, feminine, yin-self. As a man, it's easy to always be in situations that call for aggressive, rational, manipulative perspectives and skills. With Dylan I move out of that more completely than I ever have before. As a result I feel myself growing in all kinds of new ways. The clear importance of these new skills in caring for Dylan helps me respect and value them as they develop.

* * *

All of this would not be possible if I were working nine to five. That I'm not is no accident. Organizing my life to make room for a close relationship with Dylan has been a conscious deliberate process.

* * *

There's more about nine-to-five work than the scheduled hours away from home. There's the coming home tired and grouchy and tense, or being deadened by the boredom of tedious work. Whatever the spirit of my work, it carries over into the rest of my life.

* * *

I enjoy most of the time I spend with Dylan—taking care of him, playing with him, watching him change and grow. He is one of the most important parts of my life right now. There are other important parts, like my relationship with Susan, my work, being with other people. I don't want to give them up for Dylan, or him for them. There is as much total space as I have energy to clear and care for.

* * *

In struggling to define myself as a husband, I've found that I can open myself to real contact with Susan and feel good about that relationship and about myself. Now with Dylan I am in that same process of discovering new strength and energy. The last six months have been difficult for me, but this kind of growing never comes easy.

About the Editor

Louise Kapp Howe is a free-lance writer and journalist living in San Francisco. Ms. Howe was formerly the editor of *New Generation* magazine and is the editor of a collection entitled *The White Majority: Between Poverty and Affluence*.